106 - Fair
24 - April
310 - Swan, Silver
190 - Now

The Oxford Book of English Madrigals

Edited by Philip Ledger

Oxford University Press
Music Department
44 Conduit Street
London W1R 0DE

Preface

The selection of an anthology of English madrigals from what is arguably the richest period of English musical composition proved to be a task that was at once exciting and daunting.

I began with three assumptions. First, the major composers, Byrd, Gibbons, Morley, Tomkins, Weelkes, and Wilbye, would each be represented by several madrigals. Secondly, the lesser figures, and the adjective is only relative, would be represented by one or more. Into this class I placed composers such as Bennet, East, Vautor, and Ward. Thirdly, we should not, for the sake of completeness, include madrigals by minor figures if their work fell below the outstandingly high level set by their illustrious contemporaries (a notable exception was 'Sleep, fleshly birth' by Ramsey).

I was fortunate in that a colleague from King's College, Cambridge, Mr Andrew Parker, agreed to prepare new texts from the sources available, together with a critical commentary. This appears at the end of the volume for those who wish to verify instances of textual dubiety. All the tempi indications and dynamics are my own but singers and conductors should feel free to vary these according to personal taste. Editorial accidentals are indicated and these too are open to individual interpretation.

The distinguished vocal ensemble, Pro Cantione Antiqua, have recorded, under my direction, many of the madrigals from this anthology. The records are issued by Oxford University Press and illustrate the highly varied style of these wonderful pieces.

PHILIP LEDGER
General Editor

© Oxford University Press 1978

Index of composers

Index of titles

1
ALL CREATURES NOW

JOHN BENNET

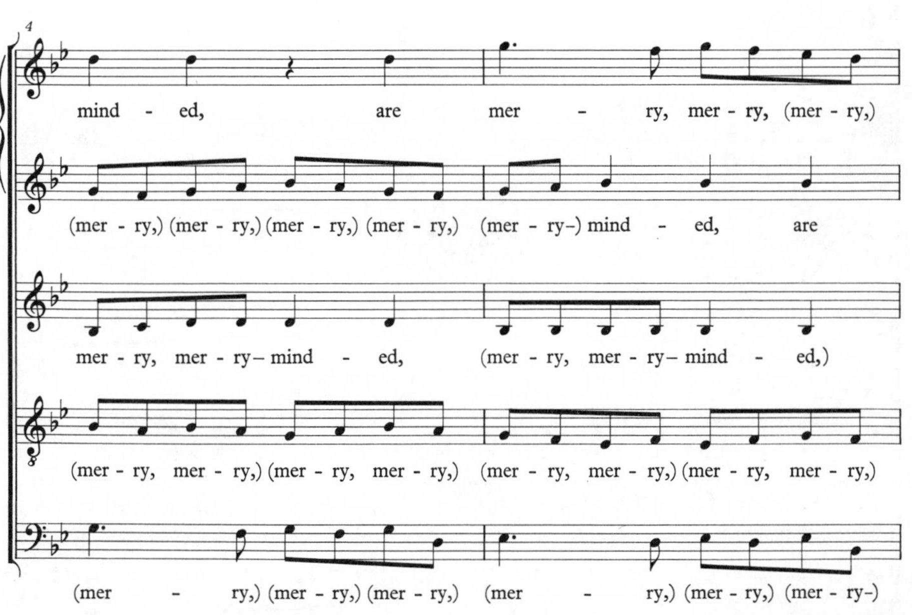

© Oxford University Press 1978

Printed in Great Britain

6
(mer - ry,) (mer - ry,) (mer - ry,) (mer - ry,) (mer - ry–) mind - ed. The
(mer - ry,) (mer - ry,) (mer - ry,) (mer - ry,) (mer - ry–) mind - ed.
(mer - ry, mer - ry – mind - - - ed.) The
(mer - ry, mer - ry,) (mer - ry, mer - ry,) (mer - ry–) mind - ed.
mind - - - - - - ed. The
9
mp
shep - herds' daugh - ters play - ing, (the shep - herds' daugh - ters
The shep - herds' daugh - ters play - ing, (the
shep - herds' daugh - ters play - ing, (the shep - herds' daugh - ters
The shep - herds' daugh - ters play - ing, (the
shep - herds' daugh - ters play - ing, (the shep - herds' daugh - ters
12
f
play - ing,) The nymphs are fa - la - la - ing,
shep - herds' daugh - ters play - ing,) The nymphs are fa - la -
play - ing,) are play - ing, are play - ing, The nymphs are fa - la - la - ing,
shep - herds' daugh - ters play - ing,) The nymphs are fa - la -
play - ing,) The nymphs are fa - la - la - ing,

15

(the nymphs are fa - la - la - ing,) the nymphs are fa - la -

- la - ing, (the nymphs are fa - la - la - ing,) (the

(the nymphs are fa - la - la - ing,) fa - la - la - la - la - ing, fa - la - la - la -

- la - ing, (the nymphs are fa - la - la - ing,) the nymphs are

(the nymphs are fa - la - la - ing,) the nymphs are fa - la -

18

- la - la - la - - - ing, Yond bu - gle was well wind - - -

nymphs are fa - la - la - - ing,) Yond bu - gle was well wind - - -

- la - la - la - - ing, Yond bu - gle was well wind - ed.

fa - la - la - la - la - la - ing, Yond bu - gle was well wind - - -

- la - la - la - - ing, Yond bu - gle was well wind - - -

22

- ed. At O - ri - a - na's pres - ence each thing smil - eth. The

- ed. At O - ri - a - na's pres - ence each thing smil - eth. The

At O - ri - a - na's pres - ence each thing — smil - eth. The

- ed. At O - ri - a - na's pres - ence each thing smil - eth. The

- ed. At O - ri - a - na's pres - ence each thing smil - eth. The

26
flowers them-selves dis - cov - er, (the flowers them-selves dis -
flowers them-selves dis - cov - er, (the flowers them-selves dis -
flowers them-selves dis - cov - er, (the flowers them - selves
flowers them - selves dis - cov - er, (the flowers them-selves dis - -
flowers them - selves dis - cov - er, (the flowers them - selves dis -
29
mf
- cov - - - er;) Birds o - ver her do ho - - -
- - cov - er;) Birds o - ver her do ho - - -
dis - cov - - - er;) Birds o - ver her do ho - - -
- cov - - - er;) Birds o - ver her do ho - - -
- cov - - - er;) Birds o - ver her do ho - - -
33
mp
- - - ver; Mu - sic the time be - guil - eth, (mu - sic the
- - - ver; Mu - sic the time be - guil - eth.
- - - ver; Mu - sic the time be - guil - eth, (mu - sic the
- - - ver; Mu - sic the time be - guil - eth, (mu - sic the
- ver; Mu - sic the time be - guil - eth.

37
mf
time be - guil - eth.) See where she comes, (see
See where she comes, (see
time be-guil - - eth.) See where she comes, (see
time be - guil - eth.) See where she comes, (see
See where she comes, (see
40
where she comes) with flower - y gar - lands crown - ed, Queen
where she comes) with flower - y gar - lands crown - ed, Queen of all
where she comes) with flower - y gar - lands crown - ed, Queen of all
where she comes) with flower - y gar - lands crown - ed,
where she comes) with flower - y gar - lands crown - ed, Queen of all
44
of all queens re - nown - ed, (queen of all
queens re - nown - ed, (queen of all queens re - - -
queens re - nown - ed, (queen of all queens re - -
Queen of all queens re - nown - ed, re -
queens re - nown - ed, (queen of all queens re -

47
f
queens re - nown - ed.) Then sang the shep -
- nown - - - ed.) Then sang the shep -
- nown - - - ed.) Then sang the shep -
- - nown - ed. Then sang the shep -
- nown - - - ed.) Then sang the shep -
51
- herds and nymphs of Di - a - na, nymphs of Di - a -
- herds and nymphs of Di - a - na, nymphs of Di - a -
- herds and nymphs of Di - a - na, nymphs of Di - a -
- herds and nymphs of Di - a - na, nymphs of Di - a -
- herds and nymphs of Di - a - na, nymphs of Di - a -
55
- na: Long
- na: Long live fair O -
- na: Long live fair O - - ri -
- na: Long live fair O -
- na: Long live fair O - ri -

59
live fair O - ri - a - na, O - ri - a -
- - ri - a - na, long live fair O - - - ri -
- a - na, long live, long
- - ri - a - - - - - na, (long live fair
- a - - - na, fair O - ri -
63
- - - na, fair O - ri - a -
- a - na, O - ri - a - na, long
live fair O - ri - a - na, fair O - ri - a - na,
O - ri - a - na,) long live fair O - ri - a - - -
- a - - - na, long (live fair O - ri - a - - -
67
- na, long live fair O - ri - a - - - na.
live fair O - ri - a - na, fair O - ri - a - na.
fair O - ri - a - - - na.
- - - na,) fair O - ri - - a - - - na.
- - - na,) fair O - ri - a - - - na.

2
ADIEU, SWEET AMARYLLIS

JOHN WILBYE

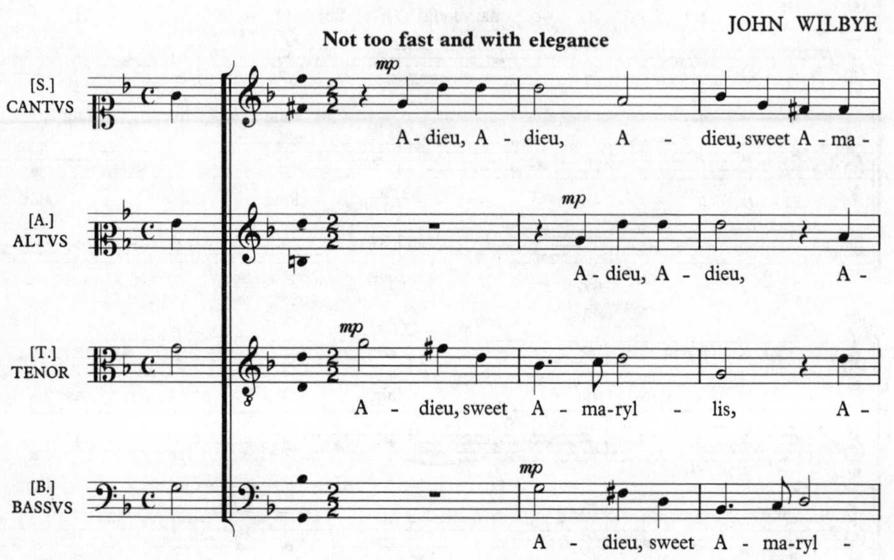

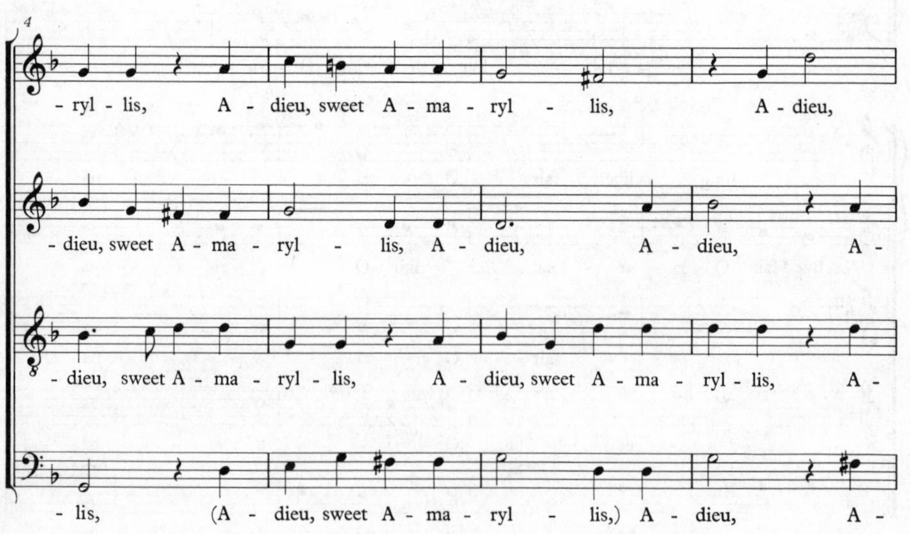

8
A - dieu, A - dieu, sweet A - ma - ryl - lis,
- dieu, A - dieu, A - dieu, sweet A - ma - ryl - lis,
mf
- dieu, A - dieu, sweet A - ma - ryl - - - lis, For
- dieu, A - dieu, sweet A - ma - ryl - - - lis,
12
mf
For since to part, to part your will
mf
For since to part, to part your will
since to part your will is,
mf
For since to part, your will
17
pp
is, O hea - vy tid - - -
pp
is, O hea - vy tid - ing,
pp
O hea - - vy tid -
pp
is, O hea - vy tid - - -

22
mf
- ing, Here is for me no bid - ing. Yet
mf
Here is for me, here is for me no bid - ing. Yet
mf
- ing, Here is for me no bid - ing. Yet once a -
mf
- ing, Here is for me no bid - ing. Yet
26
once a-gain, yet once a-gain, a - gain, ere that I part with
once a - gain, a - gain, ere that I part with
- gain, yet once a-gain, a - gain, ere that I part with
once a-gain, a - gain, ere that I part with
30
you, yet once a-gain, yet once a-gain, a - gain, ere that I
you, yet once a - gain, a - gain, ere that I
you, yet once a - gain, yet once a-gain, a - gain, ere that
you, yet once a-gain, a - gain, ere that I

34
pp
part with you, A - ma-ryl - lis, A - ma-ryl - lis,
part with you, A - ma-ryl - lis, A - ma-ryl - lis,
I part with you, A - ma-ryl - lis, A - ma-ryl - lis,
part with you, A - ma-ryl - lis, A - ma-ryl - lis,
38
sweet, A - dieu, A - dieu, A - dieu, A - dieu, sweet
sweet, A - dieu, A - dieu, A - dieu, A - dieu, sweet
sweet, A - dieu, A - dieu, A - dieu, A - dieu, A - dieu, sweet
sweet, A-dieu, A - dieu, A - dieu, A - dieu, A - dieu, sweet
42
A - ma-ryl - lis, A - ma-ryl - lis, sweet, A - dieu.
A - ma-ryl - lis, A - ma-ryl - lis, sweet, A - dieu.
A - ma-ryl - lis, A - ma - ryl - lis, sweet, A - dieu, A - dieu.
A - ma-ryl - lis, A - ma-ryl - lis, sweet, A-dieu, A - dieu.

3

ADIEU, YE CITY-PRISONING TOWERS

THOMAS TOMKINS

8

f Bet - ter are the coun - try ___ bowers, bet - ter are the

f Bet - ter are the coun - try bowers.

f Bet - ter are the coun - - - try bowers, the

f Bet - ter are the coun - try bowers, ___ the

f Bet - ter are the

11

coun - try bowers.

mf Win - ter is gone, the trees are spring - ing, ___

coun - try ___ bowers. *mf* Win - ter is gone, the trees are spring - -

(coun - try bowers.) *mf* Win - ter is gone, the trees are spring - -

coun - try bowers.

14

mf Win - ter is gone, the trees are spring - ing,

are

- - - ing, are (spring - - ing,) are

- - - ing, spring - ing, are (spring - - -

mf Win - ter is gone, the trees are spring - - -

17
are spring - - - ing; Birds on eve - ry hedge sit sing - ing,
(spring - - ing,) spring-ing; Birds on eve - ry hedge sit sing - ing,
(spring - - - ing;) Birds on eve - ry hedge sit sing - ing,
- - - ing;) Birds on eve - ry hedge sit sing - ing,
- ing, trees are spring-ing; Birds on eve - ry hedge sit sing - ing,
21
sit (sing - - - ing,)
birds (on eve-ry hedge sit sing - ing,) sit (sing - - - ing,)
birds (on eve - ry hedge) sit sing - ing, sit sing - - ing, sit
birds (on eve - ry hedge sit sing - ing,) sing - ing,
sit sing - ing, sing - ing, ‹thus› sit
25
sit (sing - - ing,) sit sing - - ing,
sit (sing - - - ing,) ‹still›
sing - - - - ing, sing - - - ing.
sit sing - - - ing, sing - ing, sit sing - - -
sing - - - ing, sit sing - - -

29
mp
sing - ing. Hark, how they chirp, (how they
mp
sit sing - ing. Hark, how they chirp,
mp
Hark, how they chirp, how (they
mp
- - ing. Hark, how they chirp,
mp
- - ing, sing - ing. Hark, how they chirp, (how they
32
chirp,) (how they chirp,) how they chirp it, (how they
how (they chirp,) (how they chirp,) (how they chirp,)
chirp,) they chirp, hark, (how they chirp,) how (they
how (they chirp,) (how they chirp,) how (they chirp,)
chirp,) (how they chirp,) how they chirp,
35
chirp,) hark, how they chirp, (how they chirp,)
hark, how they chirp, how (they chirp,) how they
chirp,) hark, how they chirp, how (they chirp,) they
how (they chirp,) how (they chirp,)
hark, how they chirp, (how they chirp,) (how they

38
(how they chirp,) they chirp, come, love, de-lay not,
chirp, how (they chirp,) how they chirp, come, love, de-
chirp, come,
(how they chirp,) (how they chirp,) how they
chirp,) (how they chirp,)(how they chirp,)
41
(come, love, de-lay not,) (come, love, de - lay
-lay not, come, (love, de-lay not,) come, (love, de-
love, (come, love,) come,
chirp, come, love, de-lay not,
44
not,)
-lay not,) de - - lay not, de-lay
love, de-lay not, de-lay not,
come, (love, de - lay not,) de-lay
come, love, de - lay not, de - lay

47 [← o = o. →]

p

Come, come, sweet love, (come, come, sweet

p

not, Come, come, sweet love, come,

p

Come, come, sweet love, sweet love,

p

not, Come, come, sweet love, sweet love,

p

not, Come, come, sweet love, sweet

51 [← o. = o →]

love,) (come, come, sweet love,) sweet love,

mf

(come, sweet love,) come, (sweet love,) O come

mf

come, (come, sweet love,) come, sweet love, O come and

mf

love, come, sweet love, come, sweet love, O come and

55

mf

O come and stay not, (O come and

O come and stay, not, stay not, O (come, and

stay not, (stay not,) come, (and stay not,

mf

come and stay not,

stay not, stay not, O (come and stay not,) stay not,

58
cresc.
stay,) and stay not, O come and
stay not,) O (come, and stay not,)
cresc.
O (come and stay not,) O
O come and stay not, O (come, and stay
cresc.
(stay not,) O come (and
61
[← o = o· →]
ff
stay, (O come and [♭] stay) not.
cresc. ff p
O come and stay not. Come, come, sweet
ff p
come, come and stay and stay not. Come, come, sweet
cresc. ff p
not,) come, O come and stay not, stay not. Come, come, sweet
ff
stay not,) and stay not.
64
p
Come, come, sweet love, (come, come, sweet love,)
love, come, (come, sweet love,) come, (come, sweet
love, sweet love, come, (come, sweet love,) come,
love, sweet love,
p
Come, come, sweet love, sweet love, come, (sweet love,) come, sweet

68
[← o·=o →]
mf
come, sweet love, O come, O come and stay not, stay
love,) sweet love, O come and stay not,
sweet love, O come and stay not, O (come, and
come and stay
love, O come and stay not, (stay not,) O (come and
72
not, O come and stay not,) (O come and
O (come and stay,) and stay, stay not,
stay not,) stay not, O come and stay not,
not, O come and stay not, O (come and
stay not, stay not,) stay not,)
75
cresc.
ff
stay) not, O come and stay not.
O (come and stay,) O come and stay not.
O come, come and stay and stay not.
stay not,) come, O come and stay not, stay not.
O come and stay not, and stay not.

4

AH, DEAR HEART

ORLANDO GIBBONS

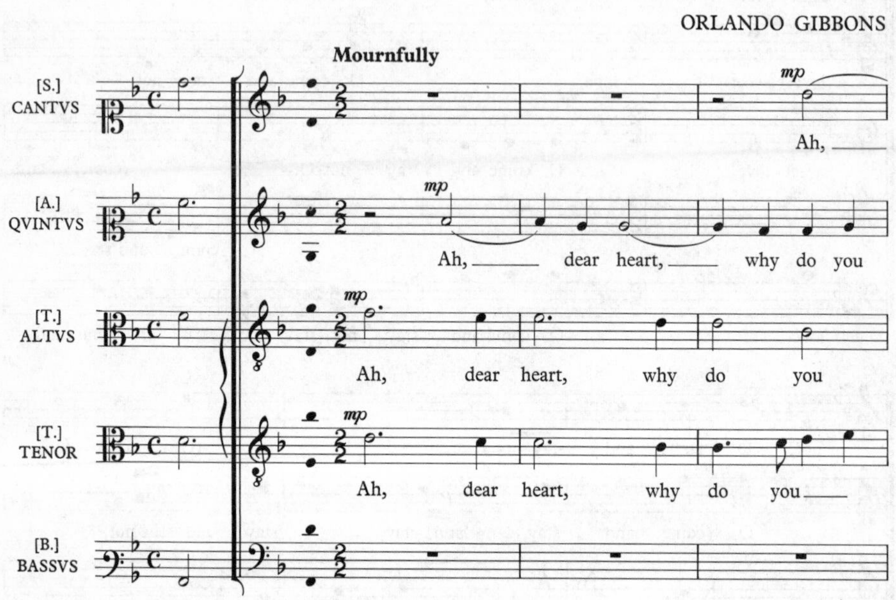

8
mf cresc.
from your eyes, your eyes, the
light that shines comes from your eyes, the (light that shines comes
cresc.
The light that shines comes from your eyes,
mf cresc.
The light that
shines comes from your eyes, the
11
(light that shines comes from your eyes,) from your
mf cresc.
from your eyes,) the (light that shines comes
shines comes from your eyes, your eyes, the (light that
light that shines comes from your
14
f
eyes. The day breaks
from your eyes,) comes from your eyes.
mf cresc.
the (light that shines comes from your eyes,) from your
shines comes from your eyes,) your eyes.
f
eyes, comes from your eyes, your eyes. The day breaks

17
not, it is my heart, To think that you and
The day breaks not, it is my heart, my
eyes. The day breaks not, it is my
The day breaks not, it is
not, it is my heart, To think that you and
20
I must part,
heart, To think
heart, To think that you and I must
my heart, To think that you and I must
I must part, to (think that you and I must
23
to (think that you and I must part.)
that you and I must part.
part, that (you and I must part.)
part, that (you and I must part.)
part,) to (think that you and I must part.)

26
mp
O stay, or else my joys will die And per -
mp
O stay, or else my_
mp
O stay,_ or else my joys will die,_ or else my
mp
O stay, or else my joys will die And
mp
cresc.
O stay, or else my joys will
29
- ish in their in - fan - cy,
_ joys will_ die
joys will_ die And per - ish in
per - ish in their_ in-fan - cy, O stay,_ or else my
die And per-ish in their in - fan - cy, and (per - ish in their
32
dim.
p
and (per - ish in their in - fan - cy.)
dim.
p
And per - ish in their in - fan - cy.
dim.
p
their in - fan - cy, and per-ish in_ their_ in - fan - cy.
dim.
p
joys will die And per - ish in their in - fan - cy.
dim.
p
in - fan - cy,) and (per - ish_ in their in - fan - cy.)

5
APRIL IS IN MY MISTRESS' FACE

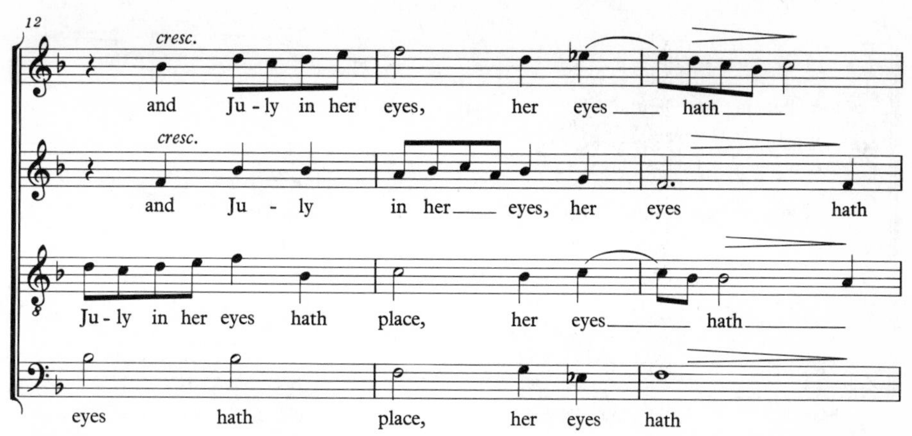
12
cresc.
and Ju - ly in her eyes, her eyes hath
cresc.
and Ju - ly in her eyes, her eyes hath
Ju - ly in her eyes hath place, her eyes hath
eyes hath place, her eyes hath

15
p
place, With - in her bo - som, with - in her bo - som is
p
place, With - in her bo - som, (with - in her bo - som) is
p
place, With - in her bo - som, with - in her bo - som is
p
place, With - in her bo - som

20
f
Sep - tem - - - - - ber, But in her heart,
Sep - tem - - - - - ber,
f
Sep - tem - - - ber, But in her heart,
f
is Sep - tem - - - ber, But in her

25
but in her heart, her heart a cold De - cem - - -
f
But in her heart, her heart a cold De - cem - - -
— her heart a cold De - cem -
heart, but in her heart a cold De - cem -
30
p
- ber, but in her heart, but in her
p
- ber, but in her heart, her heart, but in her
p
- ber, but in her heart, but in — her
p
- ber, — but in her heart,
34
heart, her heart a cold De - cem - - - ber.
heart, her heart a cold De - cem - - - ber.
heart a cold De - cem - ber.
but in her heart a cold De - cem - ber.

6
AS VESTA WAS

THOMAS WEELKES

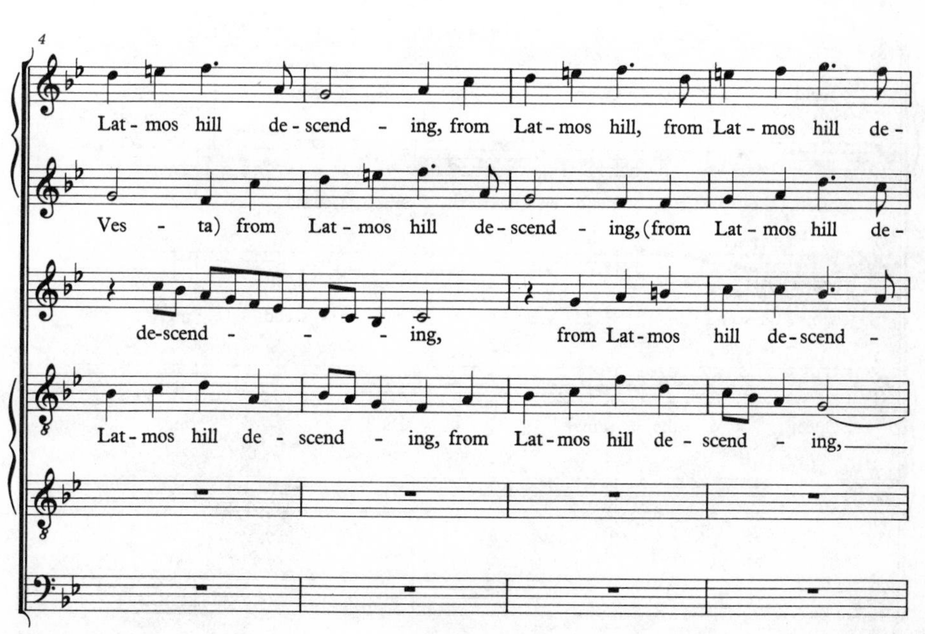

8
mp
-scend - - ing, She spied, she spied a
mp
- - scend - ing,) She spied, a maid-en
mp
- - - ing, She spied a maid - en Queen the
mp
de - scend - ing, She spied a maid - en
12
cresc.
maid - en Queen the same a-scend - - -
cresc.
Queen, (she spied a maid - en Queen) the same a-scend - -
cresc.
same a-scend - - ing, a - scend - ing, the
Queen the same a - scend - ing, the

16
- ing, a-scend - ing, the same a-scend - ing, the
- ing, a - scend - ing, the same a-scend - - -
same a-scend - - - ing, a - scend - ing, the
cresc.
same a-scend - - - ing, the same a - scend -
20
same a-scend - - - ing, At - tend - ed on by
f
- ing, a - scend - ing, At - tend - ed
same a-scend - - - ing, At - tend - ed
- ing, the same a - scend - ing, At - tend - ed
At - tend - ed

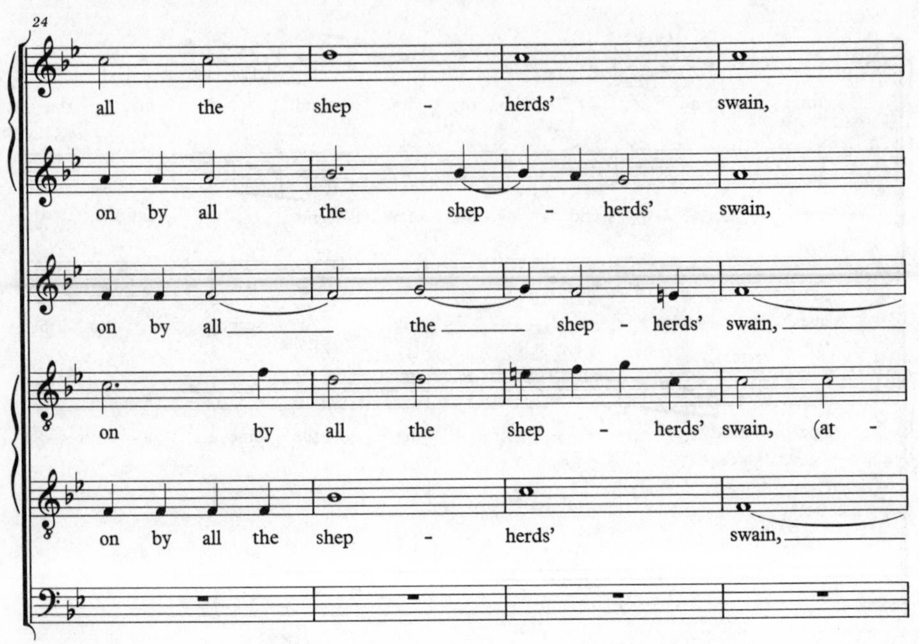

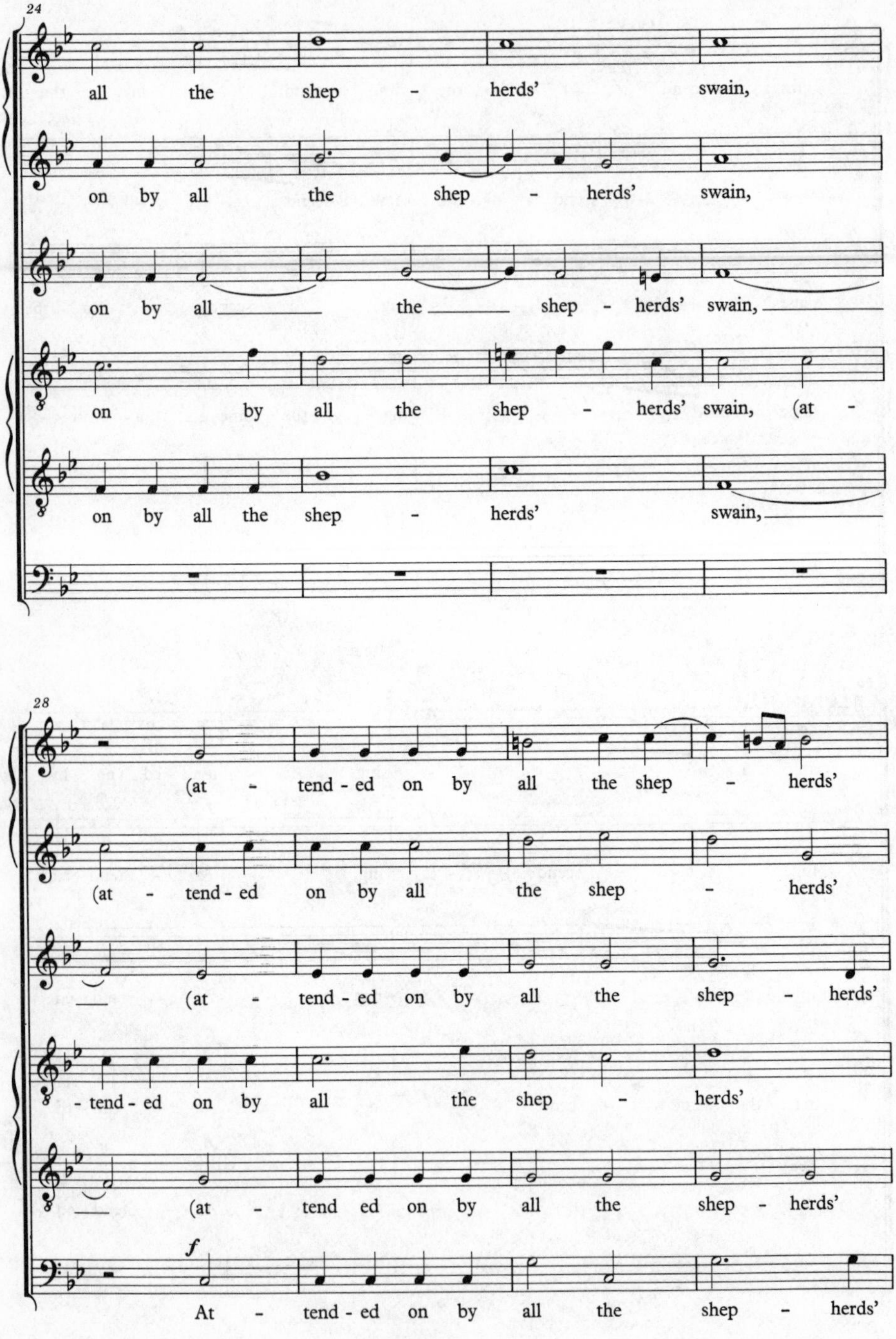

28

(at - tend - ed on by all the shep - herds'

(at - tend - ed on by all the shep - herds'

(at - tend - ed on by all the shep - herds'

- tend - ed on by all the shep - herds'

(at - tend ed on by all the shep - herds'

f

At - tend - ed on by all the shep - herds'

32

mf

swain,) To whom Di-a-na's dar - lings, dar - -

mf

swain,) To whom Di - a - na's dar -

mf

swain,) To whom Di-a-na's dar - lings, (to whom Di - a - na's

mf

swain,) To whom Di-a-na's dar - lings

mf

swain,) To whom Di - a - na's dar -

mf

swain, To whom Di-a-na's dar - lings came

36

- lings came run-ning down a-main, (came run-ning down a-main,)

- lings came run-ning down a - main, (came run-ning down a - main,)

dar - lings) came run-ning down a - main,

came run-ning down a - main, a - - - main,

- lings came run-ning down a - main, (came run-ning down a -

run-ning down a - main, (came run-ning down a - main,) came run-ning down a -

39
(came run-ning down a - -
came run-ning down a - -
(came run-ning down a - main,) (came run-ning down a - main,)
(came run-ning down a - main,) (came
- main,) (came run-ning down a - main,) a -
- main, a - main,
42
- main,) came run-ning down a - main, (came run-ning down a -
- main, (came run-ning down a - main,) (came run-ning down a -
came run-ning down a - main,
run-ning down a-main,) came run - ning down a -
- main, (came run-ning down a - main,) a - main,
(came run-ning down a - main,) came

45
mp
- main,) (came run-ning down a - main,) a - main, First
- main,) (came run-ning down a - main,) a - main, First two by two,
(came run - ning down a - main,) First two by two,
- main,) (came run - ning down a - main,) First
came down a - main,
run - ning down a - main,
49
two by two, then three by three to - ge - - -
then three by three to - ge - - -
then three by three to - ge - - -
two by two, then three by three to - ge - - -
Then three by three to - ge -
Then three by three to - ge - - -

53
p
- ther, Leav - ing their god - dess
- ther, Leav - ing their god - dess,
- ther, Leav - ing their god - dess,
- ther, Leav - ing their god dess,
- ther, Leav - ing their god - dess,
- ther, Leav - ing their god - dess,
57
mf
all a - lone, hast - ed thi - ther;
hast - ed thi ther; And
hast ed thi - ther; And
hast - ed thi ther;
hast - ed thi - ther; And
hast - ed thi - ther;

61
mf
And min - gling with the shep - herds of her
min - gling with the shep - herds of her train,
min - gling with the shep - herds of her train, of her train,
mf
And min - gling with the shep - herds of her
min - gling with the shep - herds of her train, with the shep - herds of her
mf
And min - gling with the shep - herds of her
65
f
train, With mirth - ful tunes, mirth - ful tunes her pre - sence
f
With mirth - ful tunes, (with mirth - ful tunes) her pre - sence en - ter -
f
With mirth - ful tunes, (with mirth - ful tunes) her pre - sence
f
train, of her train, With mirth - ful tunes
f
train, With mirth - ful tunes, (with mirth - ful tunes) her pre - sence en - ter -
f
train, With mirth - ful tunes her pre - sence en -

69
en - ter - tain, (her pre - sence en - ter -
- - - tain, (her pre - sence en - ter -
en - ter - tain, her pre - sence en - ter -
her pre - sence en - - ter - -
- tain, en - ter - tain, her (pre - sence en - ter-
- - ter - tain, her pre - sence en - ter -
73
- tain.) Then sang the shep - herds
- tain.) Then sang the shep - herds
- tain. Then sang the shep - herds
- tain. Then sang the shep - -
- tain.) Then sang the shep - herds
- tain. Then sang the shep - herds

77

mp

and nymphs of Di - a - na, nymphs of Di - a -

mp

and nymphs of Di - a - na, nymphs of Di - a -

mp

and nymphs of Di - a - na, nymphs of Di - a -

mp

- herds and nymphs of Di - a - na, nymphs of Di - a -

and nymphs of Di - a - na:

and nymphs of Di - a - na:

81

f

- na: Long live fair O - ri - a - na, fair O - ri - a - na,

f

- na: Long live fair O - ri - a - na, O - ri - a -

mf

- na, of Di - a - - - na: Long

f

- na: Long live fair O - ri - a -

f

Long live fair O - ri - a - na, (long live fair O -

f

Long live fair O - ri - a - na,

85
mf
long live fair O - ri - a - na, (long live fair O - ri -
mf
- na, (long live fair O - ri - a - na,)
live fair O - ri - a - na, long live fair O - ri - a -
mf
- na, (long live fair O - ri - a - na,) (long
mf
- ri - a - na,) (long live fair O - ri - a - na,) fair
sempre f
long
89
- a - na,) (long live fair O - ri - a - na,) O - ri - a -
(long live fair O - ri - a - na,) long live fair O - ri -
- na, (long live fair O - ri - a - na,) fair O - ri - a -
mp
live fair O - ri - a - na,) fair O - ri - a - na, long
O - ri - a - na, long live fair O - ri - a - na,
live fair

93
mp
- na, long live fair O - ri - a - na, (long live fair O - ri -
mp
- a - na, (long live fair O - ri - a - - -
mp
- na, long live fair O - ri - a - na, (long
live fair O - ri - a - na, live long, long live fair O - ri - a -
mp
(long live fair O - ri - a - na,) fair O - ri -
O - - - - - ri - - - - - -
97
mf
- a - na, fair O - ri - a - na, (long live fair O - ri -
mf
- na,) (long live fair O - ri - a - na,) (long live fair O - ri - a - na,)
mf
live fair O - ri - a - na,) (long
mf
- na, fair O - ri - a - na, (long live fair
mf
- a - na, long (live fair O - ri - a - na,) (long
- a - - - - - na,

101
-a-na,) fair O-ri-a-na, long live fair O-ri-
O-ri-a-na, long live fair O-ri-a-na,
live fair O-ri-a-na,) fair O-ri-a-
O-ri-a-na,) (long
live fair O-ri-a-na,) long live fair O-ri-a-na,
long
105
-a-na, fair O-ri-a-na, (fair
long live fair O-ri-a-na, fair O-ri-
-na, long live fair O-ri-a-na,
live fair O-ri-a-na,) long
(long live fair O-ri-a-na,)
live fair O-ri-

109
O - ri - a - na,) long live fair O - ri - a - na,
- a - na, long live fair O - ri - a - na, long live fair O - ri -
O - ri - a - - na, (long
live fair O - ri - a - na, (long live fair O - ri - a -
(long live fair O - ri - a - -
- a - - na, long live fair O - ri - a - na, fair
113
long live fair O - ri - a - - - - - na.
- a - na, long live fair O - ri - a - na.
live fair O - ri - a - na,) fair O - ri - a - na.
- na,) fair O - ri - a - na.
- na,) long live fair O - ri - a - - - na.
O - - - ri - a - - - na.

7
COME AWAY, SWEET LOVE

THOMAS GREAVES

8
p
la la la la la. Come a - way, sweet love, and play thee, Lest
la la la la. Come a - way, sweet love, and play thee, Lest
la la la la la la la. Come a - way, sweet love, and play thee, Lest
la, fa la la la la. Come a - way, sweet love, and play thee, Lest
la la la la. Come a - way, sweet love, and play thee, Lest
12
grief and care be - tray thee. Fa la la, fa la la la la la la la la la
grief and care be - tray thee. Fa la la la la la la la la la la la, fa
grief and care be - tray thee. Fa la la la la, fa la la, fa la la la
grief and care be - tray thee. Fa la la la la la la la la la la la
grief and care be - tray thee. Fa la la la la la la la la la, fa la
16
f
la la la la. Leave off this sad la - ment - ing And
la la la la la. Leave off this sad la - ment - ing And
la la la la la la la. Leave off this sad la - ment - ing And
la, fa la la la la. Leave off this sad la - ment - ing And
la la la la. Leave off this sad la - ment - ing And

20
più f
take thy heart's con - tent - ing. The nymphs to sport in - vite thee,
più f
p
take thy heart's con - tent - ing. The nymphs to sport in - vite thee, and
più f
take thy heart's con - tent - ing. The nymphs to sport in - vite thee,
più f
p
take thy heart's con - tent - ing. The nymphs to sport in - vite thee, and
più f
take thy heart's con - tent - ing. The nymphs to sport in - vite thee,
24
p
cresc.
and run-ning in and out, (and run-ning in and out,) (and run-ning
cresc.
run-ning in and out, (and run-ning in and out,) (and run-ning in and out,)
p
cresc.
and run-ning in and out, (and run-ning in and out,) (and run-ning in and
cresc.
run-ning in and out, (and run-ning in and out,) (and run-ning in and out,)
p
cresc.
and run-ning in and out, and run-ning in and
27
f
in and out,) (and run-ning in and out) de - lights
f
(and run-ning in and out,) (and run-ning in and out) de - lights
f
out,) (and run-ning in and out) de - lights
f
(and run - ning in and out) de - lights
f
out, (and run - ning in and out) de - lights

30

thee. Fa la la la la, fa la la la la

thee. Fa la la la la, fa la la la la la la la

thee. Fa la la la la la la la la la la, fa la

thee. Fa la la la la la la, fa la la la la la la,

thee. Fa la la la la, fa la la la la la la la la,

34

la la la, fa la la la la, fa la la la la la, fa la la

la, fa la la la la la la, fa la la la la la

la la la la la la la, fa la la la la la la,

fa la la la la, fa la la la la la la la la

fa la la la la la la la la la, fa la la

38

la la la la, fa la la la la la la. Leave

la, fa la la la, fa la la la la. Leave

fa la la, fa la la la, fa la la la la. Leave

la la la, fa la la la la la la la la la la. Leave

la la la la, fa la la la la la. Leave

42
più f
off this sad la - ment - ing, And take thy heart's con - tent - ing. The
più f
off this sad la - ment - ing, And take thy heart's con - tent - ing. The
più f
off this sad la - ment - ing, And take thy heart's con - tent - ing. The
più f
off this sad la - ment - ing, And take thy heart's con - tent - ing. The
più f
off this sad la - ment - ing, And take thy heart's con - tent - ing. The
46
p
nymphs to sport in - vite thee, and run-ning in and out, (and run-ning in and out,)
p
nymphs to sport in - vite thee, and run-ning in and out, (and run-ning
p
nymphs to sport in - vite thee, and run-ning in and out, (and run-ning in and
p
nymphs to sport in - vite thee, and run-ning in and out, (and run-ning in and out,)
p
nymphs to sport in - vite thee, and run-ning in and
50
cresc.
f
(and run-ning in and out, and run-ning in and out,) (and run-ning in and
cresc.
f
in and out, and run-ning in and out, and run-ning in and out) de -
cresc.
f
out,) (and run-ning in and out,) (and run-ning in and out) de -
cresc.
f
(and run-ning in and out,) (and run - ning in and out) de -
cresc.
f
out, (and run-ning in and out,) (and run - ning in and out) de -

53

p *poco cresc.*

out) de - lights thee. Fa la la la la, ——— fa la la la

p *poco cresc.*

- lights thee. Fa la la la la la,

p *poco cresc.*

- lights thee. Fa la la la la la la la la la

p *poco cresc.*

- lights thee. Fa la la la la la la, fa la la la la

p *poco cresc.*

- lights thee. Fa la la la la, fa la la la la la

57

la la la la la, fa la la la la la, fa la

fa la la la la la la la, ——— fa la la la la, fa la la la

la, fa la la la la la la la, fa la la

la la, ——— fa la la la la, fa la la la ———

la la la, ——— fa la la la la la la la ——— la la la,

61

cresc. *f*

la la la la la, fa — la la la, fa la la la la.

cresc. *f*

la la, fa la la ——— la la la la, fa — la la la la la la.

cresc. *f*

la la la la, ——— fa la la, fa la la la, fa la la la la.

cresc. *f*

— la la la la ——— la la la, fa la la la la la la la la la la.

cresc. *f*

fa la la la la la la, fa la la la la la.

8
COME, GENTLE SWAINS

MICHAEL CAVENDISH

8
-herds' dain - ty daugh - ters, A - dorned, a - dorned,
- herds' dain - ty daugh - ters, A - dorned with cour - te - sy and
Come, (gen - tle swains, and shep - herds' dain - ty
come - ly du - ties, Come, gen - tle swains, and
dain - ty daugh - ters, A - dorned with cour - te - sy,
12
Come, (gen - tle swains, and shep - herds' dain - ty,) dain - ty daugh - ters,
come - ly du - ties, (Come, gen - tle swains, and shep -
daugh - ters, A - dorned with cour - te - sy and) come - ly du -
shep - herds' dain - ty daugh - ters, A - dorned with cour - te - sy and
Come, gen - tle swains, and shep - herds'
16
f
A - dorn - ed, a - dorned with cour - te -
- herds' dain - ty daugh - ters,) A - dorned with cour - te -
- ties, A - dorned with cour - te -
come - ly du - ties,) A - dorned with cour - te -
dain - ty daugh - ters, A - dorned with cour - te -

20
p
cresc.
-sy, a - dorned with cour - te - sy) and come - ly
-sy, a - dorned with cour - te - sy and come - ly
-sy and come - ly du - ties, and come - ly du - ties,
-sy a - dorned with cour - te - sy and come - ly
-sy and come - ly du -
24
f
du - ties, Come, sing and joy and grace with love - ly
du - ties,
and (come - ly du - ties,) Come, sing and
du - ties, Come, sing and joy and grace with
ties, Come, sing and
28
laugh - ters, and grace with love - ly
Come, sing and joy and grace with
joy and grace with love, and grace with
love - ly laugh - ters, come, sing (and joy and
joy and grace with love, with love - ly

31
[← o = o· →]
mf
laugh - - - ters The birth - day of the
love - ly laugh - ters The birth - day of the
love - ly laugh - ters The birth - day of the
grace with love - ly laugh - ters) The birth - day of the
laugh - - - ters The birth - day of the
35
[← o· = o →]
f
beau - tiest of beau - ties. Then sang the shep - herds and nymphs
beau - tiest of beau - ties. Then sang the shep - herds and nymphs
beau - tiest of beau - ties. Then sang the shep - herds:
beau - tiest of beau - ties. Then sang the shep - herds and nymphs
beau - tiest of beau - ties. Then sang the shep - herds and nymphs
39
of Di - a - na: Long live fair O - ri - a -
of Di - a - na: Long live fair O - ri - a - na, (long
Long live fair O - ri - a - na, (long
of Di - a - na: Long live O - ri - a - na, long live fair O - ri -
of Di - a - na, of Di - a - na: Long live fair O - ri - a - na,

43
-na, (long live fair O - ri - a - na,) long live
live fair O - ri - a - na,)
live fair O - ri - a - na,)(long live fair O - ri - -
-a - na, (long live fair O - ri -
long live, long live fair O - ri - a - na,
46
fair O - ri - a - na, fair O - ri - a - -
(fair O - ri - a - na,) fair O - ri - a - - -
- a - na,) long live fair O - ri - a -
-a - na,) long live fair O - ri - a - - -
(long live fair O - ri - a - -
49
-na. Then sang the shep - herds and nymphs
-na. Then sang the shep - herds and nymphs
- na. Then sang the shep - herds:
- na. Then sang the shep - herds and nymphs
- na.) Then sang the shep - herds and nymphs
p

52
f
of Di - a - na: Long live fair O - ri - a - na, (long
of Di - a - na: Long live fair O - ri - a -
Long live fair O - ri - a - na, (long
of Di - a - na: Long live O - ri - a - na, long live fair O - ri -
of Di - a - na, of Di - a - na: Long live fair O - ri - a - na,
56
live fair O - ri - a - na,)
- na, (long live fair O - ri - a - na,) long live
live fair O - ri - a - na,) long live fair O - ri -
- a - na, (long live fair O - ri -
long live, long live fair O - ri - a - na,
59
fair O - ri - a - na, fair O - ri - a - na.
fair O - ri - a - na, fair O - ri - a - na.
- a - na, long live fair O - ri - a - na.
- a - na,) long live fair O - ri - a - na.
(long live fair O - ri - a - na.)

9
COME, SABLE NIGHT

10
mp
put on thy mourn - - - ing
stole, put (on thy mourn - ing
- ing stole,
put on thy mourn - ing stole, thy
- ing stole,
15
mf
put on thy mourn -
stole, thy (mourn - ing stole,)
stole,)(put on thy mourn - ing stole,)
put (on thy mourn - ing stole,)
mf
(mourn - ing stole,) put (on thy mourn - ing
mf
(put on thy

20
cresc.
- ing stole, put (on thy mourn - ing
mf
put (on thy mourn - - ing
mf
put (on thy mourn - ing
mf
put (on thy mourn-ing stole,) thy mourn - ing
cresc.
stole,) thy mourn - ing stole, (thy mourn - ing
cresc.
mourn - ing stole,) thy mourn - - ing
25
f p
stole,) And help A - myn - tas
stole,) And help A - myn - tas
stole,) And help A - myn - tas sad - ly
stole, And help A - myn - tas sad - ly to con - dole,
stole,) And help A - myn - tas sad -
stole, And help A - myn - tas sad - ly to con -

30
sad - ly to con -
sad -
to con - dole, sad - ly (to con-dole,) to con -
sad - ly to con - dole, (sad - ly to con - dole,)
- ly to con - dole, to con - dole, sad - ly
- dole, to con - dole,
35
cresc.
- dole, (sad - ly to con - dole,) (sad - ly to con - dole,) (sad -
- ly to con - dole, (sad - ly to con - dole,) (sad - ly to con -
- dole, sad - ly to con - dole,
(sad - ly to con - dole,) to con - dole,
(to con - dole,) to con - dole,
sad - - - ly to

40

- ly to con - dole,) to con - dole, *pp* sad -

- dole,) (sad - ly to con - *pp* dole,) (sa - ly to con -

(sad - ly to con - dole,) *pp* (sad - ly to

sad - ly to con - dole, *pp* (sad - ly

cresc. sad - ly to con - dole, con - dole, *pp* sad -

con - - - dole, *pp* to

45

- ly to con - dole. *mf* Be - hold,

- dole,) to con - dole. *mf* Be - hold,

con - - dole.) *mf* Be - hold, the sun

to con - dole. *mf* Be - hold, the sun

- ly to con - dole. *mf* Be - hold,

con - - - dole. *mf* Be - hold,

50

the sun hath

the sun hath shut his gold - en eye, (be - hold,__ the sun hath

__ hath shut _____ his gold - en eye,

__ hath shut _____ his gold - en eye, the (sun __ hath shut his

the sun __ hath shut _____

the sun __ hath shut _____

54

shut his gold - en eye, The day,__ the day is spent,

shut his gold - en eye,) The day,__ the day is spent, and shades,__

And shades,__

gold - en eye,) The day,__ the_ day is spent,

__ his gold - en eye, And shades,_____

__ his gold - en eye,_____ And

58
and shades, and shades fair lights sup - ply, and
and shades, and shades fair lights sup -
and shades fair lights sup - ply, and
and shades, and shades fair lights sup - ply, (and
and shades fair lights, fair lights sup -
shades, and shades fair
63
dim.
(shades fair lights sup - ply.)
-ply, fair (lights sup - ply.)
shades, (and shades fair lights sup - ply.)
shades fair lights sup - ply.) All things in
p
-ply, fair (lights sup - ply.) All things in sweet re-pose,
lights sup - - - ply. All things in sweet re-

67
p
All things in
p
All things in sweet re - pose,
all (things in sweet re - pose) Their la - bours
sweet re-pose,
(all things in sweet re - pose) Their la - bours
(all things in sweet re-pose,)
Their la - bours
- pose,
all (things in sweet re - pose)
Their la - bours
71
sweet re-pose,
(all things in sweet re-pose,)
(all things in
p
All things in sweet re - pose,
(all things in sweet re - pose,)
close,
all (things in sweet re-pose,)
(all things in sweet re-pose)
close,
all (things in sweet re - pose,)
(all things in sweet re-
close;
close;

75
mf
sweet re-pose) Their la - bours close; On -
(all things in sweet re - pose) Their la - bours close; On - ly A -
their la - bours close; On - ly A-myn-tas,
- pose) their la - bours close; On - ly A -
On - ly A-myn-tas,
On - ly A-myn-tas,
79
dim.
p
- ly A-myn-tas, A - myn - tas
- myn - tas, A - myn - tas, (A-myn - tas) wastes
A - myn - tas, (A - myn - tas) wastes his hours in
- myn - tas, A-myn - tas, (A - myn - tas)
(on - ly A - myn - tas,) A-myn - tas wastes his
A - myn - tas, (A - myn - tas) wastes his hours in

83
wastes
his hours in wail - ing, in wail - ing,
wail - ing, in wail - - ing, in
wastes his hours in wail - ing,
hours in wail - ing, in wail - ing,
wail - ing, in wail - ing, his
88
his hours in wail - ing, in wail - - -
wastes his hours in wail - ing,) in wail -
wail - ing, wastes (his hours in wail - - -
wastes (his hours in wail - ing,) (wastes his hours in wail -
wastes his hours in wail - ing,) in wail -
(hours in wail - - - -

93
- ing, in wail -
- ing, in wail - - - ing, in wail -
- ing,) in wail - - ing, (in wail -
- ing,) in wail - - ing, (wail - ing,)
- ing, in
- ing,) in wail - ing,
98
- - ling, (in wail - ing,)
- - ing, Whilst all his hopes do
- - ing,) Whilst all his hopes do faint, and life
Whilst all his hopes do faint, and
wail - ing, in wail - ing,
Whilst all his hopes do faint, and life is

103
mf
Whilst all his hopes do
faint, and life is fail - ing, do faint and
is fail - ing,
life is fail - ing, (whilst all his hopes do faint, and
mf
Whilst all his hopes do faint, and
fail - ing,
107
dim.
p
faint, and life is fail - ing, and (life
dim.
(life is fail - - - ing,)
p
Whilst (all his hopes do faint, and
dim.
p
life is fail - - - ing,) and life
dim.
p
life is fail - - - ing, and (life is
p
and life is

112

is fail - ing,) whilst all his hopes do faint, and life is

p

whilst all his hopes do

life is fail - ing,) (whilst all his hopes do faint, and life

is fail ing, (and life is

fail - ing,) and life is fail - ing, is

fail - - ing,

117

dim. *pp*

fail - - ing, and life is fail - ing.

dim. *pp*

faint, and life is fail - ing, and life is fail - ing.

dim. *pp*

is fail - ing,) is fail - - ing.

dim. *pp*

fail - ing,) and life is fail - ing.

dim. *pp*

fail - ing, and life is fail - ing.

pp

and life is fail - - - ing.

10
CONSTURE MY MEANING

GILES FARNABY

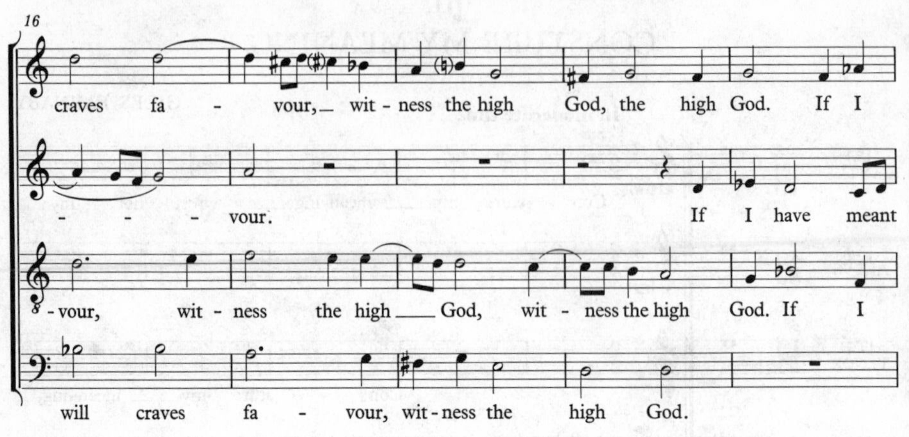
16
craves fa - vour, wit - ness the high God, the high God. If I
- - - vour. If I have meant
- vour, wit - ness the high God, wit - ness the high God. If I
will craves fa - vour, wit - ness the high God.

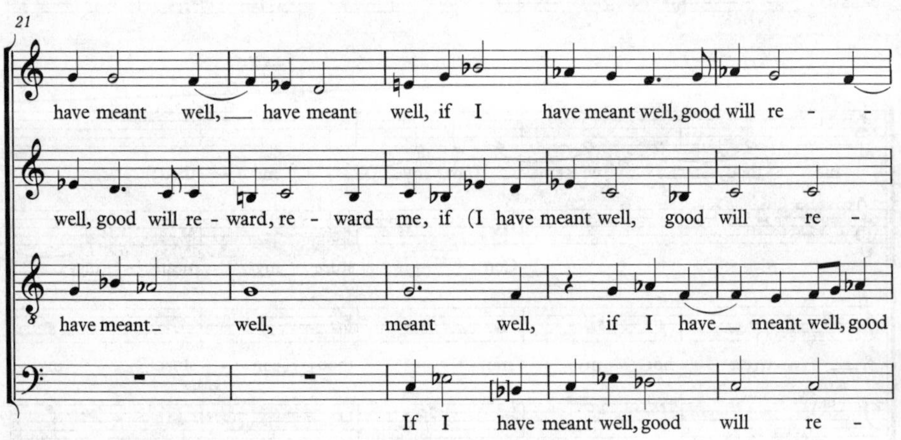
21
have meant well, have meant well, if I have meant well, good will re - -
well, good will re - ward, re - ward me, if (I have meant well, good will re -
have meant well, meant well, if I have meant well, good
If I have meant well, good will re -

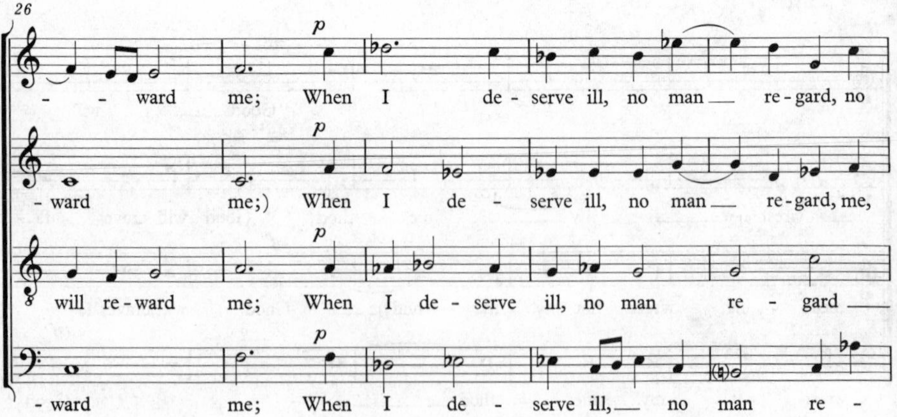
26
p
- ward me; When I de - serve ill, no man re - gard, no
- ward me;) When I de - serve ill, no man re - gard, me,
will re - ward me; When I de - serve ill, no man re - gard
- ward me; When I de - serve ill, no man re -

31
man re - gard me. What shall I say more, (what shall I say more?) speech
re - gard me. What shall I say more? speech is but blast - -
me. What shall I say more? speech is but blast - ing, speech is
- gard me. What shall I say more? speech is but blast - -
36
is but blast - ing. Still will I hope for
- ing, but blast - ing. Still will I hope for life ev - er - last - ing, still will I hope
but blast - ing. Still will I hope for life ev - er - last - ing, still will I
- ing, but blast - ing. Still will I hope for life ev - er - last - ing,
41
life ev - er - last - ing, for life ev - er - last - ing.
for life ev - er - last - ing, I hope for life ev - er - last - ing.
hope for life, still will I hope for life, hope for life ev - er - last - ing.
still will I hope for life ev - er - last - ing.
f
mp
cresc.
mf

11
COME, SIRRAH JACK, HO!

THOMAS WEELKES

14

1 | 2

f (repeat p) — *cresc. (second time)*

- day. - day. I swear that this to - bac - co Tis
clean. clean. Then those that do con - demn it, Or

f (repeat p) — *cresc. (second time)*

- day. - day. I swear that this to - bac - co Tis
clean. clean. Then those that do con - demn it, Or

f (repeat p) — *cresc. (second time)*

- day. - day. I swear that this to - bac - co Tis
clean. clean. Then those that do con - demn it, Or

17

ff (second time)

per - fect Tri - ni - da - do. By the ve - ry ve - ry Mass Ne - ver
such as not com - mend it, Ne - ver were so wise to learn Good to -

ff (second time)

per - fect Tri - ni - da - do. By the ve - ry ve - ry Mass Ne - ver
such as not com - mend it, Ne - ver were so wise to learn Good to -

ff (second time)

per - fect Tri - ni - da - do. By the ve - ry Mass
such as not com - mend it, Ne - ver were so wise;

20

ne - ver ne - ver was Bet - ter gear than is here. By the rood, for the blood, It is
- bac - co to dis - cern; Let them go pluck a crow, and not know as I do The

ne - ver ne - ver was Bet - ter gear than is here. By the rood, for the blood, It is
- bac - co to dis - cern; Let them go pluck a crow, and not know as I do The

Ne - ver was Bet - ter gear than is here.
Let them go pluck a crow, and not know,

23

1 | 2

p

ve - ry ve - ry good, tis ve - ry good. I good.
sweet of Tri - ni - da - do, Tri - ni - da - do. Then - da - do.

p

ve - ry ve - ry good, tis ve - ry good. I good.
sweet of Tri - ni - da - do, Tri - ni - da - do. Then - da - do.

p

For the blood, tis ve - ry good. I good.
know The sweet of Tri - ni - da - do. Then - da - do.

12
DAINTY FINE BIRD

ORLANDO GIBBONS

8
and my for - - - tunes are, a - las, how like thine
like thine and my for - tunes are, a - las.
like thine and my for - - - tunes are, a - las, how like thine
and my for - tunes are, a - las, how like thine
and my for - - - tunes are, a - las, how like thine
12
and my for - tunes are. mf Both
mf Both pris - oners be; and
and my for - tunes are. mf Both pris - on - ers be; and both sing - -
and my for - tunes are. mf Both pris - oners be, both
and my for - tunes are. mf Both
16
pris - oners be; and both sing - ing, thus, and
both sing - - - ing, thus, both sing - ing, thus
- ing, thus, and both
(pris - - oners be;) and
pris - oners be;

20
both sing - ing, thus, and ___ both sing - ing, thus Strive ___
Strive ___ to please her, to
sing - ing, thus, and ___ (both sing - ing, thus.)
both sing - ing, thus, (and ___ both sing - ing, thus) Strive to
and both sing - ing, thus Strive ___ to please
24
___ to please her that hath im - pris - oned us.
please her ___ that ___ hath im - pris - oned us.
f
On-ly thus we dif - fer, thou and
f
please ___ her that hath im-pris-on-ed us. On - ly thus we
f
her that hath im - pris - oned us, im - pris - oned us. On-ly thus we
28
f
On-ly thus we dif - fer, thou and I, and I, Thou liv'st
f
On-ly thus we dif - fer, thou and I, we ___ dif - fer,
I, and I,
dif - fer, on - ly thus we ___ dif - fer, ___
dif-fer, thou and I, on - ly thus we dif - fer, thou and

32
sing - ing, but I sing and die,
dim. al fine
Thou liv'st sing - ing, but I sing and die, I
dim. al fine
Thou liv'st sing - ing, but
dim. al fine
thou and I, Thou liv'st sing - ing, but I sing and
dim. al fine
I, Thou liv'st sing - - -
36
dim. al fine
thou liv'st sing - ing, but I sing and
sing and die, but I sing and die,
I sing and die, thou (liv'st sing - ing, but
die, I sing and die, thou (liv'st
- - ing, but I
40
pp [𝄐]
die, I sing and die, and die.
pp [𝄐]
I sing and die.
pp [𝄐]
I sing and die,) I sing and die.
pp [𝄐]
sing - ing, but I sing and die.)
pp 𝄐
sing and die.

13
DRAW ON, SWEET NIGHT

JOHN WILBYE

9
best friend un -
on, sweet Night,)
on, sweet Night, (draw on, sweet
(draw on, sweet Night, best friend un - to those
p
Draw on, sweet Night, best friend un - to those
14
- to those cares
mp
best friend un - to those cares That
Night,) best friend un - to those
cares,) draw on, sweet Night, best friend
cares, draw on,(sweet Night, best friend un -
p
Draw on,sweet Night, best friend un -

19
mp
That do a - rise from pain - ful me - lan -
do a - rise from pain - ful me - lan - cho - ly, from
mp
cares That do a - rise, a -
un - to those cares)
- to those cares,) un - to those cares
mp
- to those cares That
24
- cho - ly, (a - rise from pain - ful
pain - ful me - lan - cho - ly, from
- rise from pain - ful
mp
That do a - rise from pain - ful me -
mp
That do a - rise from pain - ful me - lan -
do a - rise from pain - ful me - lan -

29
me - lan - cho - ly.
mf
(pain - ful me - lan - cho - ly.) My life so ill through
mf
me - lan - cho - ly. My life so ill through
- lan - cho - ly.
mf
- cho - ly. My life so ill through
- cho - ly.
34
mf
My life so ill through
want of com - fort fares,
want of com - fort fares, my life so (ill through
mf
My life so ill through
want of com - fort fares,
mf
My life so ill through

38
want of com - fort fares,
That un - to thee, to
That un - to thee, (that un - to
want of com - fort fares,)
want of com - fort fares, That un - to thee, that (un - to
That un - to thee, (that un - to
want of com - fort fares,
42
thee I con - se - crate it whol - ly,
thee) I con - se - crate it whol - ly, that
That un - to thee I con - se - crate it whol - ly, that (un - to
thee) I con - se-crate it whol - ly,
thee) I con - se - crate it whol-ly, that (un - to
I con - se - crate it whol - ly, that

46
that (un - to thee I con - se-crate it
un - to thee, to thee I con - se - crate
thee I con - se - crate it whol - ly, that un - to thee I
that un - to thee, to thee I
thee I con - se - crate it whol - ly, it
un - to thee, to thee, I con - se -
50
whol - ly. Sweet Night, draw on,
it whol - ly. Sweet
con - se - crate it whol - ly. Sweet Night, draw on,
con - se - crate it whol - ly.
whol - ly. Sweet Night, draw on,
- crate it whol - ly.

54
(sweet Night, draw on,) O sweet Night, draw on,
Night, draw on,
(sweet Night, draw on, sweet Night, draw
p
Sweet Night, draw on, (sweet Night, draw
(sweet Night, draw

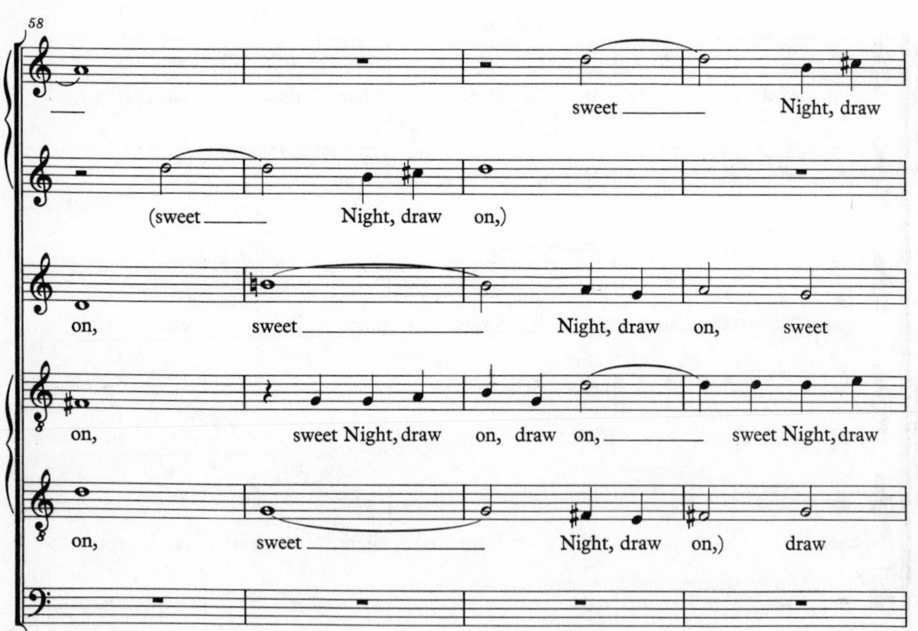
58
sweet Night, draw
(sweet Night, draw on,)
on, sweet Night, draw on, sweet
on, sweet Night, draw on, draw on, sweet Night, draw
on, sweet Night, draw on,) draw

62

on,——— (sweet ——— night, draw

(sweet night, draw on,)

night, draw on,——— (sweet ——— night, draw

on, (sweet night, draw on, (sweet ——— night, draw

on, sweet night,———

p

Sweet night, draw on,

67

on!)———

(sweet ——— night, draw on!)

on!)———

on,)——— sweet ——— night, draw on! *mf* My griefs when

——— sweet ——— night, draw on! *mf* My griefs when

draw on!——— *mf* My

72
mf
My griefs when they
mf
My griefs when they
mf
My griefs when
they be told
they be told
griefs when they be told
77
be told
To shades and dark - ness,
be told
they be told
To shades and dark - ness,
To shades and dark - ness,

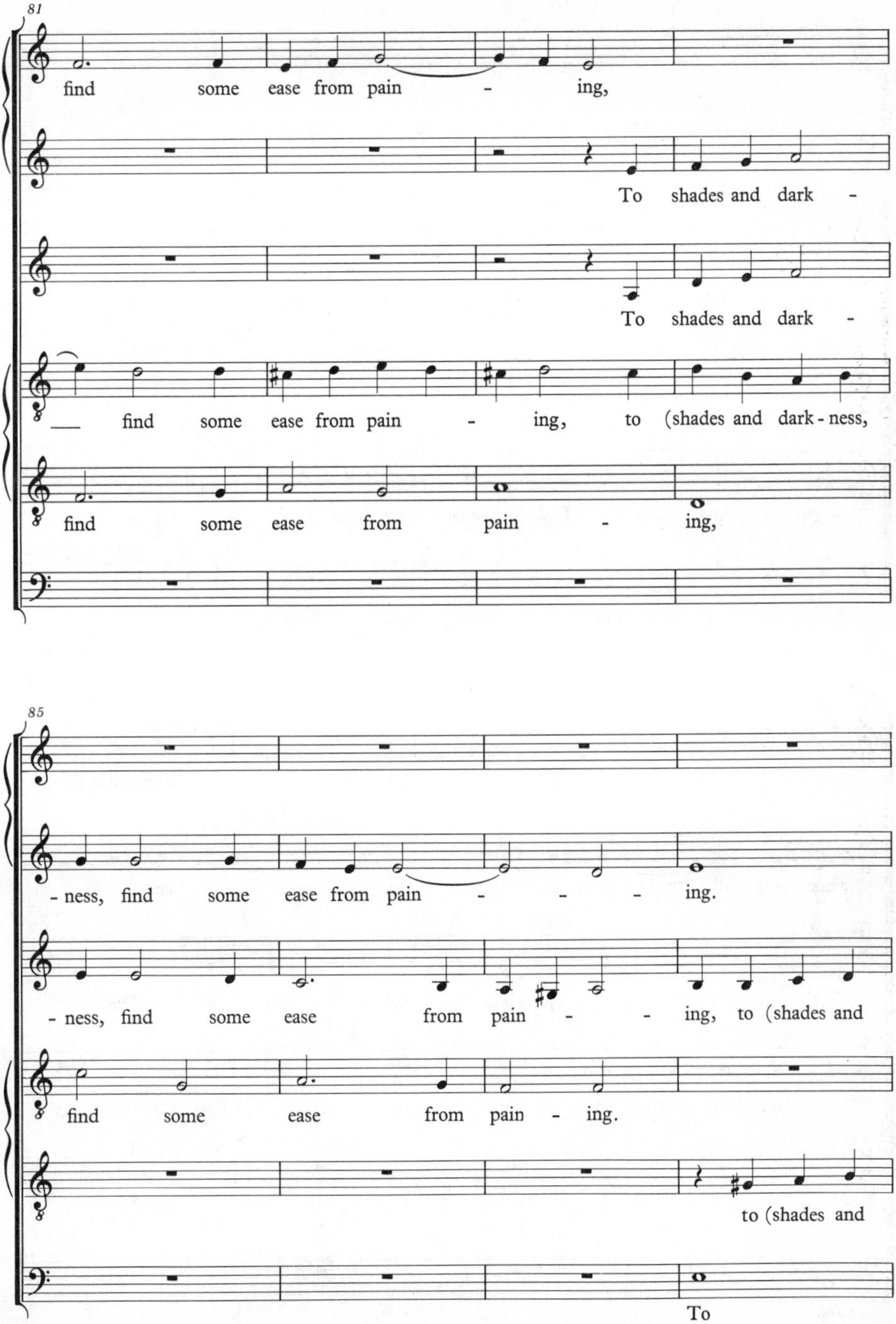

85

- ness, find some ease from pain - - - ing.

- ness, find some ease from pain - - ing, to (shades and

find some ease from pain - ing.

to (shades and

To

89
mp
And
dark - ness, find some ease from pain - - -
dark - ness, find some ease from) pain - - -
shades and dark - ness, find some ease from pain - -
93
mp
And while thou
while thou all in si - lence dost en - -
mp
- ing.) And while thou all in si - lence
mp
And while thou all in si - lence dost en -
- ing.
- ing.

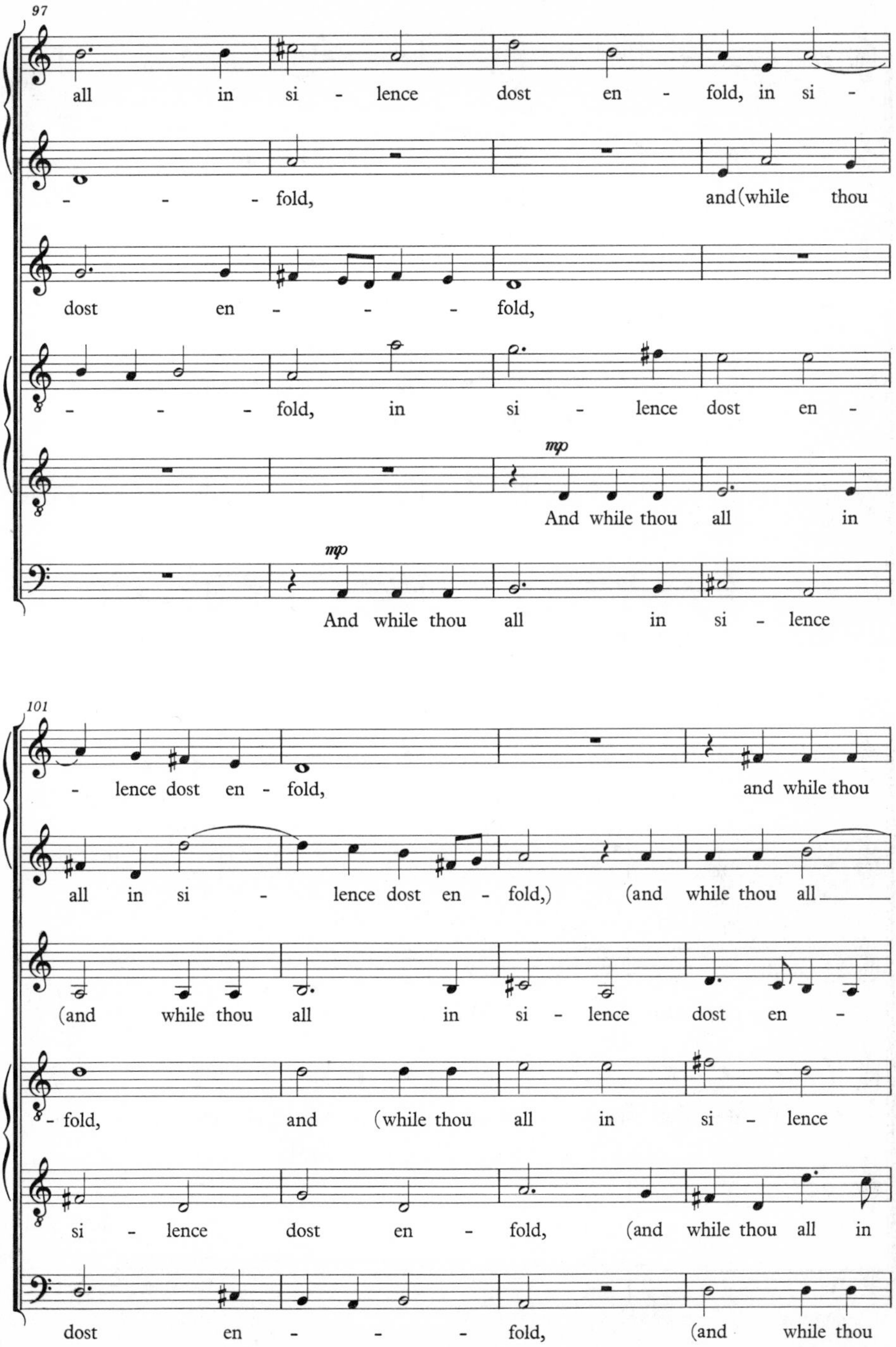

101
- lence dost en - fold, and while thou
all in si - lence dost en - fold,) (and while thou all
(and while thou all in si - lence dost en -
- fold, and (while thou all in si - lence
si - lence dost en - fold, (and while thou all in
dost en - - - fold, (and while thou

105
all in si - lence dost en - - - - -
in si - lence dost en - - - -
- fold,)
dost en - fold,) and(while thou all in si - lence dost en -
si - lence dost en - -
all in si - lence dost en - - -
109
f
- fold, I then shall have best time for my com - plain -
- fold,)
f
I then shall have best time for my com - plain - -
f
- fold,) I then shall have best time for my com - plain - ing, (for
f
- fold,) for
- fold,)

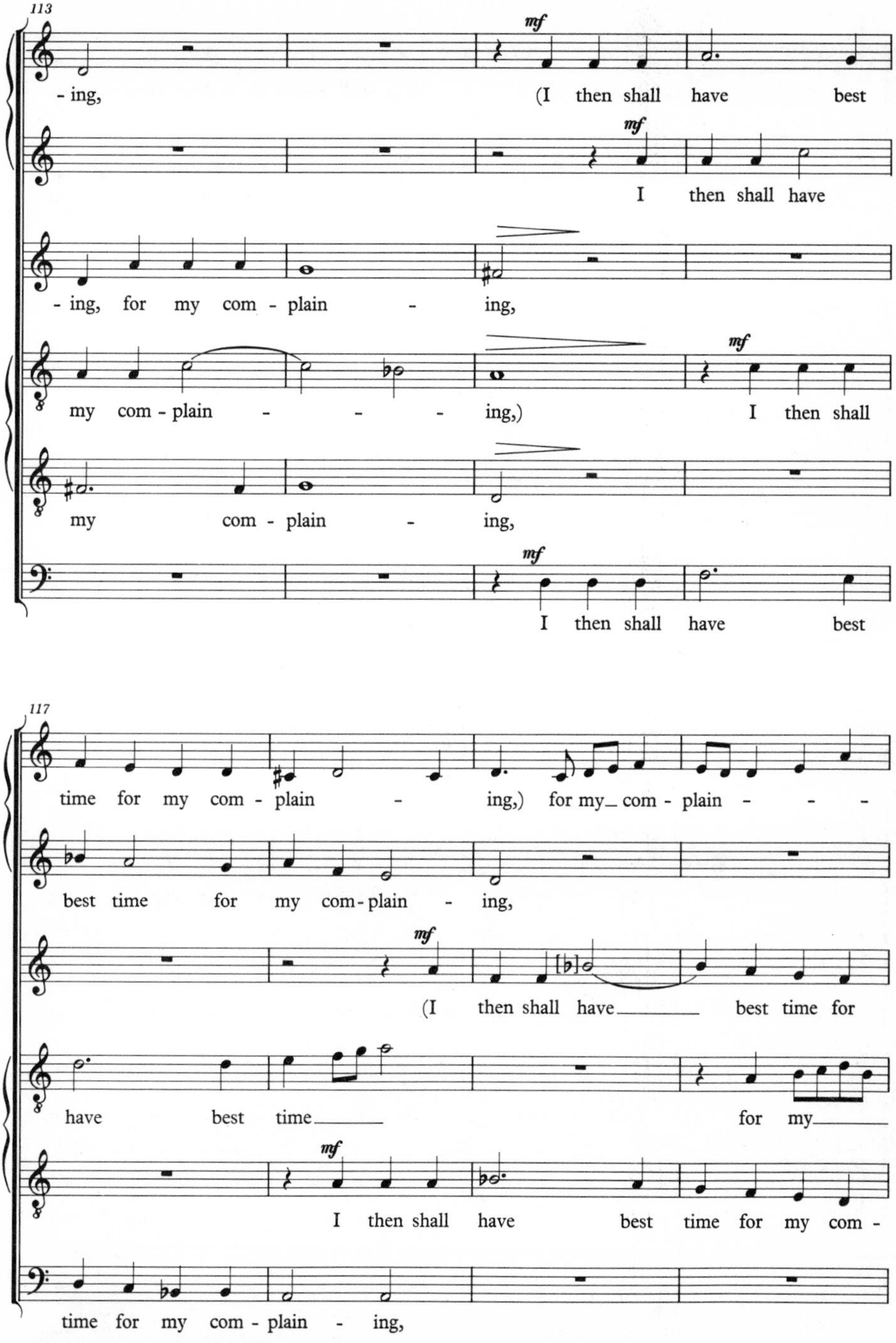
113
mf
- ing, (I then shall have best
mf
I then shall have
- ing, for my com - plain - ing,
mf
my com - plain - - - ing,) I then shall
my com - plain - ing,
mf
I then shall have best
117
time for my com - plain - ing,) for my_ com - plain - - -
best time for my com - plain - ing,
mf
(I then shall have_ best time for
have best time_ for my_
mf
I then shall have best time for my com -
time for my com - plain - ing,

121

p

- ing, ——— I then shall have best time for

p

(I then shall have best time for my com -

p

my com - plain - ing,) for

com - plain - ing,

p dim.

- plain - ing, (I then shall have best

p dim.

(I then shall have best time for) my com -

125

dim. pp[𝄐]

my ——— com - plain - - - ing.

dim. pp[𝄐]

- plain - ing,) I then shall have ——— best time for my com-plain - ing.

dim. pp[𝄐]

my com - plain - ing, shall have best time for — my com-plain - ing.

p dim. pp[𝄐]

I then (shall have ——— best time for my com-plain) - ing.

pp[𝄐]

time for my com - plain - ing.

pp[𝄐]

- plain - - - - ing.

14
FAIR NYMPHS, I HEARD ONE TELLING

JOHN FARMER

8
To beau - ti -
Di - a - na's train are hunt - ing in this chase. To beau - ti -
- na's train are hunt - ing in this chase. To beau - ti -
- a - na's train are hunt - ing in this chase. To
12
- fy the place, to(beau - ti - fy
To beau - ti - fy the place, the place, to (beau - ti -
- fy the place
- fy the place,
beau - ti - fy the place, the

16
the
place)
The fawns are run - ning, are
- fy the place,) the place The fawns are run-ning, are
The fawns are run-ning, are run - ning, the
the place The
place The fawns are
The fawns are run-ning, are run - ning, (are
20
run - ning, The
run - ning, The shep - herds their pipes tun - ing,
(fawns are run - ning,) The shep - herds their pipes
fawns are run - ning, The shep - herds
run - ning, The shep - herds their pipes
run - ning,) The

22
shep - herds their pipes tun - ing, (the
(the shep - herds their pipes tun - ing)
tun - ing, the (shep - herds
their pipes tun - ing, (the shep - herds their pipes
tun - - ing, their pipes tun - ing,
shep - herds their pipes tun - - ing, their
24
shep-herds their pipes tun - ing) To show their cun - - -
To show their cun - - -
their pipes tun - ing.)
tun - ing) To show their cun - ning, (their
tun - ing.
(pipes tun - ing.)

27
mp
- - - ning. The lambs a - maz - ed
- - - ning. The lambs a - maz - - -
The lambs a - maz - - - ed
cun - - ning.) The lambs a - maz - ed
The lambs a - maz - ed
The lambs a - maz - ed
31
leave off their graz - ing, And
- ed leave off their graz - ing, And blind
leave off their graz - ing, And blind
leave off their graz - ing, And
leave off their graz - ing, And
leave off their graz - ing, And blind their

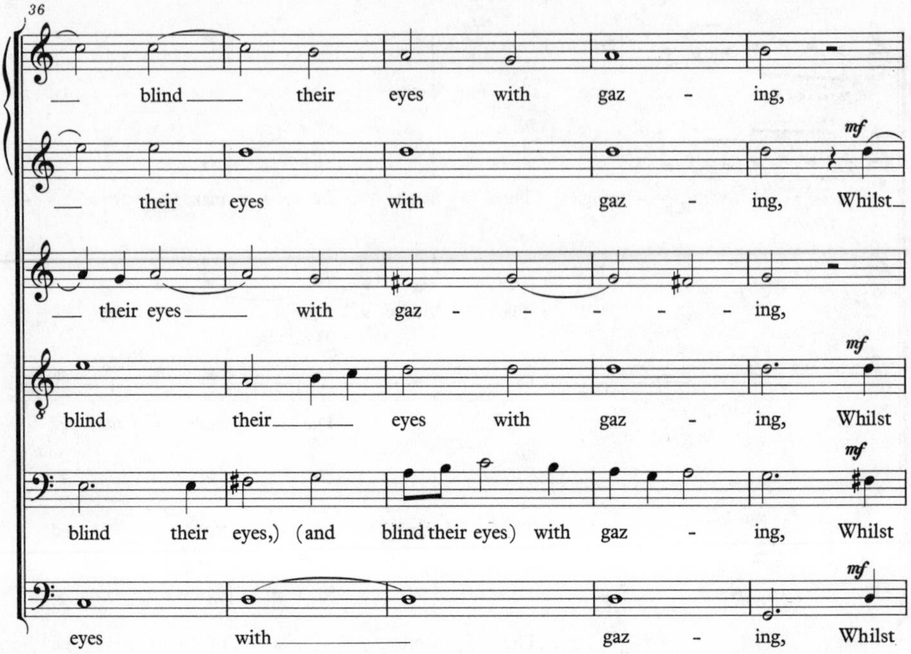

36
blind their eyes with gaz - ing,
their eyes with gaz - ing, Whilst
their eyes with gaz - - - - ing,
blind their eyes with gaz - ing, Whilst
blind their eyes,) (and blind their eyes) with gaz - ing, Whilst
eyes with gaz - ing, Whilst 
mf
41
the earth's god-dess doth draw near your pla - ces, At -
Whilst the earth's god - dess doth draw near your
the earth's god - dess doth draw near your pla - ces, pla -
the earth's god - dess doth draw near, doth draw near your pla -
the earth's god - dess, god-dess doth draw near your pla - - -
mf

45

mf At - tend - ed by the Mus - es,

- tend - ed by the Mus - es, (at - tend - ed by the

pla - ces, At - tend - ed by the Muse, (at - tend - ed by the Muse,) at -

- ces, At - tend - ed by the Muse, (at - tend - ed by the Muse,)(at -

- ces, At - tend - ed by the Mus - es, (at - tend -

- ces, At - tend - ed by the Mus - - es, (at - tend -

49

(at - tend - ed by the Mus - es) and the Gra -

Mus - es) and the ______ Gra -

- tend - ed by the Mus - es and ___ the Gra - ces, the Gra -

- tend - ed by the Muse,) at-tend - ed by the Mus - es and the ______

- ed by the Mus - es) and the Gra - ces, and Gra -

- ed by the Mus - es) and the ______ Gra -

53
- ces.
- ces, the Gra - ces. Then
- ces. Then sang the shep - herds and
Gra - ces. Then sang the shep - herds and nymphs, the shep - herds and
- ces. Then sang the shep-herds and nymphs, the shep - herds and nymphs,
- ces, the Gra - ces. Then sang the shep - herds, (then sang the shep - herds
57
Then sang the shep - herds and nymphs, the (shep -
sang the shep - herds and nymphs,
nymphs, and nymphs, then (sang the shep - herds and
nymphs, then sang the shep - herds,
then sang the shep-herds, (then sang the shep - herds,)
and nymphs,)
(then sang the

60
- herds and nymphs,) and nymphs of Di - a - -
(then sang the shep - herds and nymphs) of Di - a - -
nymphs,) the shep - herds and nymphs of Di - a - -
then (sang the shep - herds) and nymphs of Di - a - -
(then sang the shep-herds) and nymphs of Di - a - -
shep - herds and nymphs) of Di - a - -
63
- na: Long live fair O - ri - a -
- na: Long live fair O - ri - a - na,
- na: Long live fair O - ri - a - na, (long live fair O - ri - a -
- na: Long live fair O - ri - a - na, O-ri-a -
- na: Long live fair O - ri - a -
- na:

67

– na, long live, long live fair O - ri - a - na,

(long live fair O - ri - a - na,)

– na,) long live fair O - ri - a - na, (long live fair O - ri - a -

– na, long live fair O - ri - a - na, long (live fair

– na, (long live fair O - ri - a - -

Long live fair O - ri - a - na,

71

(long live fair O - ri - a - na.)

long live fair O - ri - a - - na.

– na,) O - ri - a - na, long live fair O - ri - a - na.

O - ri - a - na,) (long live fair O - ri - a - na.)

– na, fair O - ri - a - na, long___ live fair O - ri - a - na.

(long live fair O - ri - a - - na.)

15
FLORA GAVE ME FAIREST FLOWERS

JOHN WILBYE

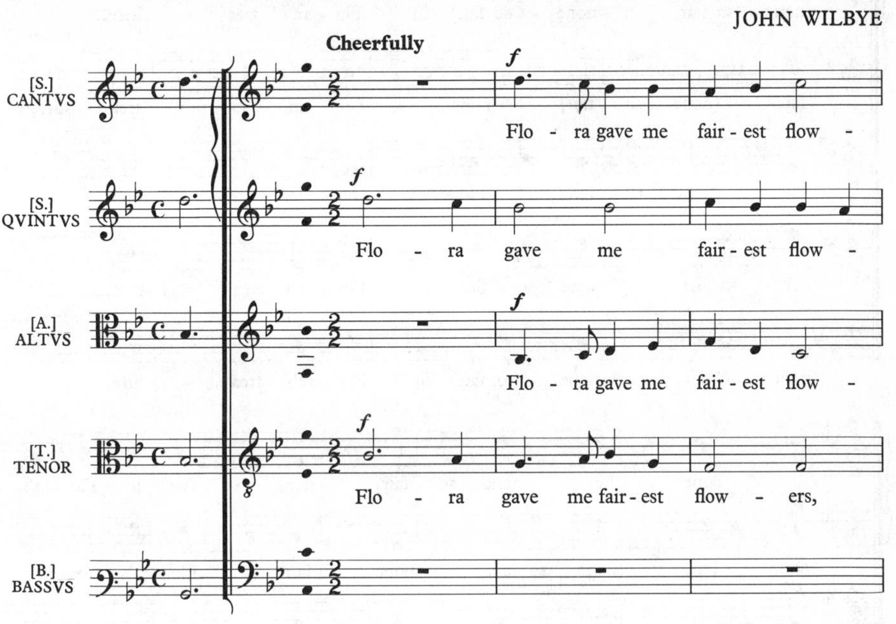

8
(none so fair, none - so fair) in Flo - ra's trea - sure,
fair, (none so fair, none so fair) in Flo - ra's trea - sure,
fair, (none so fair) in Flo - ra's trea - sure,
(none so fair, none so fair) in Flo - ra's trea - sure,
(none so fair, none so fair) in Flo - ra's trea - sure,
12
p
none so fair, (none so fair, none so fair) in Flo - ra's
none so fair, (none so fair, none so fair) in Flo - ra's trea -
none so fair, (none so fair) in Flo - ra's trea -
none so fair, (none so fair) in Flo - ra's trea -
none so fair, (none so fair, none so fair) in Flo - ra's trea -
16
mf
trea - sure. These I placed on Phyl - lis' bow - ers,
- sure. These I placed on Phyl - lis' bow - ers,
- sure. These
- sure. These I placed on Phyl - lis' bow - ers, (these
- sure. These

20

f She was pleased, (she was pleased, she was pleased,) and

f She was pleased, (she was pleased, she was pleased,) and

___ I placed on Phyl - lis' bow - ers, *f* She was pleased, and

___ I placed on Phyl - lis' bow - ers,)

___ I placed on Phyl - lis' bow - ers,

24

she my plea - sure, she was pleased, (she was pleased,

she my plea - sure, she was pleased, (she was pleased,

she my plea - sure, she was pleased, (she was

f She was pleased, (she was pleased,) she was___

f She was pleased, she was

28

she was pleased,) and she my plea - sure. *mp* Smil - ing mea-dows

she was pleased,) and she my plea - sure. *mp* Smil - ing mea - dows

pleased,) and she my plea - sure.

___ pleased, and she my plea - sure.

pleased, and she my plea - sure.

32
seem to say: Come ye wan-tons, here to play, smil-ing
seem to say: Come ye wan-tons, here to play,
mp
Smil-ing mea-dows seem to say: Come ye wan-tons, here to
mp
Smil-ing mea-dows seem to say: Come ye wan-tons,
mp
Smil-ing mea-dows seem to
36
cresc.
mea-dows seem to say: come ye wan-tons, here to play, come
cresc.
smil-ing mea-dows seem to say: come ye wan-tons,
cresc.
play, smil-ing mea-dows seem to say: come ye wan-tons,
cresc.
here to play, (come ye wan-tons, here to play,) come
cresc.
say: Come ye wan-tons, here to play, come ye wan-tons,
40
f
here to play, come ye wan-tons, here to play, to play, come ye
f
here to play, come ye wan-tons, here to
f
here to play, come ye wan-tons, here to play, to
f
here to play, come ye wan-tons,
f
here to play, come ye wan-tons, here to play,

43
wan - tons, here to play, (come ye wan - tons, here to play, come ye
play, to play, (come ye wan - tons, here to play, to play,)
play, (come ye wan - tons, here to play,) come here to play,
here to play, to play, come ye wan - tons, here to play,
come ye wan - tons, here to play, come here to play,
46
wan - tons, here to play,) to play, come ye wan - tons, here to
come ye wan - tons, here to play, to play, come ye
come ye wan - tons, here to play, to play, (come ye wan - tons,
come ye wan - tons, here to play, to
come ye wan - tons, here to play, (come ye wan - tons,
49
play, to play, come, come ye wan - tons, here to play.
wan - tons, here, come, come ye wan - tons, here to play.
here to play,) come, come ye wan - tons, here to play.
play, come ye wan - tons, come ye wan - tons, here to play.
here to play,) come, come ye wan - tons, here to play.

16
FAIR PHYLLIS I SAW

10
gone,
But af-ter her lov -
gone,
But af-ter her lov - er,
knew not, they knew not whi-ther she was gone,
But af-ter her
shep - herds knew not whi-ther she was gone,
But af-ter
13
- er, her lov - er, but af - ter her lov - er
A - myn-tas
her lov - er, but af - ter her lov - er
A - myn - tas
lov - er, her lov - er,
but af - ter her lov-er A - myn-tas
her lov - er,
but af - ter her lov-er A - myn-tas
17
hied.
p
Up and down he wan - dered,
hied.
p
Up and down,
up and down he
p
hied. Up and down he wan - dered, up and down,
up and
hied.
p
Up and down he wan - dered, he

20
up (and down he wan-dered,) up (and down he wan-dered,)
wan - dered, up and down he wan - dered, up and down he
down he wan - dered, up (and down he wan - dered,) up (and
wan - - dered, up and
24
cresc.
up and down he wan - dered, up and down he wan - - -
cresc.
wan - dered, up and down he wan - dered, he wan -
cresc.
down he wan - dered,) up and down he wan-dered, up (and down he wan -
cresc.
down he wan - - -
27
f
mf
- dered whilst she was miss - ing; When he found
f
mf
- dered whilst she was miss - ing; When he found
f
mf
- dered) whilst she was miss - ing; When he found
f
mf
- dered whilst she was miss - ing; When he found

31
[← 𝅗𝅥 = 𝅗𝅥. →]
[← 𝅗𝅥. = 𝅗𝅥 →]
[← 𝅗𝅥 = 𝅗𝅥. →]
her, O, then they
her, O, then they fell a - kiss-ing, O, then they
her, O, then they fell a - kiss-ing, O, (then they
her, O, then they fell a - kiss-ing, O, then they
36
[← 𝅗𝅥. = 𝅗𝅥 →]
fell a - kiss - ing, a - kiss - ing, O, then they fell a -
fell a - kiss - ing, a - kiss - ing, O, (then they fell a -
fell a - kiss - ing,) a - kiss - ing, O, then they fell a -
fell a - kiss - ing, a - kiss - ing, O, then they fell a -
41
- kiss - ing, up and down he wan-dered,
- kiss - ing,) up and down, up and down he
- kiss-ing, up and down he wan - dered, up and down, up and
- kiss - ing, up and down he wan - dered, he

44
up (and down he wan - dered,) up (and
wan - dered, up and down he wan - dered, up
down he wan - dered, up (and down he wan - dered,)
wan - - dered, up
47
cresc.
down he wan - dered,) up (and down he wan - dered,) up and down
cresc.
and down he wan - dered, up and down he wan - - -
cresc.
up (and down he wan - dered,) up and down he wan-dered,
cresc.
and down he
50
f
he wan - - dered whilst she was
f
- dered, he wan - dered whilst she was
f
up (and down he wan - dered) whilst she was miss - ing;
f
wan - - - dered whilst she was miss - ing;

53
miss - ing; When he found her,
miss - ing; When he found her, O, then they
When he found her, O, then they
When he found her, O, then they
57
O, then they fell a -
fell a - kiss - ing, O, then they fell a -
fell a - kiss - ing, O, (then they fell a -
fell a - kiss - ing, O, then they fell a -
61
- kiss - ing, a - kiss - ing, O, then they fell a - kiss - ing.
- kiss - ing, a - kiss - ing, O, then they fell a - kiss - ing.
- kiss - ing,) a - kiss - ing, O, then they fell a - kiss - ing.
- kiss - ing, a - kiss - ing, O, then they fell a - kiss - ing.

17
FYER, FYER!

THOMAS MORLEY

Forcefully

8
p
Fa la la la la la la la la la, fa la la la la la la.
ff
Fy-er, fy -
O, I burn
p
Fa la la la la la la___ la la la, fa la la la la la.
ff
Fy-er, fy -
O, I burn
la, fa la la la la la la, fa la la la la la.
la la la la la, fa___ la la la la la la la, fa la la la la la.
la la la la la la la la la la la la, fa la la la la la.
13
mf
- er! (fy-er, fy - er!) fy-er, fy - er! (fy-er, fy - er!) my
me! O, I burn me! O, I burn me! O, I burn me! a -
mf
- er! (fy-er, fy - er!) fy-er, fy - er! (fy-er, fy - er!) my
me! O, I burn me! O, I burn me! O, I burn me! a -
ff
mf
Fy-er, fy - er! (fy-er, fy - er!) fy-er, fy - er! my heart!
O, I burn me! O, I burn me! O, I burn me! a - las!
ff
mf
Fy-er, fy - er! (fy-er, fy - er!) fy-er, fy - er! my heart!(my
O, I burn me! O, I burn me! O, I burn me! a - las! a -
ff
mf
Fy-er, fy - er! (fy-er, fy - er!) fy-er! fy - er! my heart!
O, I burn me! O, I burn me! O, I burn me! a - las!

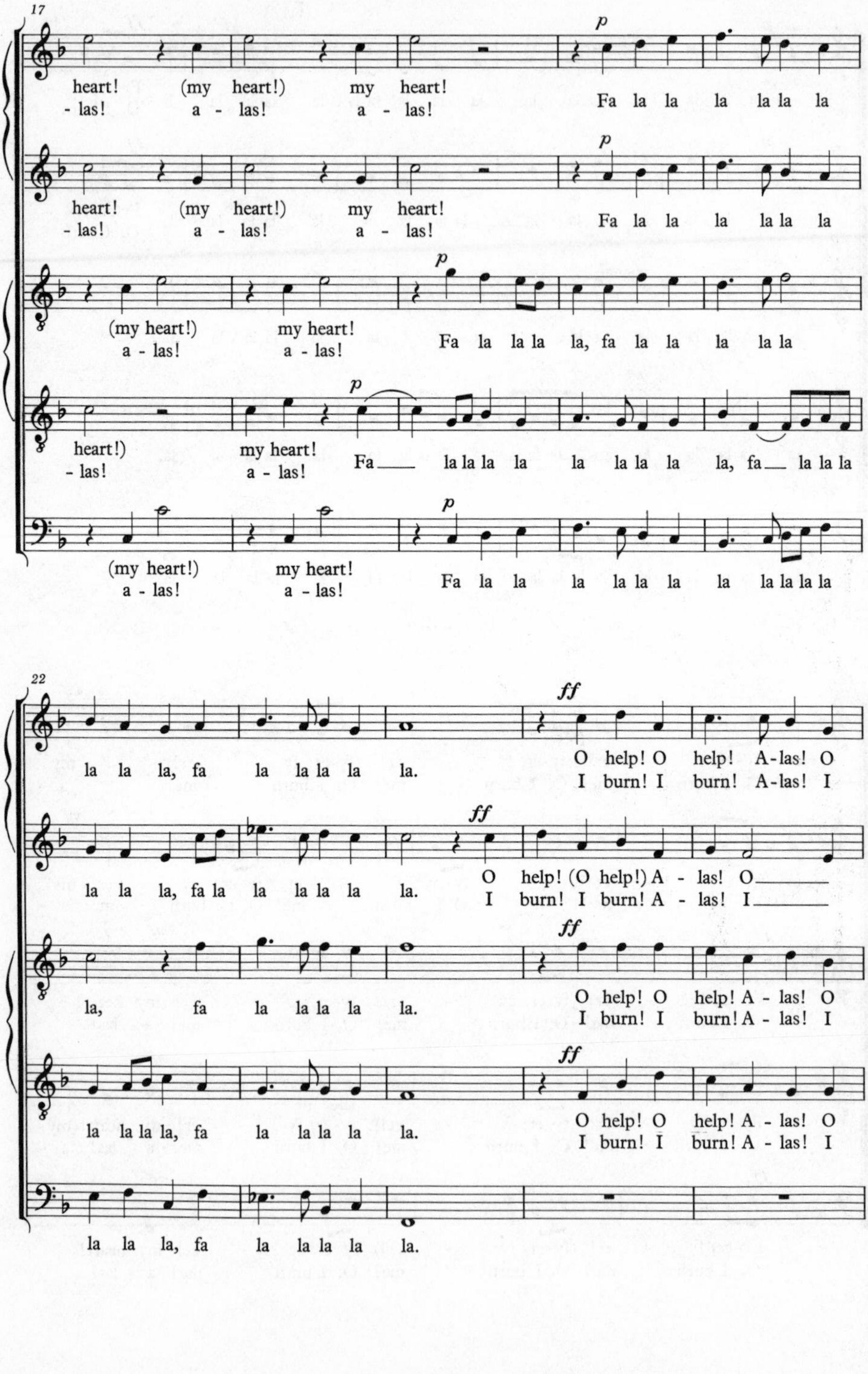

17

heart! (my heart!) my heart! Fa la la la la la la
-las! a - las! a - las!

heart! (my heart!) my heart! Fa la la la la la la
-las! a - las! a - las!

(my heart!) my heart! Fa la la la la, fa la la la la la
a - las! a - las!

heart!) my heart! Fa___ la la la la la la la la la, fa___ la la la
-las! a - las!

(my heart!) my heart! Fa la la la la la la la la la la la
a - las! a - las!

27

help! Ay me! Ay me!
burn! Ay me! Ay me!

help! Ay me! Ay me! I
burn! Ay me! Ay me! will

help! Ay me! Ay me! I
burn! Ay me! Ay me! will

help! Ay me! Ay me! I
burn! Ay me! Ay me! will

Ay me! Ay me! I
Ay me! Ay me! will

32

I sit and cry me, And call for
will none come quench me? O cast, cast

sit and cry me,
none come quench me?

sit and cry me, And call for help, a-las, but
none come quench me? O cast, cast wa-ter on, a-

sit and cry me, And call for help, a-las, but
none come quench me? O cast, cast wa-ter on, a-

sit and cry me,
none come quench me?

36

help, a-las, but none comes nigh me! (and call for help, a - las,
wa - ter on, a - las, and drench me, O cast, cast wa - ter on,

And call for
O cast, cast

none comes nigh me! (and call for help, a - las,
-las, and drench me, O cast, cast wa - ter on,

none comes nigh me! (and
-las, and drench me, O

And call for help, a - las, but none comes
O cast, cast wa - ter on, a - las, and

40

but none comes nigh me!)
a - las, and drench me.

help, a-las, but none comes nigh me!
wa - ter on, a - las, and drench me.

but none comes nigh me!) but none comes nigh me!
a – las and drench me, a - las, and drench me. Fa

call for help, a - las, a - las, but none comes nigh me!)
cast, cast wa - ter on, a - las, a - las, and drench me. Fa la la la

nigh me! but (none comes nigh me!)
drench me, a - las, and drench me. Fa la la la

44
f
Fa la la la la la la, fa la la la la la la,
f
Fa la la la la la la la la, fa la
la la la la la la la la, fa la la, fa la la la la la la la la la la la
la la la la la, fa la la la la la la la la la la la,
la la la la la la, fa la la la
48
dim.
fa la la la la la la la la la la la la la la
dim.
la la la la la la la la la la la la la la, fa la la la, fa
dim.
la, fa la la la, fa la la la la la la, fa la la
dim.
fa la la la la la la la la la la la, fa la, fa la la la
dim.
la la la, fa la la la la la la la la,
52
p
f
la la la, fa la la la la la la la, fa la la la la. O I
p
la la la la la, fa la la la la la la, fa la la la.
p
la la la la la, fa la la la la la la.
p
la la la la la la, fa la la la la la la la.
p
fa la la la la, fa la la la.

57

help! O help! A - las! O help! Ay me!
burn! I burn! A - las! I burn! Ay me!

O help! O help! A-las! O help! Ay me!
I burn! I burn! A-las! I burn! Ay me!

O help! O help! A - las! O help! Ay me!
I burn! I burn! A - las! I burn! Ay me!

O help! O help! A - las! O help! Ay me!
I burn! I burn! A - las! I burn! Ay me!

Ay me!
Ay me!

62

Ay me! I sit and cry me,
Ay me! will none come quench me?

Ay me! I sit and cry me,
Ay me! will none come quench me?

Ay me! I sit and cry me, And call for
Ay me! will none come quench me? O cast, cast

Ay me! I sit and cry me, And call for
Ay me! will none come quench me? O cast, cast

Ay me! I sit and cry me,
Ay me! will none come quench me?

67

And
O

And call for help, a - las, but none comes nigh me! (and call for
O cast, cast wa - ter on, a - las, and drench me, O cast, cast

help, a - las, but none comes nigh me! (and call
wa - ter on, a - las, and drench me, O cast,

help, a - las, but none comes nigh me!
wa - ter on, a - las, and drench me,

And call for help, a -
O cast, cast wa - ter

71

call for help, a - las, but none comes nigh
cast, cast wa - ter on, a - las, and drench

help, a - las, but none comes nigh
wa - ter on, a - las, and drench

for help, a - las, but none comes nigh me!) but none comes nigh
cast wa - ter on, a - las, and drench me, a - las, and drench

(and call for help, a - las, a - las, but none comes nigh me!)
O cast, cast wa - ter on, a - las, a - las, and drench me.

- las, but none comes nigh me! but (none comes nigh
on, a - las, and drench me, a - las, and drench

75
me!
me. Fa la la la la la la la la, fa la
me!)
me. Fa la la la la la la la, fa la la la la la la,
me!
me. Fa la la la la la la la la, fa la la, fa la la la la la la la la la la
Fa la la la la la la la la, fa la la la la la la la la la la la la,
me!)
me. Fa la la la la la la la la la, fa la la la
80
la la la la la la la la la la la la la, fa la la la, fa la la la la
fa la la la la la la, fa la la la la la la la la la la la la la, fa
la, fa la la la la, fa la la la la la la, fa la la la la la la
fa la la la la la la la la la la, fa la la la la la la, fa la la
la la la, fa la la la la la la la la,
85
la, fa la la la la la la, fa la la la.
la la la la la la la, fa la la la la la la la la la la la la.
la, fa la la la la la la la la la la la la.
la la, fa la la la la la, fa la la la la la.
fa la la la la, fa la la la.

18
HARD BY A CRYSTAL FOUNTAIN

THOMAS MORLEY

8
(hard by a crys - tal fount - - - - -
(hard by a crys - tal fount - - - - -
(hard by a crys - tal fount - - - - -
crys - - - tal fount - - - - -
12
mp
- ain) O - ri - a - na the bright, (O - ri -
mp
- - - - ain O - ri - a - na the bright,
mp
- - - ain) O - ri - a - na the
mp
- - - ain O - ri - a - na the bright

16
p
pp
- a - na the bright) lay down a - sleep - ing, lay
(O - ri - a - na the bright lay
bright lay down a - sleep - - ing, lay
lay down a - - - sleep - ing, (lay
20
f
(down a - - - sleep - ing.) The
down a - sleep - - - - - ing. The
(down a - sleep - - - - - ing.) The
down a - sleep - - - - - ing.)
The
The birds they fine - ly

24
birds they fine - ly chirp - ed, (the birds they fine - ly chirp - ed,)
birds they fine - ly chirp - ed, (the
birds they fine - ly chirp - ed, (the birds they fine - ly chirp - ed,) the
f
The birds they fine - ly chirp - ed,
birds they fine - ly chirp - ed, (the
chirp - ed, (the birds they fine - ly chirp - ed,) (the birds they fine - ly
28
the birds they fine - ly chirp - ed, (the
birds they fine - ly chirp - ed,) the birds they fine - ly chirp - ed,) (the
birds they fine - ly chirp - ed, (the birds they fine - ly chirp - ed,) (the
the birds they fine - ly chirp - ed,) (the
birds they fine - ly chirp - ed,) the
chirp - - - ed,) the

32

mp

birds they fine - ly chirp - ed,) the winds were

mp

birds they fine - ly chirp - ed,) the winds were

mp

birds they fine - ly chirp - ed,) the

mp

birds they fine - ly chirp - ed,) the winds were

mp

(birds they fine - ly chirp - ed,) the winds were

mp

birds they fine - ly chirp - ed, the winds were

37

still - ed, Sweet -

still - - - - - ed,

winds were still - - - - - - ed,

still - - ed, were still - ed,

still - ed, (the winds were still - ed,) Sweet - ly with

still - - - - - ed,

41
cresc.
- ly with these ac - cent - ing, (sweet - ly with
Sweet - ly with these ac - cent - - -
cresc.
Sweet - ly with these ac - cent - ing, (sweet-
Sweet - ly with these ac - cent - ing,
cresc.
these ac - cent - ing, (sweet - ly with these ac -
Sweet - ly with these ac - cent - ing,
45
these ac - cent - - - ing) the air was
cresc.
- - ing, (sweet - ly with these ac - cent - ing)
- ly with these ac - cent - ing) the air was
cresc.
(sweet - ly with these ac - cent - ing) the air was
- cent - ing, (sweet - ly with these ac - cent -
cresc.
(sweet - ly with these ac - cent - ing) the

49
f *f* *f* *f*
fill - - - - - - ed. This__
__ the air was fill - - - ed. This__
fill - - - - - - ed. This__
fill - ed, (the air was fill - - - ed. This__
- ing) the air was fill - ed.
air was fill - - - - - ed.
53
f *f*
__ is that fair______ whose head a crown de - serv - eth Which Heaven for
__ is that fair______ whose head a crown de - serv - eth
__ is that fair______ whose head a crown de - serv - eth
__ is that fair______ whose head a crown de - serv - eth
Which Heaven for
Which

57
her re - serv - eth, (which Heaven for
Which Heaven for her re - serv - eth, (which
Which Heaven for her re - serv - eth, re - serv - eth,
Which Heaven for her re - serv - eth, (which
her re - serv - eth, (which Heaven for her re - serv - eth,) (which
Heaven for her re - serv - eth, (which Heaven for her re -
61
her re - serv - - - eth.) Leave, shep - herds,
Heaven for her re - serv - - - eth.) Leave, shep - herds,
(which Heaven for her re - serv - eth.) Leave, shep - herds,
Heaven for her re - serv - - - eth.) Leave, shep - herds,
Heaven for her re - serv - - - eth.)
- - - serv - - - eth.)

65
your lambs keep - ing, leave, shep - herds, your lambs keep - ing
mp
your lambs keep - ing, leave, shep - herds, your lambs keep - ing Up -
your lambs keep - ing, leave, shep - herds, your lambs keep - ing
your lambs keep - ing
Leave, shep - herds, your lambs keep - ing
Leave, shep - herds, your lambs keep - ing
69
mp
Up - on the bar - ren mount - ain,
- on the bar - ren mount - ain, (up - on the
mp
Up - on the bar - ren mount - -
mp
Up - on the bar - ren mount - ain, (up - on the bar - ren
mp
Up - on the bar - ren mount -
mp
Up - on the bar - ren

73
(up - on the bar - ren
bar - ren mount - ain,) the bar - ren mount - ain, up - on (the
- ain, (up - on the bar - ren mount - ain,)
mount - ain,) the (bar - ren mount - ain,)
- ain, (up - on the
mount - ain, the (bar - ren mount - ain,)
77
mount - ain,) the (bar - ren mount - -
bar - ren mount - - - - - -
(up - on the bar - ren mount - - - -
(the bar - ren mount - -
bar - ren mount - ain,) the (bar - ren mount - - - -
up - on (the bar - ren mount - - - -

[← o = o. →]

81

mf

– ain,) And, nymphs, at – tend on her and leave your

– ain,) And, nymphs, at – tend on her and leave your

– ain,) And, nymphs, at – tend on her and leave your

– ain,)

– ain,) And, nymphs, at – tend on her and leave your

– ain,)

85

bow – ers, For she the shep – herds' life main – tains and

bow – ers.

bow – ers, For she the shep – herds' life main – tains and

For she the shep – herds' life main – tains and

bow – ers.

For she the shep – herds' life main – tains and

[← o· = o →]

89

you - ers. Then sang the shep - herds and nymphs, nymphs

Then sang the shep - herds and nymphs, nymphs

you - ers. Then sang the shep - herds and nymphs, nymphs

you - ers. Then sang the shep - herds and nymphs, nymphs

Then sang the shep - herds and nymphs, (then

you - ers. Then sang the shep - herds and nymphs, nymphs

93

of Di - a - na, (nymphs of Di -

of Di - a - na, (nymphs of Di - a - - -

of Di - a - na, (nymphs of Di - a - -

of Di - a - na, (nymphs of Di - a - na,) Di -

sang the shep - herds and nymphs,) and nymphs of Di -

of Di - a - na, (nymphs of Di - a - - -

97
- a - - na:)
- - - na:)
- - - na:) Long live fair O - ri - a - na, fair
- a - - na: Long live fair O - ri - a - - - na, (long live
- a - - na:
- - - na:) Long live fair O - ri - a - - - na, fair
101
Long (live fair O - ri - a - - -
Long live fair O - ri -
O - ri - a - na, (long live fair
fair O - ri - a - na,) long live fair O - ri - a - -
Long live fair O - ri - a - na,
O - ri - a - na,

105
- na,) long live fair O - ri - a - - - na,
- a - - - na, (long live fair O - ri - a -
O - ri - a - - na,)
- na, (long live fair O - ri - a - - - na,) (long live fair O - ri -
(long live fair O - ri - a - na,) (long
long (live fair O - ri - a - - - na,) fair O - ri -
109
(long live fair O - ri - a - na,)
- - na,) fair O - ri - a - na,
long live fair O - ri - a - na,) mp (long live fair O - ri -
- a - na,) fair O - ri - a - na, mp long (live fair O - ri - a -
live fair O - ri - a - na,
- a - - - na, mp long live fair O - ri - a -

113
mp
long live fair O - ri -
- a - na,) fair O - ri - a - na,
- - na,) fair O - ri - a - na, long live fair
mp
long live fair O - ri - a -
- - na, fair O - ri - a - na,
117
mp
long (live fair O - ri - a - - - na,)
mf
long (live fair
- a - - - na,
mf
(long live fair O - ri - a - -
mf
long (live fair O - ri - a - - - na,)
O - ri - a - na, (long live fair O - ri - a - - - na,)
mf
- na,
mf
long (live fair O - ri -
mf
long (live fair O - ri - a - - -

121
f
O - ri - a - na,) long live fair O - ri - a - na,
- - na,)
(long live fair
long (live fair O - ri - a - na,)
(long live fair O - ri - a - na,) (long live fair O - ri - a - na,)
- a - na, fair O - ri - a - na, long live fair O - ri -
- na, fair O - ri - a - - - - - - -
125
[𝄐]
(long live fair O - ri - a - - - - - na.)
O - ri - a - - - na,) fair O - ri - a - na.
fair O - ri - a - - na.
(long live fair O - ri - a - - - - na.)
- a - na, fair O - ri - a - na.
- - - - - - - - - na.

19
HARK, ALL YE LOVELY SAINTS

THOMAS WEELKES

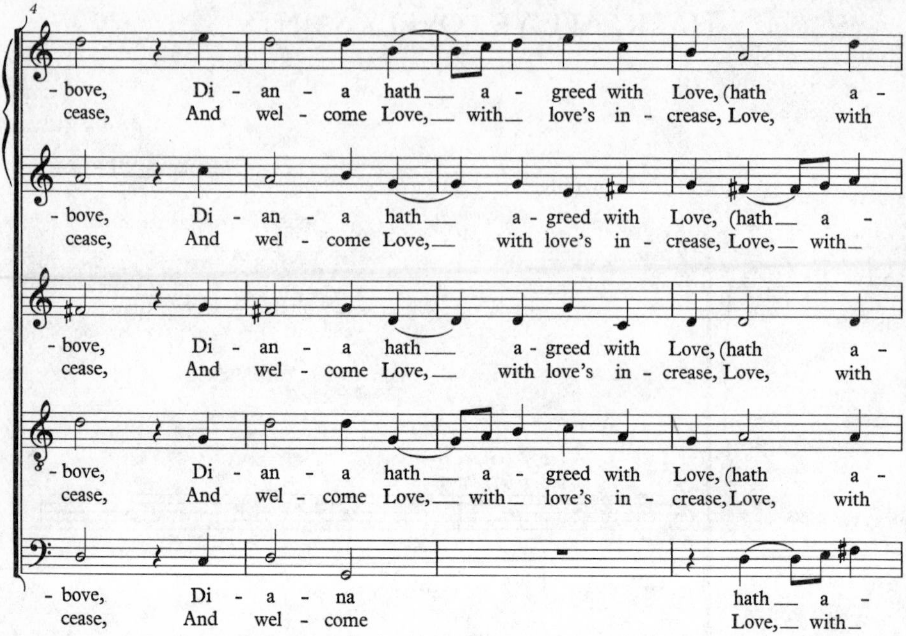

4

- bove, Di - an - a hath___ a - greed with Love, (hath a -
cease, And wel - come Love,___ with___ love's in - crease, Love, with

- bove, Di - an - a hath___ a - greed with Love, (hath___ a -
cease, And wel - come Love,___ with love's in - crease, Love,___ with___

- bove, Di - an - a hath___ a - greed with Love, (hath a -
cease, And wel - come Love,___ with love's in - crease, Love, with

- bove, Di - an - a hath___ a - greed with Love, (hath a -
cease, And wel - come Love,___ with___ love's in - crease, Love, with

- bove, Di - a - na hath___ a -
cease, And wel - come Love,___ with___

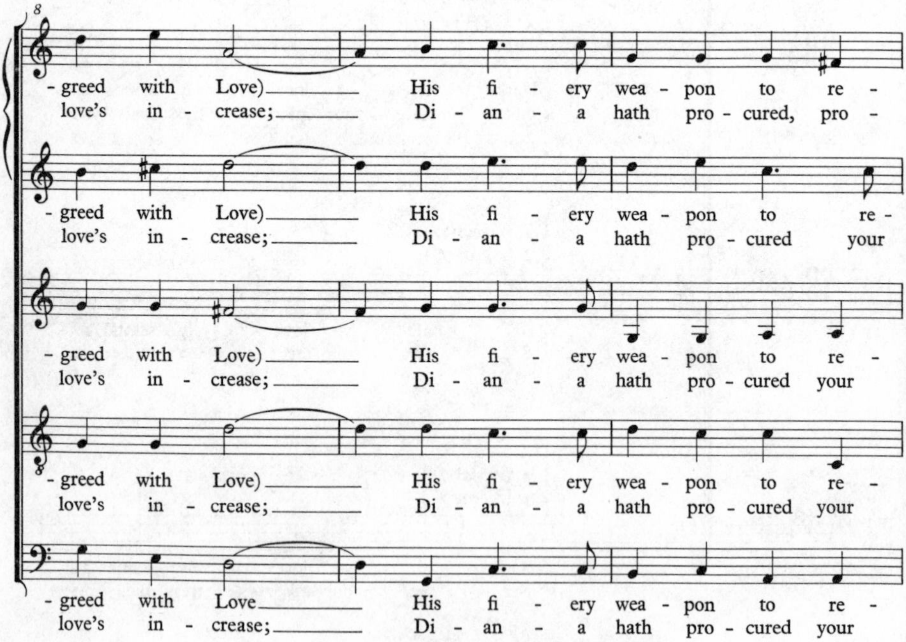

8

- greed with Love)___ His fi - ery wea - pon to re -
love's in - crease;___ Di - an - a hath pro - cured, pro -

- greed with Love)___ His fi - ery wea - pon to re -
love's in - crease;___ Di - an - a hath pro - cured your

- greed with Love)___ His fi - ery wea - pon to re -
love's in - crease;___ Di - an - a hath pro - cured your

- greed with Love)___ His fi - ery wea - pon to re -
love's in - crease;___ Di - an - a hath pro - cured your

- greed with Love___ His fi - ery wea - pon to re -
love's in - crease;___ Di - an - a hath pro - cured your

11

- move, to re - move. Fa la la la la la la la la
- cur - ed your peace.

- move. Fa la la la la la la la la la la la la la la
peace.

- move. Fa la la la la la la la la la la la
peace.

- move. Fa la la la la la la la la, fa la la la la la la la,
peace.

- move. Fa la la la la la la la la, fa la la la la
peace.

15

1

v.1 *p*
v.2 *f*

la, fa la la la la la la la la la la. Hark,
See,

la la la la la, fa la la la la la la la la. Hark,
See,

la, fa la la la la la la la la la la. Hark,
See,

fa la la la la la la la la la la. Hark,
See,

la la la la la la la la la la. Hark,
See,

2
18
v.1 f (repeat p)
v.2 mf (repeat pp)
sustained
la. Do you not see How they a - gree? Then cease, fair
Cu-pid hath sworn His bow for - lorn To break and
v.1 f (repeat p)
v.2 mf (repeat pp)
sustained
la. Do you not see How they a - gree? Then cease, fair
Cu-pid hath sworn His bow for - lorn To break and
v.1 f (repeat p)
v.2 mf (repeat pp)
sustained
la. Do you not see How they a - gree? Then cease, fair
Cu-pid hath sworn His bow for - lorn To break and
v.1 f (repeat p)
v.2 mf (repeat pp)
sustained
la. Do you not see How they a - gree? Then cease, fair la -
Cu-pid hath sworn His bow for - lorn To break and burn,
v.1 f (repeat p)
v.2 mf (repeat pp)
sustained
la. Do you not see How they a - gree? Then cease, fair
Cu-pid hath sworn His bow for - lorn To break and
22
la - dies; why weep ye, (why
burn, ere la - dies mourn, la -
la - dies; why weep ye, (why
burn, ere la - dies mourn, la -
la - dies; why weep ye,
burn, ere la - dies mourn,
- - dies; why weep ye,
ere la - dies mourn,
la - dies; why weep ye, (why
burn, ere la - dies mourn, la -

27

p (staccato)

— weep ye?) Fa la la la la la, fa la la la la la — la la,
- dies mourn.

p (staccato)

— weep — ye?) Fa la la la la la, fa la la la la la — la la,
- dies — mourn.

p (staccato)

(why weep ye?) Fa la la la la la, fa la la la la la la la la,
la - dies mourn.

p (staccato)

(why weep ye?) Fa la la la la la, fa la la la la la la la la la,
la - dies mourn.

p (staccato)

weep ye?) Fa la la la la la, fa la la la la la la la,
- dies mourn.

32

1 v.1 p v.2 pp 2 [fermata]

f

fa la la la la la, fa la la la la la la la la la. Do you / Cu-pid la.

f

fa la la la la la, fa la la la la la la la. Do you / Cu-pid la.

f

fa la la la la la, fa la la la la la la la la la. Do you / Cu-pid la.

f

fa la la la la la, fa la la la la la — la la la. Do you / Cu-pid la.

f

fa la la la la la, fa la la la la la la la. Do you / Cu-pid la.

20
LADY, WHEN I BEHOLD

JOHN WILBYE

11
mf
the ro - ses sprout - ing, (the ro - ses sprout - ing,) Which
mf
the ro - ses sprout - ing, (the ro - ses sprout - ing,) Which
mf
the ro - ses sprout - ing, (the ro - ses sprout - ing,) Which
mf
the ro - - - ses sprout - ing, Which

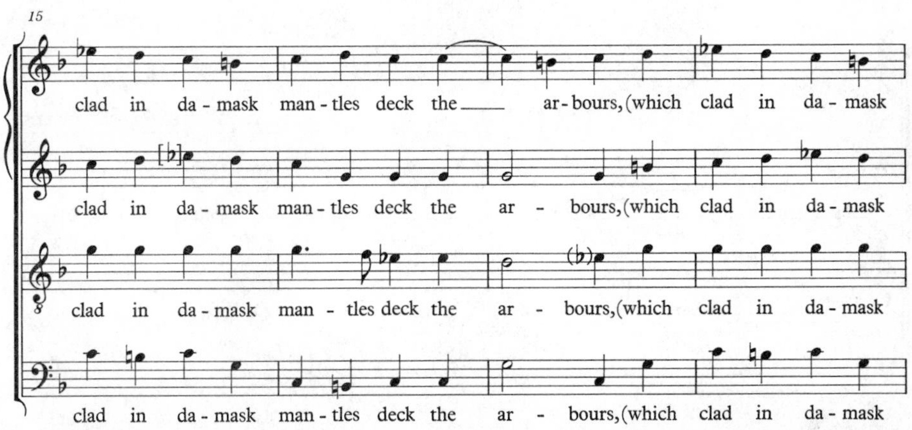
15
clad in da - mask man - tles deck the ar - bours, (which clad in da - mask
clad in da - mask man - tles deck the ar - bours, (which clad in da - mask
clad in da - mask man - tles deck the ar - bours, (which clad in da - mask
clad in da - mask man - tles deck the ar - bours, (which clad in da - mask

19
p
man - tles deck the ar - bours,) And then be - hold your
p
man - tles deck the ar - - - bours,) And then be -
p
man - tles deck the ar - - - bours,) And then be - hold your
man - tles deck the ar - - - bours,)

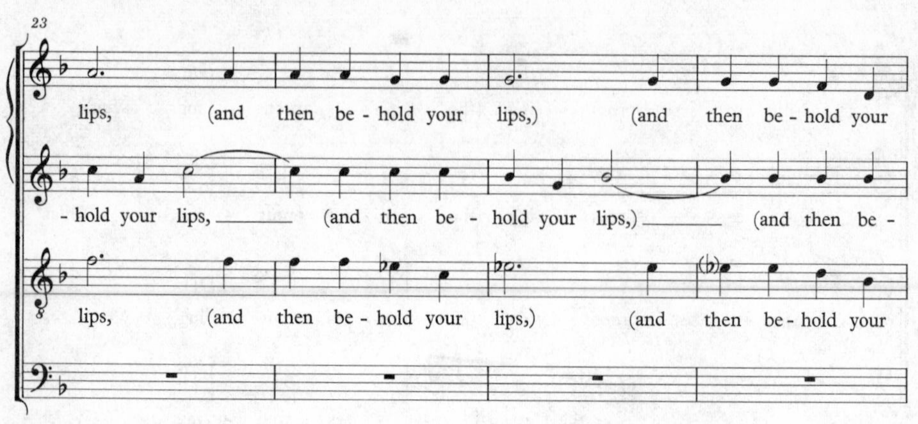
23
lips, (and then be - hold your lips,) (and then be - hold your
- hold your lips, (and then be - hold your lips,) (and then be -
lips, (and then be - hold your lips,) (and then be - hold your

27
lips) where sweet Love har - - - bours, My eyes
- hold your lips) where sweet Love har - bours, My
lips) where sweet Love har - - - bours,
p
My eyes pre -

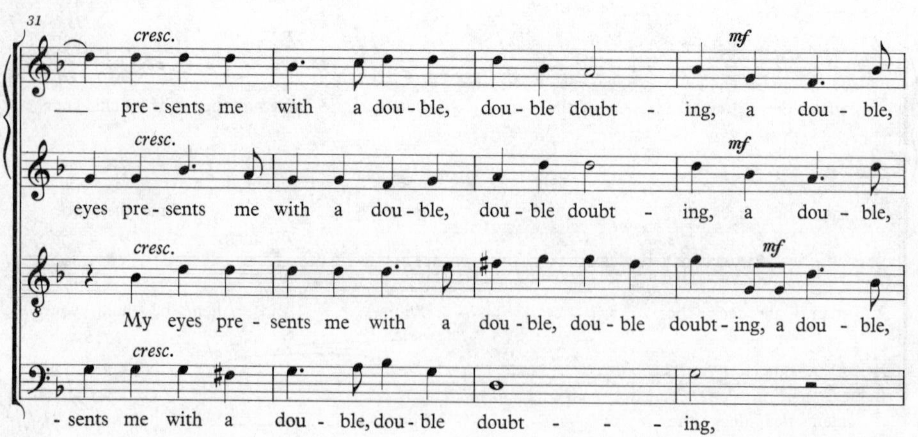
31
cresc.
mf
pre - sents me with a dou - ble, dou - ble doubt - ing, a dou - ble,
cresc.
mf
eyes pre - sents me with a dou - ble, dou - ble doubt - ing, a dou - ble,
cresc.
mf
My eyes pre - sents me with a dou - ble, dou - ble doubt - ing, a dou - ble,
cresc.
- sents me with a dou - ble, dou - ble doubt - - - ing,

35
mf
dou - ble doubt - ing, my eyes pre - sents me with a dou - ble,
dou - ble doubt - ing, my eyes pre - sents me with a dou - ble,
dou - ble doubt - ing, my eyes pre - sents me with a dou - ble,
(my eyes pre - sents me with a dou - ble, dou - ble
39
f
dou - ble doubt - ing. For, view - ing both a - like, hard -
dou - ble doubt - ing. For, view - ing both a -
dou - ble doubt - ing. For, view - ing both a -
doubt - - - ing.) For, view - ing both a -
43
- ly my mind sup - po - - - ses
- like, hard - ly my mind sup - po - ses
- like, hard - ly my mind sup - po - ses Whe - ther the
- like, hard - ly my mind sup - po - ses

47
Whe-ther the ro - ses be your lips, or your lips the ro - ses,
Whe-ther the ro - ses be your lips, or your lips the ro - ses,
ro - ses be your lips, or your lips the ro - - -
Whe-ther the ro - ses be your lips,
51
(whe-ther the ro - ses be your lips, or your lips the ro -
(whe-ther the ro - ses be your lips, or your lips the ro -
- ses, (whe-ther the ro - ses be your lips, or your lips the ro -
(whe-ther the ro - ses be your lips,) or your lips the ro -
55
mp
- ses.) For, view - ing both a - like, hard -
mp
- ses.) For, view - ing both a-like, hard - ly my
mp
- ses.) For, view - ing both a - like, hard -
mp
- ses. For, view - ing both a - like, hard -

59
-ly my mind sup-po - ses
mind_ sup - po - - - ses
-ly my mind sup-po - ses Whe-ther the ro-ses be your
-ly my mind sup-po - ses Whe-ther the ro-ses
63
Whe-ther the ro-ses be your lips, or your lips the ro-ses,
Whe-ther the ro-ses be your lips, or your lips the ro-ses,
cresc.
lips, or your lips the ro - - - ses, (whe-ther the
cresc.
be your lips, (whe-ther the ro-ses
67
cresc.
mf [𝄐]
(whe-ther the ro-ses be your lips, or your lips the ro - ses.)
cresc.
mf [𝄐]
(whe-ther the ro-ses be your lips, or your lips the ro - ses.)
mf [𝄐]
ro-ses be your lips, or your lips the ro - ses.)
mf [𝄐]
be your lips,) or your lips the ro - ses.

21
I LOVE, ALAS, I LOVE THEE

THOMAS MORLEY

8
my dain - ty dar - ling, (my dain - ty dar - -
my dain - ty dar - ling, (my dain - ty dar -
love thee,) my dain - ty dar - ling, (my dain - ty dar -
love thee,) my dain - ty dar - ling, (my dain - ty dar -
love thee,) my dain - ty dar - ling, (my dain - ty dar -
12
- ling.) I love, a - las, I love, thee, (I love, a - las, I
- ling.) I love, a - las, I love, thee, (I love, a -
- ling.) I love, a - las, I love thee,
- ling.) I love, a - las, I love thee,
- ling.) I love, a - las, I love thee,
17
love, a - las, I love thee,) my dain - ty dar -
- las, I love thee,) my dain - ty dar -
(I love, a - las, I love thee,) my dain - ty dar -
(I love, a - las, I love thee,) my dain - ty dar -
(I love, a - las, I love thee,) my dain - ty dar -

21
- ling, (my dain - ty dar - - ling.)
- ling, (my dain - ty dar - ling.) Come kiss me then, come kiss
- ling, (my dain - ty dar - ling.) Come kiss me
- ling, (my dain - ty dar - ling.) Come kiss me then, come
- ling, (my dain - ty dar - ling.) Come kiss me
25
Come kiss me then, (come kiss me then,) come kiss me, A -
me, (come kiss me then, come kiss me,) A - ma -
then, come kiss me, A - ma - ryl - - -
kiss me, (come kiss me then, come kiss me,)
then, come kiss me, (come kiss me then, come kiss me,) A - ma -
29
- ma - ryl - lis, (A - ma - ryl - lis,) More love - ly than sweet
- ryl - lis, (A - ma - ryl - lis,) More love - ly than sweet
- lis, (A - ma - ryl - lis,) More love - ly than sweet
A - ma - ryl - - - lis, More love - ly than sweet_
- ryl - lis, More love - ly than sweet
f
mp
mf

33
Phyl - lis, (more love - ly than sweet Phyl - lis,) more love - ly than sweet
Phyl - lis, (more love - ly than sweet Phyl - lis,) more love - ly than sweet
Phyl - lis, (more love - ly than sweet Phyl - lis,) more love - ly than sweet
Phyl - lis, (more love - ly than sweet Phyl - lis,) more love - ly than sweet
Phyl - lis more love - ly than sweet
37
Phyl - lis, (more love - ly than sweet Phyl - - - lis.)
Phyl - lis, (more love - ly than sweet Phyl - - - lis.) Come kiss me
Phyl - lis, (more love - ly than sweet Phyl - - - lis.)
Phyl - lis, (more love - ly than sweet Phyl - - - lis.) Come
Phyl - lis, (more love - ly than sweet Phyl - - - lis.)
41
Come kiss me then, (come kiss me then,) come kiss
then, come kiss me, (come kiss me then, come kiss
Come kiss me then, come kiss me, A - ma -
kiss me then, come kiss me, (come kiss me then, come
Come kiss me then, come kiss me, (come kiss me then, come kiss

45
mp
mf
me, A - ma - ryl - lis, (A - ma - ryl - lis,) More
mp
mf
me,) A - ma - ryl - lis, (A - ma - ryl - lis,) More
mf
- ryl - - lis, (A - ma - ryl - lis,) More
mp
mf
kiss me,) A - ma - ryl - - - - - lis, More
mp
mf
me,) A - ma - ryl - lis, More
49
p
f
love - ly than sweet Phyl - lis, (more love - ly than sweet Phyl - lis,) more
p
f
love - ly than sweet Phyl - lis, (more love - ly than sweet Phyl - lis,) more
p
f
love - ly than sweet Phyl - lis, (more love - ly than sweet Phyl - lis,) more
p
f
love - ly than sweet_ Phyl - lis, (more love - ly than sweet Phyl - lis,) more
f
love - ly than sweet Phyl - lis, more
53
love - ly than sweet Phyl - lis, more love - ly than sweet Phyl - - lis.
love - ly than sweet Phyl - lis, more love - ly than sweet Phyl - - lis.
love - ly than sweet Phyl - lis, more love - ly than sweet Phyl - - - lis.
love - ly than sweet Phyl - lis, more love - ly than sweet Phyl - - lis.
love - ly than sweet Phyl - lis, more love - ly than sweet Phyl - - lis.

22
LEAVE, ALAS, THIS TORMENTING

THOMAS MORLEY

Passionately

[S.] CANTVS

[A.] ALTVS — *mf* Leave, a - las,

[T.] QVINTVS — *mf* Leave, a - las, this ___ tor - ment -

[T.] TENOR — *mf* Leave, a -

[B.] BASSVS

4

ALTVS: this tor - ment - - ing, (leave, ___ a - las,

QVINTVS: - - - ing, tor - - ment - - - ing, leave,

TENOR: - las, this tor - ment - - ing, (leave, a -

BASSVS: *mf* Leave, ___ a - las,

9
mf
Leave, ___
this tor - ment - - ing) and strange an -
a - las, this tor - ment - - ing and strange an -
- las, this tor - ment - - - - ing) and strange an -
this tor - ment - - - - - ing and strange an -
14
___ a - las, this tor - ment - - ing,
- guish, leave, ___ a - las, this tor - ment - -
- guish, leave, ___ a - las, this tor -
- guish, (and strange an - guish,) leave, ___ a - las, this ___
- guish, and (strange an - - guish,) leave, ___
19
(leave, ___ a - las, this tor - ment - - - -
- ing, (leave, ___ a - las, this tor - ment - -
- ment - - ing, tor - ment - - - -
___ tor - ment - ing, ___ tor - ment - - ing
___ a - las, this tor - ment - - - -

24
- ing) and strange an - - - - - guish,
f
- ing) and strange an - - - - - guish, Or
f
- ing and strange an - guish, Or
f
and strange an - guish, Or
f
- ing and strange an - guish, Or
28
f
Or kill my heart op - press - -
kill my heart op - press - ed, (or kill my heart op - press - -
kill my heart op - pressed, or kill my heart op-press - - -
kill my heart op-press - - ed, or kill my heart op - pressed.
kill my heart op - pressed.
32
mp
- ed. A - las, it skill not, (a - las, it skill
mp
- ed.) A - las, it skill not, (a - las, it skill
mp
- ed. A - las, it skill not, (a - las, it skill
mp
mf
A - las, a - las, it skill not, (a - las, it skill not!) For
mp
A - las, it skill not, (a - las, it skill

36
mf
not!)
For thus I will not, (for thus I will
not!)
For thus I will not,
not!) For thus I will not, for thus I will
thus I will not, (for thus I will not,) I will
not!) For thus I will not, (for thus I will
40
[← o = o· →]
[← o· = o →]
not,) Now con-tent - ed, Then tor - ment -
Now con-tent - ed, Then tor - ment -
not, Now con-tent - ed, Then tor - ment -
not, Now con - tent - ed, Then tor - ment -
not,) Now con - tent - ed, Then tor - ment -
44
- ed, Live in
- ed, Live in love and
- ed, Live in love and lan
- ed,
- ed, Live in love and

49
love and lan - - guish, (live in love and lan -
lan - - guish, (live
- guish, (live in love and lan - -
Live in love and lan - guish,
lan - guish, (live in love and lan - guish,)
54
cresc.
- guish,) live in love and lan - - -
in love and lan-guish,) live in
- guish,) live in love and lan - - -
(live in love and lan - - guish,) live in
live in love and
59
1
2
f
mf
- - - - - guish. - guish.
love and lan - guish. - guish.
guish, and lan - guish. For - guish.
love and lan - guish. For thus I will - guish.
lan - - - guish. For thus I - guish.

23
LULLABY, MY SWEET LITTLE BABY

WILLIAM BYRD

9

lul - la lul - la - by, lul - la

lul - la - by, lul - la

- by, lul - la, lul - la

lul - la lul - la - by, la,

- la - by, la, lul - la lul - la - by.

14

lul - la - by. *mp* My sweet lit - tle ba - -

lul - la - by. *mp* My

lul - la - by. *mp* My sweet lit - tle ba - by,

lul - la lul - la - by. *mp* My sweet lit -

mp My sweet lit - tle ba - - -

18

- by, (my sweet lit - tle ba - - -

sweet lit - tle ba - by, my

ba - - by, my sweet lit - tle ba - by, ba -

- tle, lit - tle ba - - - by, my

- by, my sweet lit - tle ba - - -

22
mf
- by,) my sweet lit - tle ba - by, what
mf
sweet lit - tle ba - by, what mean - -
mf
- - - by, what mean - est thou
mf
sweet lit - tle ba - by, what mean - est
mf
- by, what mean - - - est thou to
26
dim. p
mean - est thou to cry? Lul - la lul - la -
dim. p
- est thou to cry? Lul -
dim. p
to cry? Lul - la lul - la - by,
dim. p
thou to cry?
dim. p
cry, to cry? Lul - la
30
mf
- by, la lul - - la, lul - la lul - la -
mf
- la lul - la - by, lul - la
mf
la, lul - la lul - la - by,
mf
Lul - la lul - la - by, lul - la - by,
mf
lul - la - by, la lul - la, lul - la lul - la - by,

34
dim.
- by, la lul - la lul - la - by,
p
lul - la - by, la, lul - la lul - la -
dim. p
la lul - la lul - la - by, la, lul - la, lul - la lul - la -
p
- by, la lul - la -
dim.
la lul - la - by,
38
p
la lul - la, la lul - la - by,
- by, la lul - la, la
- by, la lul - la lul - la - by, la lul -
- by, la lul - - la, la
p
la lul - la - by, la lul - la
42
pp
la lul - la - by, la lul - la - by,
pp
lul - la - by, la lul - la - by,
pp
- la - by, la lul - la lul - la -
pp
lul - la - by, la lul - la lul - la - by,
pp
lul - la, la lul - la lul - la, la lul - la - by,

46
lul - la - by. My sweet lit - tle ba - by, ba -
lul - la - by. My sweet lit - tle ba - - -
- by. My sweet lit - tle ba - - by, sweet
lul - la - by. My sweet lit - tle ba - by,
lul - la - by. My sweet lit - tle
50
[← o = o. →]
mp
- - - by. Be still, my
- - - by.
ba - - by. Be still,
ba - - by. Be still, my bless - ed
ba - - by. Be still, my bless - ed
54
bless - ed babe, my bless - ed babe,
Be still, my bless - ed babe,
my bless - ed babe, my bless - ed babe, though cause
babe, bless - ed babe, be still, my bless - ed
babe, bless - ed babe, be still, my bless - ed

58

though cause thou hast to mourn, though cause thou

though cause thou hast to mourn,

thou hast to mourn, to mourn, Whose blood most

babe, though cause thou hast to mourn, to

babe, though cause thou hast to mourn, Whose

62

hast to mourn, Whose blood most in - no -

Whose blood most in - no-cent to shed

in - no - cent to shed

mourn, Whose blood most in - no - cent the cru - el king

blood most in - no-cent to shed, to

66

-cent to shed the cru - el king hath sworn, the cru-el

the cru - el king hath sworn,

the cru - el king hath sworn, (the cru - el king

hath sworn, hath sworn, the cru -

shed the cru - el king hath sworn,

70
king hath sworn. And lo, a - las, be -
And lo, a - las, be -
hath sworn.) And lo, a - las, be -
- el king hath sworn. And lo, a - las, be - hold,
hath sworn. And lo, a - las, be -
74
- hold, what slaugh - ter he doth make,
- hold, what slaugh - ter he doth
- hold, be - hold, what slaugh - ter he doth
what slaugh - ter he doth make, he doth make, he
- hold, what slaugh - ter he doth make,
78
Shed - ding the blood of in - fants all,
dim.
make, Shed - ding the blood of
make, Shed - ding the blood of in - fants all,
dim.
doth make, Shed - ding the blood of, of in -
what slaugh - ter he doth make, Shed - ding the

82
dim.
mp
of in - fants all, sweet Sa-vi - our, for thy
in - fants all, sweet Sa - vi-our, for thy
sweet Sa-vi - our, for thy
- fants all, sweet Sa - vi - our, for thy
blood of in - fants all, sweet Sa-vi - our, for thy
86
f
sake, for thy sake. A King, a King is born,
sake. A King is born, they
sake, for thy sake. A King is born, they
sake, for thy sake. A King is born, they
sake, for thy sake. A King is born, they
90
they say, which King this king would
say, which King this king would
say, which King this king would kill, would
say, which King this king would kill, would
say, which King this king would kill, would

94
p
kill. O woe, woe, woe, O woe,
p
kill. O woe, O
p
kill. O woe, and woe - ful hea - vy day, O woe, and
p
kill. O woe, woe, O woe, woe, O woe,
p
kill. O woe, O woe, O woe, woe,
99
and woe - ful, and woe - ful hea - vy day, hea -
woe, and woe - ful hea - vy day,
mf
woe - ful hea - vy day, when wretch -
mf
and woe - ful hea - vy day, when wretch -
O woe, and woe - ful hea - vy day, hea -
103
mf
- vy day, when wretch - es have
mf
when wretch - es have their will, (when wretch -
- es have their will, have their will, have their will,
- es have their will, have their will, when wretch - es have
mf
- vy day, when wretch - es have their will, have their will,

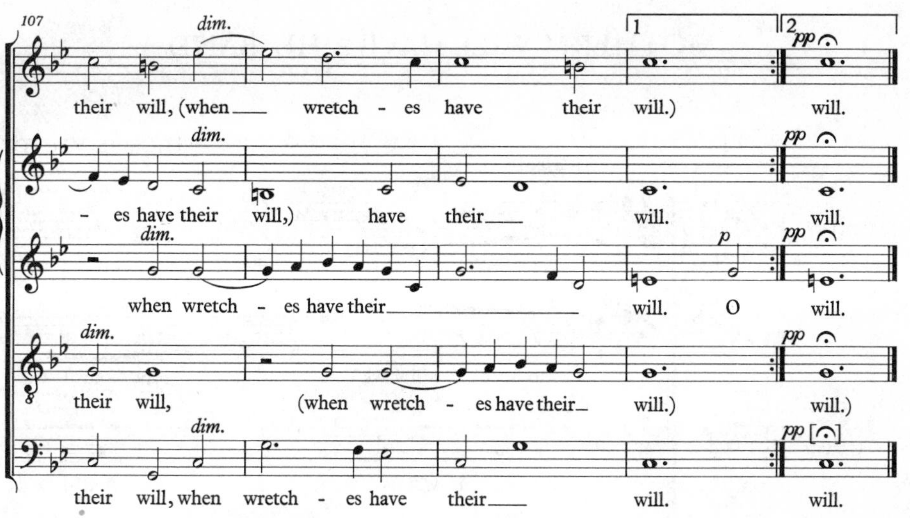

2. Lulla la, lulla lulla lullaby.
My sweet little baby, what meanest thou to cry?
Three kings this King of kings to see are come from far,
To each unknown, with offerings great, by guiding of a star.
And shepherds heard the song which angels bright did sing,
Giving all glory unto God for coming of this King,
Which must be made away, king Herod would him kill.
O woe, and woeful heavy day, when wretches have their will.

3. Lulla la, lulla lulla lullaby.
My sweet little baby, what meanest thou to cry?
Lo, lo, my little babe, be still, lament no more.
From fury shalt thou step aside, help have we still in store.
We heavenly warning have some other soil to seek,
From death must fly the Lord of life, as lamb both mild and meek.
Thus must my babe obey the king that would him kill.
O woe, and woeful heavy day, when wretches have their will.

4. Lulla la, lulla lulla lullaby.
My sweet little baby, what meanest thou to cry?
But thou shalt live and reign as Sibyls have foresaid,
As all the Prophets prophesy, whose mother, yet a maid
And perfect virgin pure, with her breasts shall upbreed
Both God and man, that all hath made, the Son of heavenly seed,
Whom caitiffs none can 'tray, whom tyrants none can kill.
O joy, and joyful happy day, when wretches want their will.

24
MOTHER, I WILL HAVE A HUSBAND

THOMAS VAUTOR

6
one, have one, In spite of her, of her that will have none. John a
one, have one, In spite of her, of her that will have none. John a
one, In spite of her, of her that will have none. John a
one, In spite of— her, of— her— that will have none.
one, In spite of her, of her that will have none.
10
Dun should have had me long ere this, John (a Dun should have had me
Dun should have had me long ere this, John (a Dun should have had me
Dun should have had me long ere this, John (a Dun should have had me
John (a Dun should have had me
John (a Dun should have had me
13
long ere this,) He said I had good lips to kiss, to kiss, to (kiss, to
long ere this,) He said I had good lips to kiss, to kiss, to kiss, (to
long ere this,) He said I had good lips to kiss,
long— ere this,) He said I had good lips to— kiss, to
long ere this,) He said I had good lips to kiss, to
mp
f

16
kiss, to kiss, to kiss,) to kiss. Mo-ther, I will sure have
kiss,)(to kiss,)(to kiss,) (to kiss.) Mo-ther, I will sure have
to kiss, to kiss, (to kiss.) Mo-ther, I will sure have
kiss, (to kiss.) Mo - ther, I will sure have
kiss, to kiss. Mo - ther, I will sure have
19
one, In spite of her that will have none. For I have
one, In spite of her that will have none.
one, In spite of her that will have none. For I have heard 'tis
one.
one, In spite of her that will have none. For
22
heard 'tis trim, 'tis trim, for (I have heard 'tis trim,) for (I have heard 'tis
For I have heard 'tis trim, 'tis trim, for (I have heard 'tis
trim, for (I have heard 'tis trim,) for (I have heard 'tis
For I have heard 'tis trim, 'tis trim, for (I have heard 'tis
I have heard 'tis trim when

25
trim) when folks do love, By good Sir John I swear now I will
trim) when folks do love, By
trim) when folks do love, By good Sir John I swear now I will
trim) when folks do love, By good Sir John now I will
folks do love, By good Sir John I swear now I will
28
prove, now (I will prove,) by (good Sir John I swear)
good Sir John I swear now I will prove, by (good Sir John I swear)
prove, by good Sir John now I will prove, by good Sir John I
prove, now (I will prove,) I, by good Sir
prove, now (I will prove,) by (good Sir John I swear)
31
now (I will prove.) For Mo-ther, I will
now (I will prove.) For Mo-ther, I will
swear now I will prove. For Mo-ther, I will sure have
John I swear I will prove. For Mo-ther, I will sure have
now (I will prove.) For Mo-ther, I will sure have

34
cresc.
ff
sure have one, have one, (have one,) In spite of her that
sure have one, have one, have one, In spite of her that
one, have one, (have one, have one,) In spite of her__ that__
one, have one, (have one, have one,) In spite of her that
one, have one, (have one, have one,) In spite of her that
37
[← 𝅗𝅥 = 𝅗𝅥. →]
f
will have none.
will have none. To the town there -
__ will__ have none. To the town there -
will have none. To the town there -
will have none. To the town there -
41
f
To the town there - fore will I gad,
- fore will I gad, to (the town there -
- fore will I gad, will (I gad,) will (I gad,) will I
- fore will I gad, will I gad, will (I gad,) will (I
- fore will I gad, will I

45

to the (town there - fore will I gad,) To

- fore will I gad,) will I gad, will (I gad,) To

gad, (will I gad,) To

gad,) will (I gad,) will I gad, will (I gad,) To

gad, will (I gad,) will I gad, will (I gad,) To

49

get me a hus - band good or bad, to

get me a hus - band good or bad, to

get me a hus - band good or bad, to

get me a hus - band good or bad, to

get me a hus - band good or bad, to

53

(get me a hus - band good or bad.)

(get me a hus - band good or bad.)

(get me a hus - band good or bad.)

(get me a hus - band good or bad.)

(get me a hus - band good or bad.)

57
f
Mo-ther, I will have a hus - band, And I will have him out of
Mo-ther, I will have a hus - band, And I will have him out of
Mo-ther, I will have a hus - band, And I will have him out of
Mo-ther, I will have a hus - band, And I will have him out of
Mo-ther, I will have a hus - band, And I will have him out of
60
hand. Mo-ther, I will sure have one, have one, In spite of her that
hand. Mo-ther, I will sure have one, have one, In spite of her, in
hand. Mo-ther, I will sure have one, have one, In spite of her,
hand. Mo-ther, I will sure have one, have one, In spite of
hand. Mo-ther, I will sure have one, In spite of her,
64
will, in spite of her that will have none.
spite of her that will, that will have none.
in spite of her that will have none.
her that will, in spite of her that will have none.
that will have none.

25
MUSIC DIVINE

10
di - vine, (mu - sic
(mu - sic di - vine, di - vine,)
di - vine,) di - vine,
- vine, di - vine, di -
mu - sic
(mu - sic di - vine, di - vine,)
15
di - vine, di - vine,)
(mu - sic di - vine, di -
di - vine, di - vine, di - vine,
-vine, mu - sic, mu - sic di - vine, di -
(di - vine, di - vine,) di - vine,

20
mf
pro-ceed - ing from a - bove,
mf
- vine,) di - vine, pro - ceed- ing from a - bove,
mf
mu - sic (di - vine, di - vine,) pro - ceed-ing from a -
mf
- vine, di - vine, di - vine, pro-ceed - ing
mf
mu - sic di-vine, di - vine, di - vine, pro -
mf
mu - sic di - vine, di - vine, pro-ceed - ing from a - bove,
25
(pro-ceed - ing from a - bove,) from a -
(pro - ceed - ing from a - bove,) from a -
- bove, (pro - ceed - ing from a - bove,) from a-bove,
from a - bove, (pro-ceed - ing from a-bove,) a -
- ceed - ing from a - bove, (from a - bove,) from a -
a - bove, (pro-ceed - ing from a - bove,)

29
p
-bove, (from a - bove,) Whose sa - cred sub - ject oft - en - times is
p
-bove, from a - bove,) Whose
p
Whose sa - cred sub - ject oft - en - times is
p
-bove, from a - bove, Whose sa - cred sub - ject, sub - ject oft - en - times is
p
-bove, a - bove, Whose
p
from a - bove, Whose sa - cred sub - ject oft - en - times is
33
love, oft - en - times, oft - en, oft - en - times is love, is love, oft -
sa - cred sub - ject oft - en - times is love, oft - en - times is
love, oft - en - times is love,
love, oft - en - (times is love,) (oft - en - times is
sa - cred sub - ject oft - en - times is love, is love, (oft - en - times is
love, oft - en - times is love,

37
- en-times is love, In this ap - pears
love, In this ap - pears
(oft - en-times is love,) In this ap - pears, ap - pears
love,) In this ap - pears her heaven -
love,) is love, In this ap - pears her heaven - ly
(oft - en-times is love,) In this ap - pears her heaven - ly
42
her heaven - ly har - - -
her heaven - ly har - - -
her heaven - ly har - mo - ny,
- ly har - mo - ny, (her heaven - ly har - mo - ny,)
har - - - mo - ny,
har - - - mo - ny,

46
- - mo - - - ny, her har - mo - -
- - - - mo-ny, har - mo-ny,
her heaven - ly, her
her har - mo - ny
her heaven-
her (heaven - ly har - mo - ny,)
(her heaven - ly har - -
50
- ny,
her (heaven - ly har - - - - - mo -
her (heaven - ly har - - - - - mo -
heaven-ly har - mo - ny, (her heaven - ly har - mo - ny,)
- ly har - mo - ny,
her heaven - ly har - - - mo -
- - - mo - ny,) her heaven - ly, her heaven-ly, heaven-ly har - mo -

54
mp
-ny, Where tune - ful con - cords, tune - ful con - cords
mp
-ny,) Where tune - ful con - cords, tune - ful con - cords
mp
Where tune - ful con - cords, tune - ful con - cords
mp
Where tune - ful con - cords, (tune - ful con - cords)
mp
-ny, Where tune - ful con - cords, tune - ful con-cords
mp
-ny, Where tune - ful con - cords, (tune - ful con - cords,
59
sweet - ly do a - gree, a - gree, (sweet - ly do a-gree,)
sweet - ly do a-gree, sweet - ly do a - gree, (sweet -
sweet - ly sweet - ly do a-gree, a - gree,
sweet - ly do a - gree, (a - gree,) (a -
sweet - ly, sweet - ly do a - gree, sweet - ly (do a -
sweet - ly do a - gree, (sweet - ly do a-gree,) (sweet - ly

64

(sweet - ly a-gree,) do a-gree, do a-

- ly do a - gree,) (sweet - ly do a - gree,) a-

sweet - ly do a - gree, (sweet - ly do a - gree.)

- gree,) sweet - ly do a-

- gree,) (sweet - ly do a-gree,) a-gree.

do a-gree,) thus sweet - ly do a - gree, a-

69

- gree. *mf* And

- gree. *mf* And yet in

mf And yet in

- gree. *mf* And yet in this her slan-der is un - just, un-just,

mf And yet in this her slan-der, slan-der is un - just,

- gree. *mf* And yet in this her slan-der, slan-der is un - just,

74
yet in this her slan - der is un - just, her (slan - der is un -
this her slan - der is un - just, her slan - der is un - just,
this her slan - der is un - just, her
(her slan - der is un -
her slan - der is un - just,
her (slan - der is un - just,) (her
79
f
- just,) her slan - der is un - just, is (un - just,) To
her (slan - der is un - just,)
f
(slan - der is un - just,) is un - just, To
f
- just,) To call that love
f
her (slan - der is un - just,) un - just, To
f
slan - der is un - just,) To call that love

84
call that love which is in-deed but lust,
f
which is in-deed but lust, to
call that love, love, to (call that love,)
which is but lust, to (call that love,)
call that love, to
which is in-deed but lust, to
89
mp
to (call
call that love, love which is in-deed but lust,
mp
to
mp
which is in - deed but lust, to call that love
to (call that love,) which (is in-deed but lust,
mp
(call that love,) which is in-deed but lust, to call that love which
mp
(call that love) which is but lust, to

94
f
that love which is in - deed but lust,) to (call that love which
call that love which is in - deed but lust,
f
which is in-deed but lust, which (is in-
mp
f
which is in - deed, in-deed but lust, which (is
f
is but lust, to (call that love,)
f
(call that love) which is but lust, which
99
is but lust, which is in - deed but lust.
f
to (call that love) which is in - deed but lust.
- deed but lust,) which is in - deed but lust.
in-deed but lust,) is in - deed but lust.
love which is in - deed but lust.
is but lust, which is in - deed but lust.

26
MY BONNY LASS SHE SMILETH

THOMAS MORLEY

3
When she my heart be - guil - eth.
O how my heart it burn - eth!
When she my heart be - guil - eth.
O how my heart it burn - eth!
When she my heart be - guil - eth.
O how my heart it burn - eth!
Fa la la la
When she my heart be - guil - eth.
O how my heart it burn - eth!
Fa la la la la
When she my heart be - guil - eth.
O how my heart it burn - eth!
Fa la la la
6
Fa la la la la la la, fa la la la la la, fa la la
Fa la la la la la la la la, fa la la
la la la, fa la la la, fa la la la la, fa la la
la la, fa la la la la la la la la, fa la
la la la, fa la la la, fa la la la la, fa la la

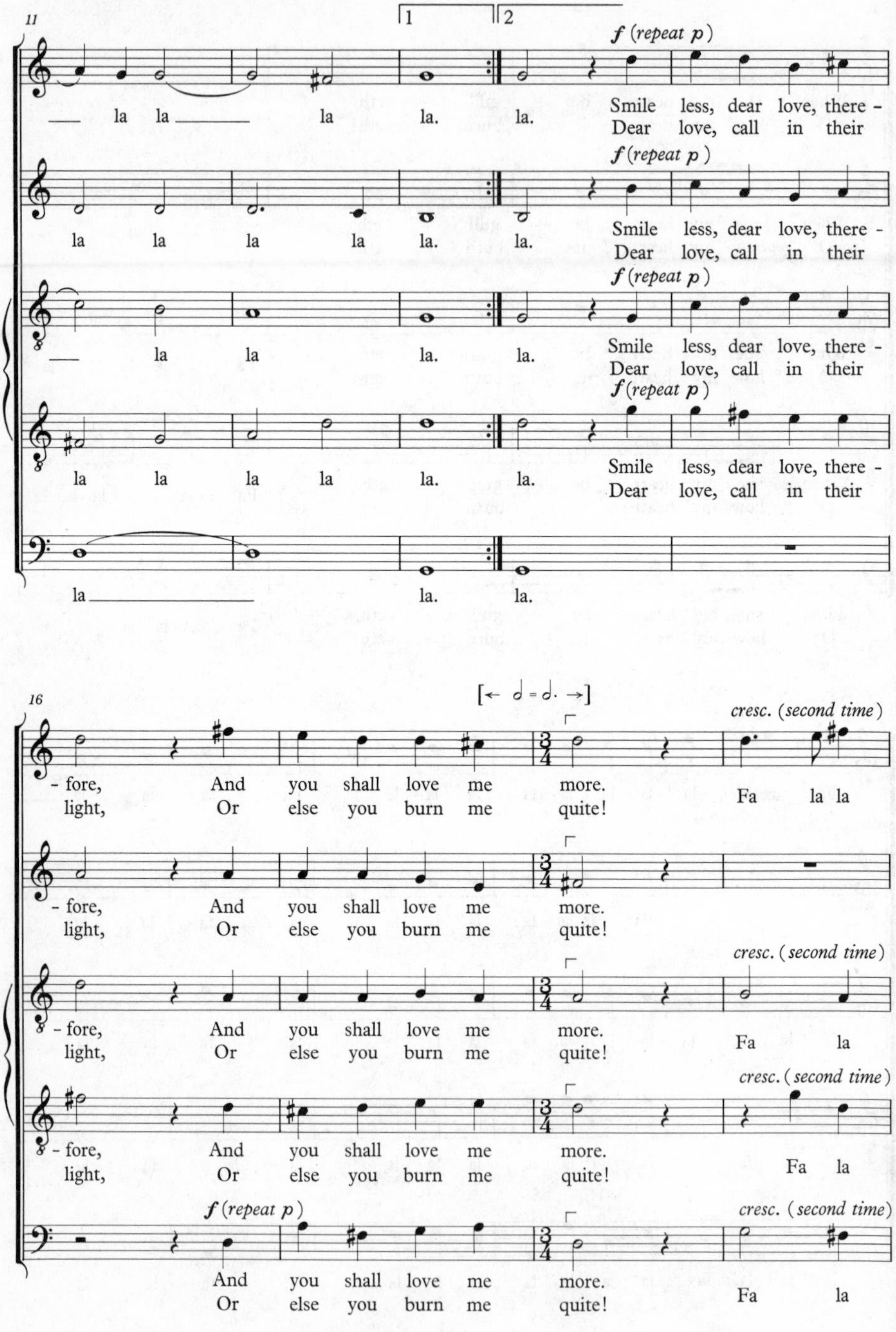

16

[← 𝅗𝅥 = 𝅗𝅥. →]

cresc. (second time)

- fore, And you shall love me more. Fa la la
light, Or else you burn me quite!

- fore, And you shall love me more.
light, Or else you burn me quite!

cresc. (second time)

- fore, And you shall love me more. Fa la
light, Or else you burn me quite!

cresc. (second time)

- fore, And you shall love me more. Fa la
light, Or else you burn me quite!

f (repeat p) cresc. (second time)

And you shall love me more. Fa la
Or else you burn me quite!

20
la la la, fa la la la, fa la la
cresc. (second time)
Fa la la la la la la la, fa la la la
la, fa la la la, fa la la, fa la la la la la la
la la la la la la la la la, fa
la la la la la la la la, fa la la la

25
1
2
la la la la la la. Smile Dear la.
la la la la la la la. Smile Dear la.
la la la la la la la la. Smile Dear la.
la la la la la la. Smile Dear la.
la la la la la la la. la.
p
f

27
NOW IS THE MONTH OF MAYING

THOMAS MORLEY

p (*repeat* *f*) 2. The Spring, clad all in gladness,
Doth laugh at Winter's sadness, fa la,
p (*repeat* *f*) And to the bagpipe's sound
The nymphs tread out their ground. Fa la.

f (*repeat* *ff*) 3. Fie then! why sit we musing,
Youth's sweet delight refusing? fa la, [*repeat* fa la *pp*]
f (*repeat* *ff*) Say, dainty nymphs, and speak,
Shall we play barley-break? Fa la. [*repeat* fa la *pp cresc.*]

28

O CARE, THOU WILT DESPATCH ME

(The first part)

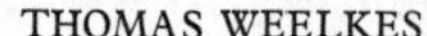

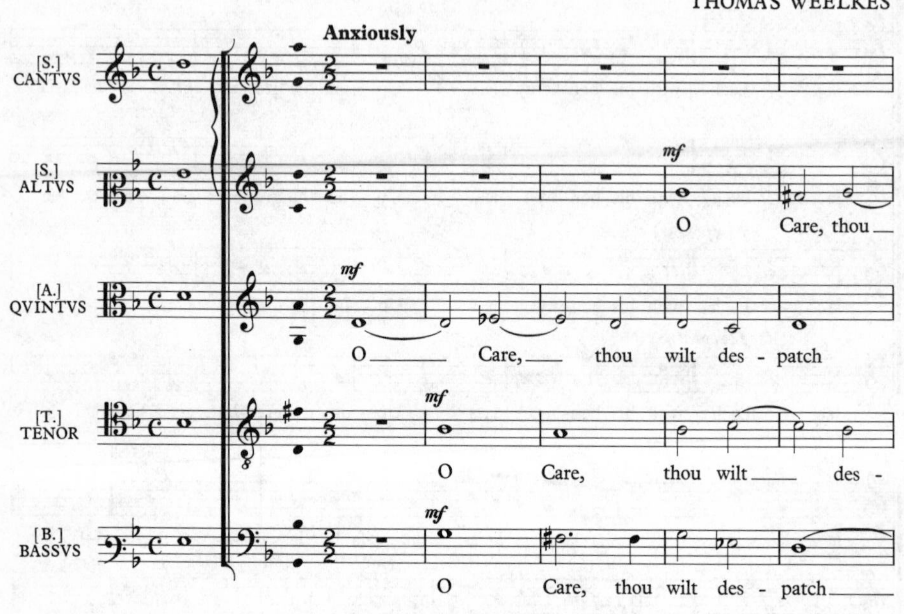

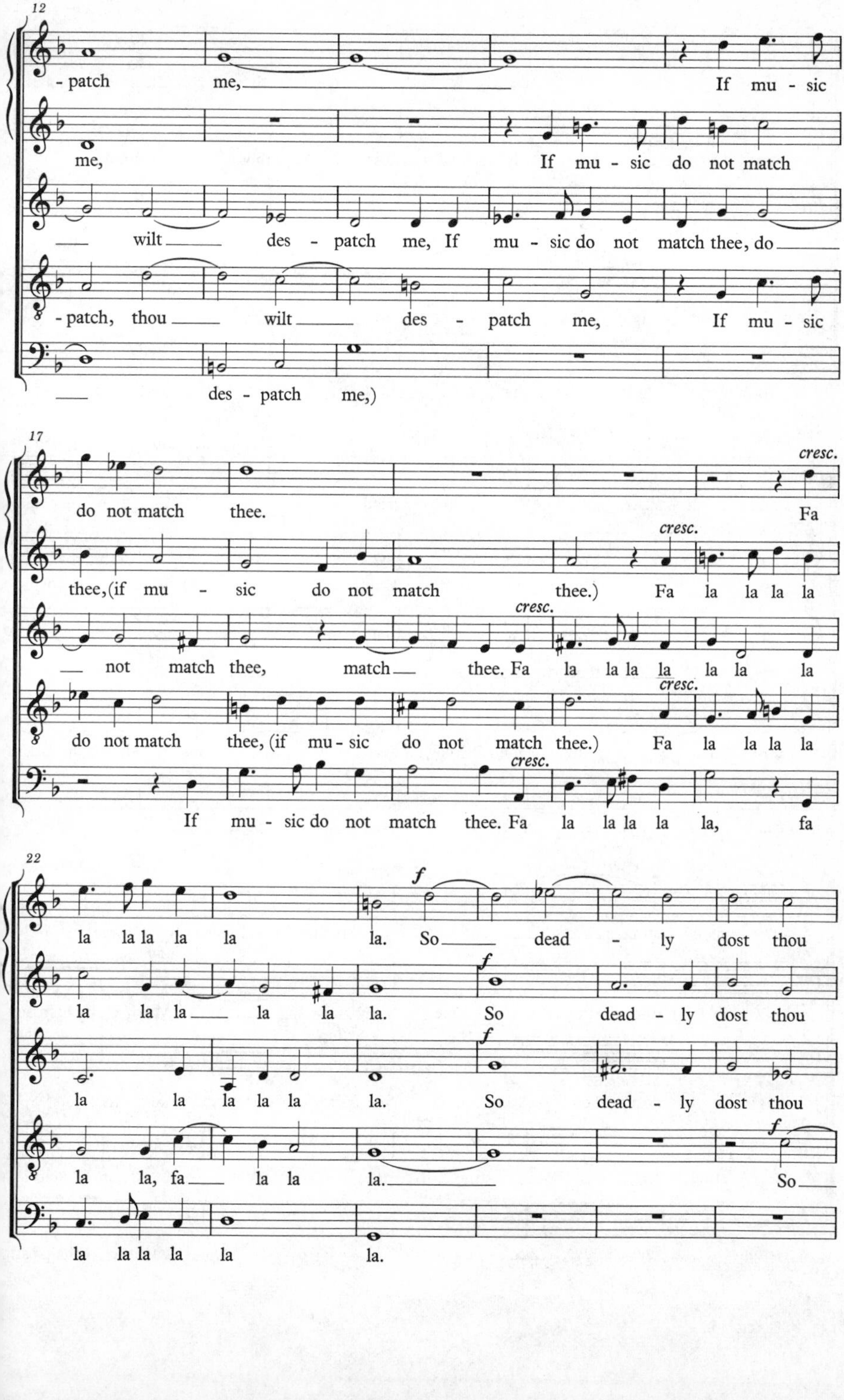

12
-patch me, If mu - sic
me, If mu - sic do not match
wilt des - patch me, If mu - sic do not match thee, do
-patch, thou wilt des - patch me, If mu - sic
des - patch me,)
17
cresc.
do not match thee. Fa
cresc.
thee,(if mu - sic do not match thee.) Fa la la la la
cresc.
not match thee, match thee. Fa la la la la la la la
cresc.
do not match thee, (if mu- sic do not match thee.) Fa la la la la
cresc.
If mu - sic do not match thee. Fa la la la la la, fa
22
f
la la la la la la. So dead - ly dost thou
f
la la la la la la. So dead - ly dost thou
f
la la la la la la. So dead - ly dost thou
f
la la, fa la la la. So
la la la la la la.

28
sting me, (so dead - ly dost thou sting
sting, so dead - ly (dost thou sting,)
sting, so dead - ly dost thou sting
dead - ly, so dead - - ly
f
So dead - ly (so
34
me, so dead - - ly dost
so dead - ly dost thou sting me, (so dead -
me, dost thou sting me, so dead - - -
dost thou sting me, (so dead - ly dost thou
dead - ly) dost thou
40
mf
thou sting me, Mirth on-ly help can bring me,
mf
- ly dost thou sting me, sting me, Mirth on-ly help can
mf
- ly dost thou sting me, Mirth on-ly help can bring me,
mf
sting me,) dost thou sting me, Mirth on-ly help
mf
sting me, Mirth on-ly help can

45
(mirth on-ly help can bring,) mirth on-ly help can bring me, (mirth
bring me, (mirth on-ly help can bring me,) mirth
(mirth on-ly help can bring me,) can bring
can bring me, mirth on-ly help can
bring me, (mirth on-ly help can
48
on-ly help can bring me,) mirth on-ly help can bring me.
on-ly help can bring, mirth on-ly help can bring me, mirth on-ly help can
me, (mirth on-ly help can bring me,) can
bring me, (mirth on-ly help can bring me. Fa
bring me,) mirth on-ly help can bring me. Fa la la la la
51
Fa la la la la la la, fa la la la la la.
bring me. Fa la la la la la, fa la la la la la la la la la la la la.
bring me. Fa la la la la la la la.
la la la la la, fa la la la la la la, fa la la la la la la la la.
la la la la la.

29
HENCE, CARE, THOU ART TOO CRUEL
(The second part)

THOMAS WEELKES

At the same speed

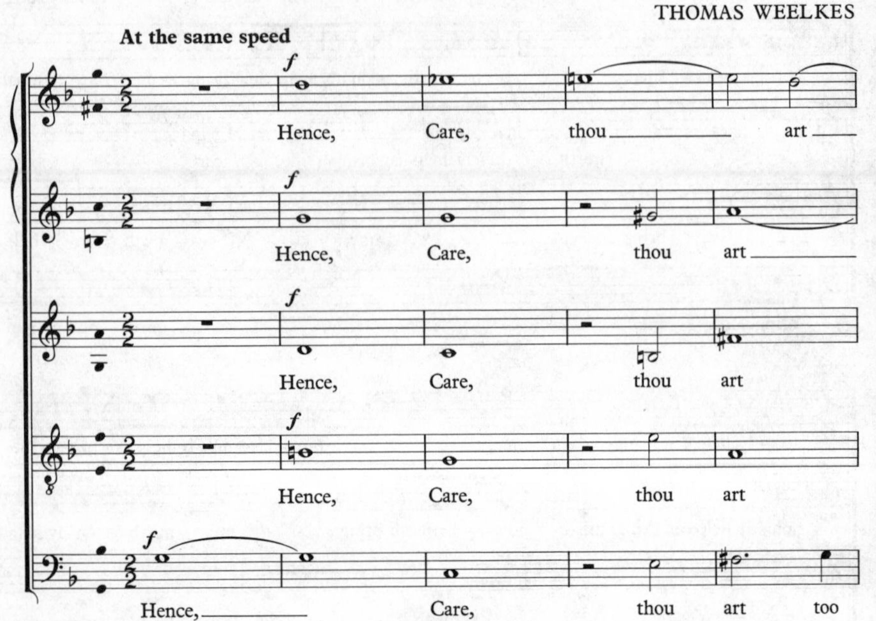

12
too cru - el, too cru - - - el,
- el, (thou art too cru - el,)
art too cru - - el, (thou art too cru - el,) Come,
too, too cru - el, thou art too cru - el, Come,
art too cru - - - el,)
18
Come, mu - sic, sick man's jew - el,
Come, mu - sic, come, mu - sic, sick
mu - sic, sick man's jew - el, (come, mu - sic,
mu - sic, come, come, mu - sic,
Come, mu - sic, sick man's jew - el, sick
24
sick man's jew - - - el. Fa la la la la la, fa la la la la
man's jew - - - el. Fa la la la la la la la,
sick man's jew - - el.) Fa la la la la la, fa la la la
sick man's jew - - el. Fa la la la la la, fa la la la la
man's jew - - - el. Fa la la la la la la

29
la, fa la la la la la la la la la la la la.
fa la la la la, fa la la la la la. His
fa la la la la la, fa la la la la la la la la la. His
la la la la la la, fa la la la la la. His force had
la, fa la la la la la la la la.
34
His force had well nigh slain me, slain
force had well nigh slain me, slain me, (his
force had well nigh slain me, (his
well nigh slain me, slain me, (his
His force had well nigh slain
40
force had well nigh slain me, But thou must
force had well nigh slain me,) But
force had well nigh slain me,)
force had well nigh slain me,) But
me, had well nigh slain me,

45
now sus-tain me, but thou must now sus - tain me,
thou must now sus-tain me, but thou must now sus-
But thou must now sus-tain me,
thou must now sus - tain me, sus - tain me, but thou must
But thou must
49
but thou must now sus-tain me, now sus - tain
- tain me, sus - tain me, but thou must now sus-tain
(but thou must now sus-tain me,) now sus-tain
now sus-tain me. Fa
now sus-tain me. Fa
53
me. Fa la la la la la la la la la la.
me. Fa la la la la la la la, fa la la la la.
me. Fa la la la la la la la, fa la la.
la la la la la la, fa la la la.
la la la la la la la la la la.

30
OUT FROM THE VALE

JOHN WARD

10
deep de - - - spair, of deep de - spair
— of deep de - spair, from (the vale of deep
out (from the vale of deep
vale of deep de - spair,) (out from the vale of deep
- spair, out (from the vale of
vale of deep de - spair, of deep
15
p
With mourn - ful
— de - spair) With mourn - ful
— de - spair) With mourn - ful tunes I fill the
de - spair) With mourn - ful
deep de - spair) With mourn - ful tunes I fill the
— de - spair With mourn - ful tunes I fill the

19
tunes I fill the
tunes I fill the air, with(mourn - ful tunes I fill the
air, with(mourn - ful tunes I fill the air,) I fill the
tunes I fill the air, (with mourn - ful tunes I fill the air,) I fill the
air, with(mourn - ful tunes I fill the air,)(with mourn-ful tunes I fill the
air, with(mourn - ful tunes I fill the air,) I fill the
23
mf
air, with mourn - ful tunes I fill the air, I fill the
mf
air,) with (mourn - ful tunes
mf
air, with mourn - ful tunes I fill the air, (with mourn - ful
mf
air, with(mourn - ful tunes I fill the air,)
mf
air,) with mourn - ful tunes I fill the
mf
air, I fill the air, with mourn - ful

27
dim.
air, with(mourn - ful tunes I fill the air,) with mourn - ful
I fill the air,) with(mourn - ful
tunes I fill the air,) with mourn - ful tunes I fill the air, with(mourn-ful
(with mourn - ful tunes I fill the air,) I fill the air, with(mourn-ful
air, (with mourn - ful tunes I fill the air,) I fill the air, with(mourn - ful
tunes I fill the air, I fill the air, with(mourn - ful
31
mf
tunes I fill the air,) To sa - tis - fy my rest -
tunes I fill the air,) To sa - tis - fy my rest -
tunes I fill the air,)
tunes I fill the air,)
tunes I fill the air,) To
tunes I fill the air,) To

35
mf
mf
- less ghost, my rest - less ghost, to
- less ghost, my rest - less ghost,
To sa - tis - fy my rest -
To sa - tis - fy my rest -
sa - tis - fy my rest - less ghost,
sa - tis - fy my
39
(sa - tis - fy my rest - less ghost,)
to (sa - tis - fy my
- less ghost, my rest - less ghost,
- less ghost, my rest - less ghost,
to (sa - tis-fy my
rest - less ghost, to sa - tis - fy my

43
to (sa - tis - fy my
rest - less ghost,) to sa - tis - fy
to (sa - tis -
to sa - tis - fy my rest - less ghost, to
rest - less ghost,) to (sa - tis - fy my rest - -
rest - less ghost, to (sa - tis - fy my
47
rest - less ghost, Which
my rest - less ghost,) Which Daph - ne's cru - el -
- fy my rest - less ghost,) Which Daph - ne's cru - el -
(sa - tis - fy my ghost,) Which
- - less ghost,) Which Daph - ne's cru - el -
rest - less ghost,) Which Daph - ne's cru - -

52
Daph - ne's cru - el - ty, which Daph -
- ty hath lost, hath lost, (which Daph -
- ty hath lost, which
Daph - ne's cru - el - ty hath lost, hath
- ty, which Daph - ne's cru - el -
- el - ty hath lost, which
57
- ne's cru - el - ty hath lost, ⟨her⟩ cru - el -
- ne's cru - el - ty hath lost,) ⟨her⟩ cru -
Daph - ne's cru - el - ty hath lost, which (Daph - ne's
lost, (which Daph - ne's
- ty hath lost, hath lost, (which Daph - ne's
Daph - ne's cru - el -

62

dim. *mp*
- ty hath ___ lost. O'er hills and dales in her dull ears,

dim. *mp*
- el - ty hath lost. O'er hills and

dim. *mp*
cru - el - ty hath lost.) O'er hills and dales in her dull

dim. *mp*
cru - el - ty hath lost.) O'er hills and dales in her dull

dim. *mp*
cru - el - ty hath lost.) O'er hills and dales in

dim. *mp*
- ty hath lost. O'er hills and dales in

67

o'er (hills and dales in her dull ears,) o'er_ hills and dales in her dull

dales in her dull ears, o'er_ hills and dales in her dull ears,

ears, o'er (hills and dales in her dull ears,)(o'er hills and ___ dales in

ears, dull ears, o'er (hills and dales in her dull ears,) (o'er

her dull ears, dull ears, o'er (hills and dales in her dull ___ ears,

her dull ears,

71
mf
ears, in her dull ears I'll send
(o'er hills and dales in her dull ears) I'll send
her dull ears,) in her dull ears
hills and dales in her dull ears) I'll send
o'er hills and dales in her dull ears
o'er (hills and dales in her dull ears) I'll send
75
f
my notes, my notes with bit-
my notes, my notes with bit-
I'll send my notes with
my notes, (I'll send my notes
I'll send my notes
my notes with

80
dim. al fine
- ter tears, with bit - ter tears,
dim. al fine
- ter tears, with (bit - ter tears,)
dim. al fine
bit - - - ter tears, with (bit - ter
f
dim. al fine
with bit - ter tears, with bit -
f
dim. al fine
with bit - - - ter tears, (with bit -
dim. al fine
bit - - - ter tears, with bit - - - ter
85
pp
with bit - ter tears, bit - ter tears.
pp
with bit - ter tears, with bit - ter tears.
pp
tears, with bit - - ter tears.
pp
- ter tears, with bit - ter tears.
pp
- ter tears,) with bit - ter, bit - ter tears.
pp
tears, with bit - - - ter tears.

31
O WHAT SHALL I DO?

JOHN WILBYE

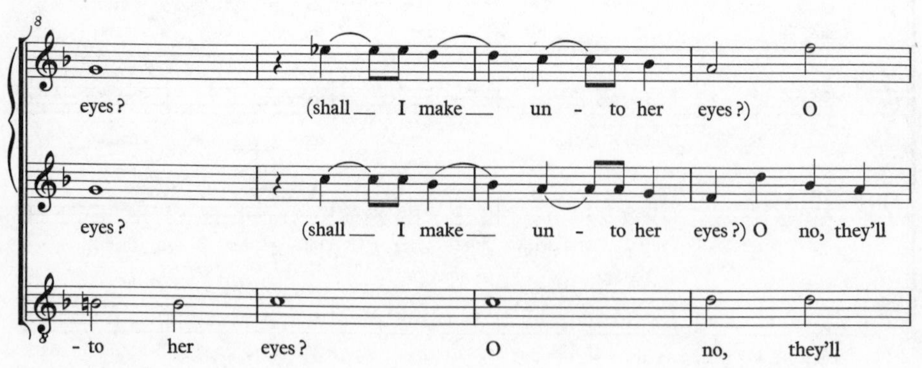

12
no, they'll burn me. Shall I seal up my
burn me. Shall I seal up my eyes and speak my
burn me. Shall I seal up my eyes and speak my
16
eyes and speak my part? Then in a flood of tears, (then in a flood of
part?
Then in a flood of
part, and speak my part? Then in a flood of tears, (then
19
tears, then in a flood of tears) I drown my
tears, (then in a flood of tears) I drown my
in a flood of tears) I drown my
22
mp
cresc.
f
heart. For tears being stopped will swell, will swell,
heart. For tears being stopped will swell, will swell,
heart. For tears being stopped will swell, will swell,

26
for
30
will swell for scope, Though they o'er - flow love, life and
will swell for scope, Though they o'er - flow love, life, love, life
scope, Though they o'er - flow
34
hope. By Beau - ty's eye I'll choose to
and hope. By Beau - ty's eye I'll choose to die, I'll choose to
love, life and hope. By Beau - ty's eye I'll choose to
38
die. At thy feet I fall, fair
die. At thy feet I fall, fair crea - ture rich
die. At thy feet I fall, fair crea - ture
mf

42
crea - ture rich in beau - ty; And for pi - ty
in beau - - ty; And for pi - ty call; O kill not
rich in beau - ty; And for pi - ty call, for
46
mp
call, for pi - ty call; O kill not
mp
love and du - ty, O kill not
mp
pi - ty call; O kill
50
love and du - ty, (O kill not
love and du - ty, (O kill not
not love and du - -
54
cresc.
love and du - ty, O kill not
cresc.
love and du - ty, O kill not
cresc.
- - - ty, (O kill

58
love and du - ty, O kill not
love and du - ty, O kill not
not love and du - - -
62
love and du - ty.) Let thy smooth tongue fan
love and du - ty.) Let thy smooth tongue fan on my sense
- - - ty.) Let thy smooth tongue fan on my
66
on my sense thy breath, To stay thine eyes from
thy breath, To stay thine eyes from
sense thy breath, To stay thine eyes from
69
burn - ing me to death.
burn - ing me to death. But if mer - cy
burn - - ing me to death. But if

72
f
But if mer - cy be ex -
be ex - il - - - ed From a thing so fair
mer - cy be ex - il - ed From a thing so
76
- il - ed From a thing so fair com - pil - - -
com - pil - - - ed, (from a
fair com - pil - - - - - - -
80
- ed, (from a thing so fair com - pil - - - ed,) Then
thing so fair com - pil - - - - - ed,) Then
- ed, (from a thing so fair com - pil - - - ed,) Then
p
84
pa - tient - ly By thee I'll die, I'll die.
pa - tient - ly By thee I'll die.
pa - tient - ly By thee I'll die.

32
O YES! HAS ANY FOUND A LAD?

13
pur - ple wings fair paint - ed, (fair paint - ed,) (fair paint -
pur - ple wings fair paint-ed, (fair paint - ed,) paint -
pur - ple wings fair paint - ed, fair paint - ed, (fair paint-ed,)
pur - ple wings fair paint - ed, fair paint - ed, (fair paint -
17
mp
- ed,) In na - ked beau - ty clad, in
- ed, In
In na - ked beau - ty clad, in beau - ty clad,
- ed,) In na - ked beau -
21
na - ked, na - ked beau - ty clad, in (na-ked,) na - ked, (na - ked
na - ked beau - ty clad, in
in na - ked, na - ked beau - ty
- ty clad, beau - ty clad, in na - ked beau - ty

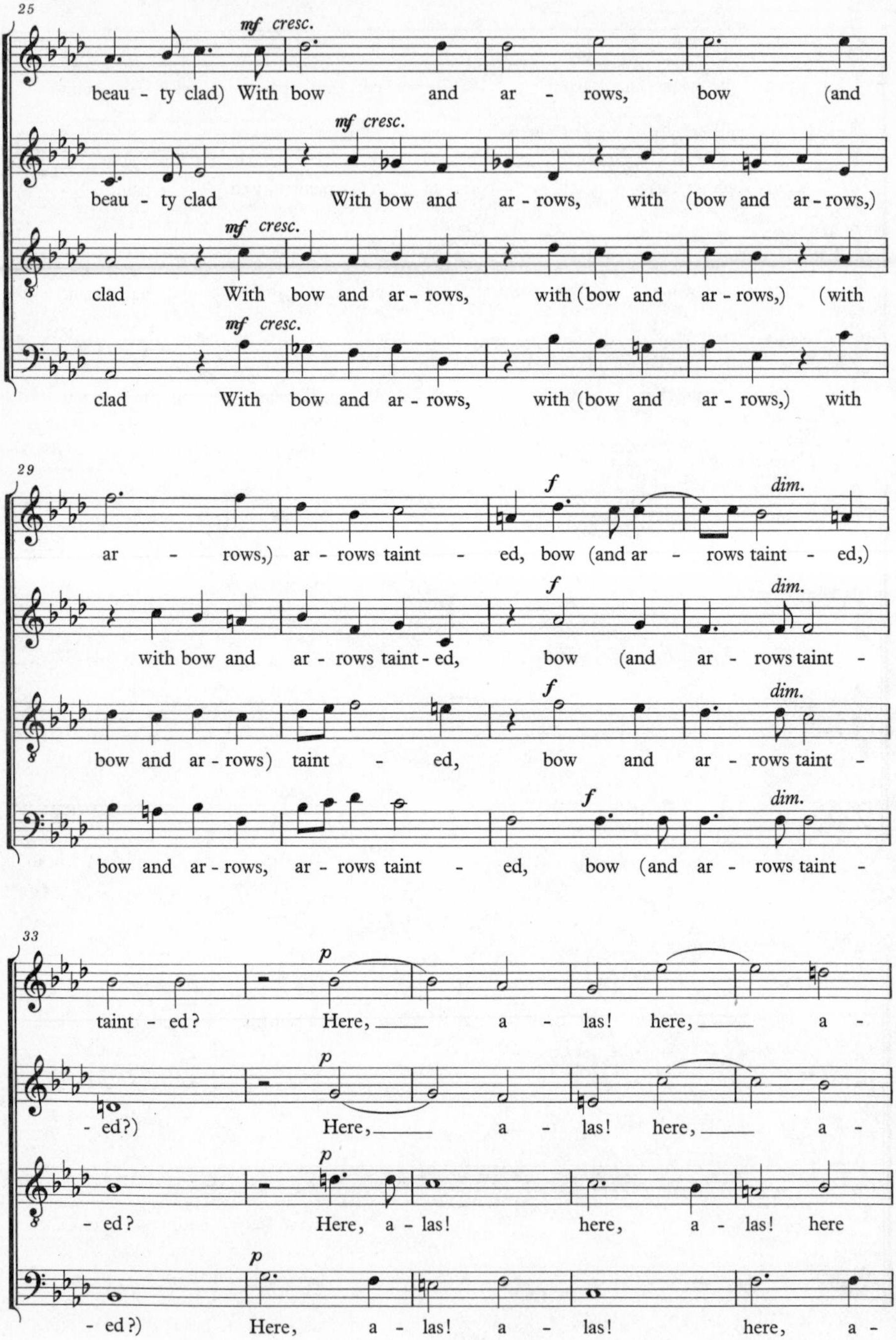

25

mf cresc.

beau - ty clad) With bow and ar - rows, bow (and

mf cresc.

beau - ty clad With bow and ar - rows, with (bow and ar - rows,)

mf cresc.

clad With bow and ar - rows, with (bow and ar - rows,) (with

mf cresc.

clad With bow and ar - rows, with (bow and ar - rows,) with

29

f *dim.*

ar - rows,) ar - rows taint - ed, bow (and ar - rows taint - ed,)

f *dim.*

with bow and ar - rows taint - ed, bow (and ar - rows taint -

f *dim.*

bow and ar - rows) taint - ed, bow and ar - rows taint -

f *dim.*

bow and ar - rows, ar - rows taint - ed, bow (and ar - rows taint -

38
-las! here close, here close he li - - -
-las! here close, here close he li - eth, he
close, here close he li - - - - -
-las! here close, here close
42
f
- - - - - eth; Take him quick be-fore he
li - eth; Take him quick be-fore he
- - - - - eth; Take him quick be-fore he
he li - eth;
46
fli - eth, be-fore he fli - eth,
fli - - - - - eth, fli-eth, fli-eth, Take him
fli - - - - - eth, be - fore
Take him

49
pp
Take him
quick be - fore he fli - - - - - eth, Take (him
pp
he fli - - - - - eth, Take (him
pp
quick be - fore he fli - - - - - eth,
53
quick be - fore he fli - eth, fli - - -
quick be - fore he) fli - eth, fli - - -
quick be - fore he fli - - - - - - -
56
f
- - - eth, Take him quick be - fore he fli - -
- - - eth,
f
- - - eth) be - fore he fli - -
f
Take him quick be - fore he fli - -

60
- - - eth, be - fore he
f
be - fore, be - fore he
- - - eth, be - fore he fli -
- - - - - - eth, he
63
fli - eth, take him quick be - fore he fli - -
fli - eth, be-fore he fli - eth, be - fore he
- eth, be - fore he fli - eth, be - fore he fli -
fli - - eth,
66
- eth, be - fore he fli - - - eth.
fli - eth, be-fore he fli - eth, fli - - - eth.
- eth, be - fore he fli - eth.
be - fore he fli - - - eth.

33
O THAT THE LEARNED POETS

ORLANDO GIBBONS

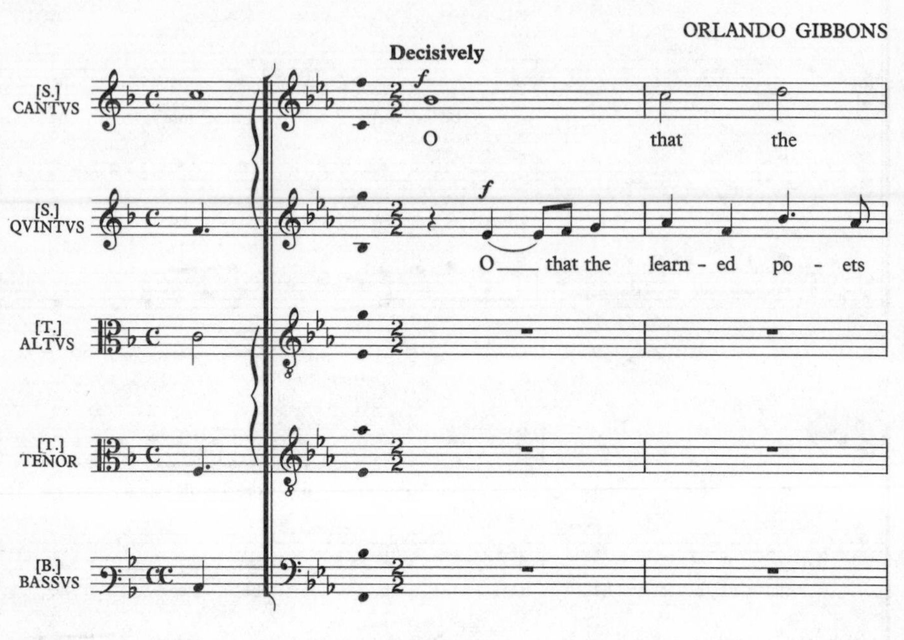

7

time, O (that the learn-ed,) learn-ed po - ets of this time,

learn - ed po - ets,) O (that the learn-ed po-ets

po-ets of this time,) the learn-ed po-ets of this

time, the (learn - ed po - ets of this

11

this time, of this time, of this

of this time,) the learn - ed po - ets of this

O that the learn-ed po-ets of this time,

time, O (that the

time,) O that the learn-ed po-ets

15

time, Who in a love - sick

time, Who in a love-sick line so well can speak,

O that the learn-ed po-ets of this time, Who

learn - ed po - ets of this time,)

of this time, of this time,

19
line so well can speak, who (in a love-sick
who (in a love-sick line,) who (in a love-sick
in a love-sick line, who in a love - sick line so well can speak,
Who in a love-sick line so well can speak, who
Who in a love-sick line, who
23
line so well can speak,) who in a
line so well can speak,) so well can speak, who
who (in a love-sick line
(in a love - sick line
(in a love - sick line) so well, so
26
love - - sick line so well can speak,
(in a love-sick line so well can speak,) Would
mf
so well can speak,)
so well can speak,) Would not
mf
well can speak, Would not con -
mf

29

mf

Would not con - sume good ___ wit, con -

not con - sume good wit in hate - ful rhyme, con - sume

mf

Would not con - sume,

con - sume good wit in hate - ful rhyme, would

- sume good wit in hate - ful rhyme,

33

- sume good wit ___ in hate-ful rhyme, good (wit in

(good wit ___ in hate-ful rhyme,) good (wit ___ in hate - ful

would

(not con - sume good wit,) good (wit in hate - ful rhyme,)

36

hate - ful rhyme,) ___ good (wit ___ in hate - ful

rhyme,) in hate - ful rhyme, But with deep

not con - sume good wit in hate - ful rhyme,

good wit ___ in hate - ful rhyme, in hate - ful ___

good (wit in hate - ful rhyme,) But

39
cresc.
rhyme,) But with deep care some bet - ter
cresc.
care some bet - ter sub - - ject find, But (with
cresc.
But with deep care some
cresc.
rhyme, But with deep care some bet -
cresc.
with deep care some bet - ter
43
sub - ject find, some (bet - ter
deep care some bet - ter sub -
bet - ter sub - ject find, some (bet - ter sub - ject
- ter sub - ject find, but (with
sub - ject find, some (bet - ter sub - ject
47
f
sub - ject find.) For if their mu-sic please in earth -
f
- ject find.) For if their mu - sic
f
find.) For if their mu-sic please in earth - ly things,
f
deep care some bet - ter sub - ject find.) For
f
find,) For

50
- ly things, in (earth - ly things,) for (if their mu - sic
please, for (if their mu -
their mu-sic please in earth - ly things,
if their mu-sic please in earth - ly things, in earth - ly things,
if their mu-sic please in earth - ly things, for (if, for if their mu-sic
53
please in earth - ly,) earth - ly things, please in earth - ly,
- sic please) in earth - ly things, for (if their mu-sic
for (if their mu-sic please in earth - ly
in (earth-ly things,)
please in earth - ly things,)
56
earth - ly things,
please in earth - ly things,) in earth - ly things, in earth -
things,) for if their mu-sic please in earth - ly things, in earth - ly
for (if their mu-sic please in earth - ly things,)
sustained
for (if their mu-sic please in earth - ly things,) How would

59
sustained
How would it sound if strung with
sustained
- ly things, How would it sound if
sustained
things, How would it sound if strung with heaven-ly,
sustained
in earth - ly things, How would it sound if strung with heaven-ly
it sound if strung with heaven - ly strings,
63
heaven - ly strings, how would it sound if strung with
strung with heaven - ly strings, how (would it sound if
heaven - ly strings, how would it
strings, if (strung with heaven - ly strings,)
with heaven - ly strings,
67
heaven - ly strings, heaven - ly strings?
strung with heaven - ly strings?)
sound if strung with heaven - ly strings?
if strung with heaven - ly strings?
if strung with heaven - ly strings?

34
POOR IS THE LIFE

MICHAEL EAST

8
kiss - es, Which end in end - less plea - sure, which (end in end - less
kiss - es, Which end in end - less plea - sure, which (end in
kiss - es, Which end in end - less plea - sure, which end in
mf
Which end in end - less plea - sure, in plea - sure, which
- - es, Which end in end - less plea - sure,
kiss - es, Which end in
12
plea - sure.) O, then, if this be
end - less plea - - - sure.) O, then, if this be
end - less plea - - - sure. O, then, if this be
(end in end-less plea - - - sure.) O, then, if this be
in plea - sure. O, then, if this be
end - less plea - - - sure. O, then, if this be
mp
f

17
[← o.=o →]
so, O, (then, if this be so) Shall I a vir - gin
so, O, (then, if this be so) Shall I a vir - gin
so, O, (then, if this be— so) Shall I a vir - gin
so, O, (then, if this be so)
so, O, (then, if this be— so)
so, O, (then, if this be so)
22
die? Fie no, no, no! fie no, no, no!
die? Fie no, no, no, no, no, no, no, no! shall I a vir - gin
die? Fie no, no, no, no! fie no, no, no! shall (I a vir - gin
Fie no, no, no! fie no, no, no! shall I a vir - gin
Fie no, no, no, no! fie no, no, no!
Fie no, no, no! fie no, no, no!

26
fie no, no, no! fie no, no, no!
die? Fie no, no, no! fie no, no, no!
die?) Fie no, no, no! fie no, no, no!
die? Fie no, no, no! fie no, no, no! shall I a vir - gin
Fie no, no, no, no! fie no, no, no! shall I a vir - gin
Fie no, no, no! fie no, no, no! shall I a vir - gin
30
fie no, no, no! fie no, no, no! O, then, if
fie no, no, no! fie no, no, no, no, no! O, then, if
fie no, no, no! fie no, no, no, no, no! O, then, if
die? Fie no, no, no! fie no, no, no, no, no! O, then, if
die? Fie no, no, no! fie no, no, no, no, no, no! O, then, if
die? Fie no, no, no! fie no, no, no! O, then, if

35

p mp

this be so, O, then, if this be so Shall

this be so, O, (then, if this be so) Shall

this be — so, O, then, if this be — so Shall

this be — so, O, (then, if this be so)

this be so, O, (then, if this be — so)

this be — so, O, (then, if this be so)

40

f

I a vir - gin die? Fie no, no, no! fie no, no, no!

I a vir - gin die? Fie no, no, no, no, no, no, no, no! shall

I a vir - gin die? Fie no, no, no, no! fie no, no, no! shall

Fie no, no, no! fie no, no, no! shall

Fie no, no, no, no! fie no, no, no!,

Fie no, no, no! fie no, no, no!

44
f
fie no, no, no! fie no, no, no!
f
(I a vir - gin die?) Fie no, no, no! fie no, no, no!
f
(I a vir - gin die?) Fie no, no, no! fie no, no, no!
f
mp
I a vir - gin die? Fie no, no, no! fie no, no, no! shall
f
mp
Fie no, no, no, no! fie no, no, no! shall
f
mp
Fie no, no, no! fie no, no, no! shall
48
[← o = o· →]
f
fie no, no, no, no! fie no, no, no, no!
f
fie no, no, no, no! fie no, no, no, no!
f
fie no, no, no! fie no, no, no!
f
(I a vir - gin die?) Fie no, no, no, no, no, no, no, no, no, no!
f
I a vir - gin die? Fie no, no, no! fie no, no, no!
f
I a vir - gin die? Fie no, no, no! fie no, no, no!

35
QUICK, QUICK, AWAY, DISPATCH!
(The first part)

MICHAEL EAST

Quite fast and with clear diction

6

-ring - ing, bells (are now a - ring - ing,)

Bells are now a - ring - ing, bells (are now a -

Bells are a - ring - ing, bells (are a - ring - ing,)

-ring - ing, bells are a - ring - ing,

-ring - ing, bells (are a - ring - ing,) bells are a -

Bells are a - ring - ing, bells are a -

10

[← o·=o →]

-ring - ing,)

dim. *p*

bells are a - ring - ing, bells (are a - ring - ing,) Maids

dim. *p*

bells are a - ring - ing, are a - ring - ing, a - ring - ing, Maids

dim.

-ring - ing, bells (are a - ring - ing,) a - ring - ing,

dim.

-ring - ing, bells are a - ring - ing, a - ring - ing,

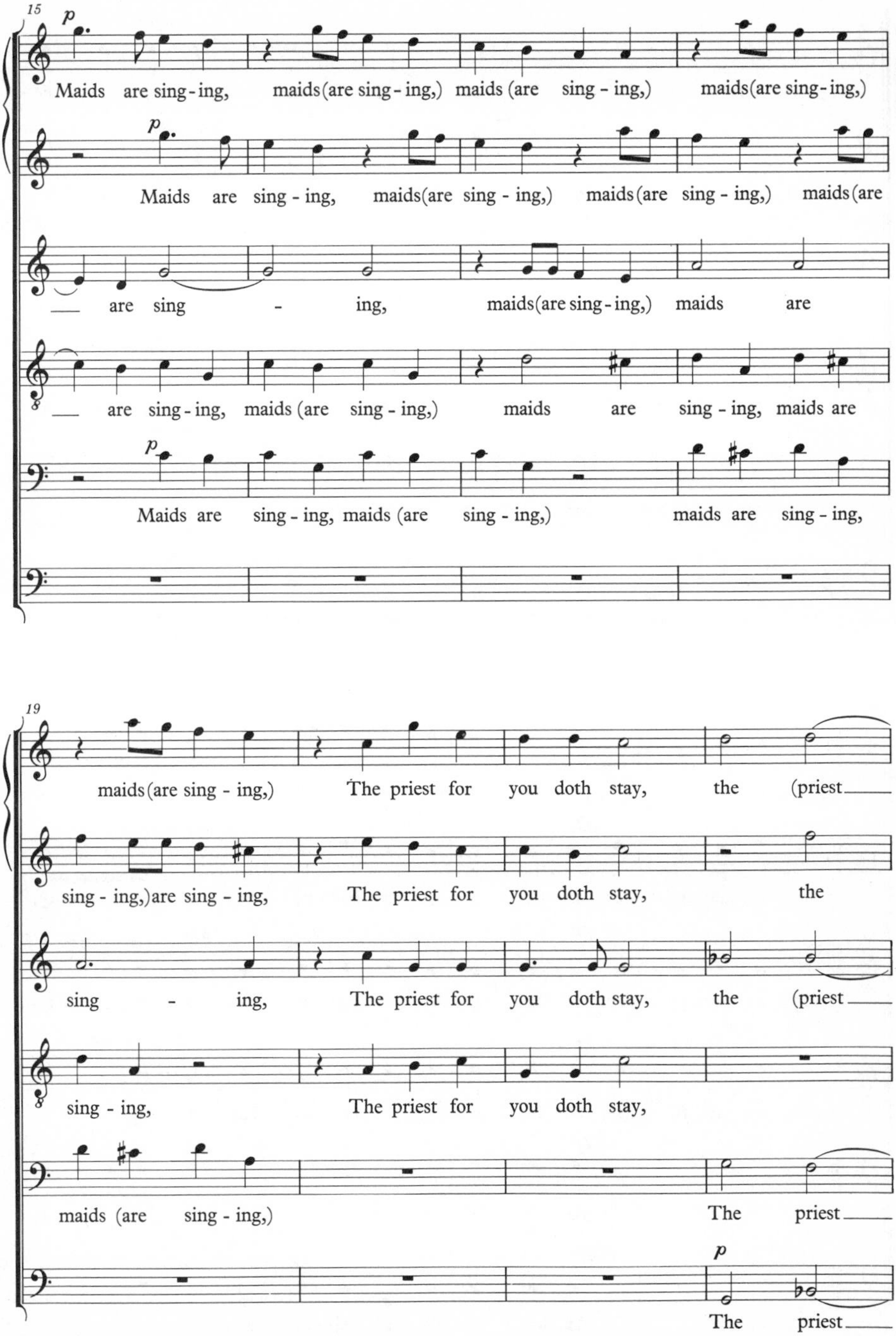

19

maids (are sing-ing,) The priest for you doth stay, the (priest —

sing-ing,) are sing-ing, The priest for you doth stay, the

sing - ing, The priest for you doth stay, the (priest —

sing-ing, The priest for you doth stay,

maids (are sing-ing,) The priest —

p

The priest —

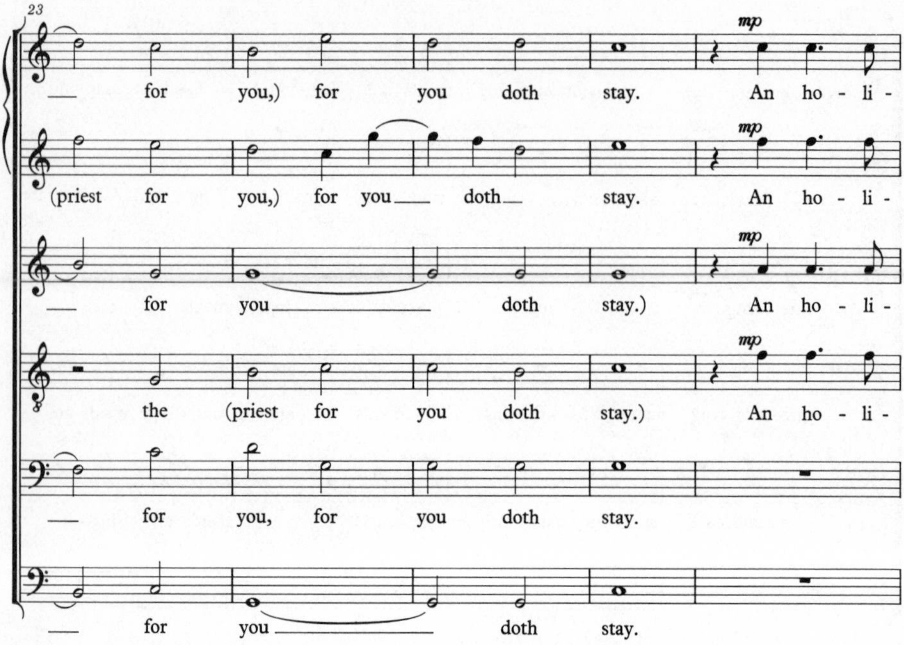
23
mp
for you,) for you doth stay. An ho - li -
(priest for you,) for you doth stay. An ho - li -
for you doth stay.) An ho - li -
the (priest for you doth stay.) An ho - li -
for you, for you doth stay.
for you doth stay.

28
ff
mp
- day, a hap - py day, an (ho - li - day, a hap - py day,) a mer-ry, mer-ry,
- day, a hap - py day, an (ho - li - day, a hap - py day,) a mer-ry, mer-ry,
- day, a hap - py day, an (ho - li - day, a hap - py day,) a mer-ry, mer-ry,
- day, a hap - py day, an ho - li - day, a hap - py, hap - py day,
An ho - li - day, a mer-ry, mer-ry,
An ho - li - day, a hap - py day,

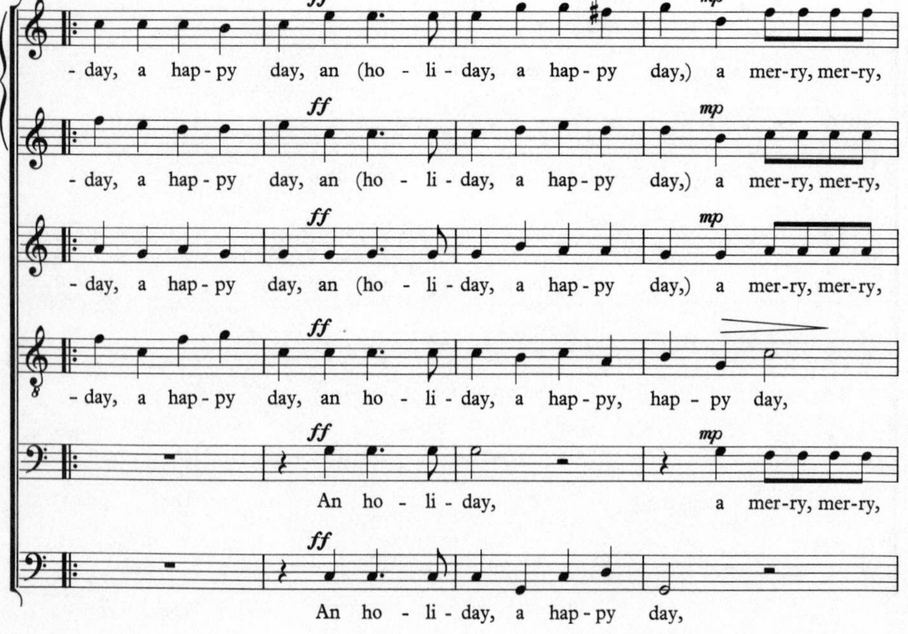

32

ff f
mer - ry day, a (mer-ry, mer-ry, mer - ry day!) The first of

ff f
mer - ry day, a (mer-ry, mer-ry, mer - ry day!) The

ff f
mer - ry day, a (mer-ry, mer-ry, mer - ry day!) The last of no-thing,

ff f
a mer-ry, mer-ry, mer - ry day! The last of no-thing,

f
mer - ry day! The last of no-thing

ff f
a mer-ry, mer-ry, mer - ry day! The last of no-thing,

36

mp
some - thing. Be nim-ble, nim-ble, quick, a - way!

mp
first of some - thing. Be nim-ble, nim-ble, quick, a - way!

mp mf
first of some - thing. Be nim-ble, nim-ble, quick, a-way, be

mp mf
first of some - thing. Be nim-ble, nim-ble, quick, a - way, be

mf
first of some - thing. Be

mf
Be

39

mp

quick, quick, quick, quick, a - way,

mp

quick, quick, quick, quick, a - way,

mp

(nim-ble, nim-ble, quick, a - way!) quick, quick, quick, quick, a - way,

mp

(nim-ble, nim-ble, quick, a - way!) quick, quick, quick, quick, a - way,

nim-ble, nim-ble, quick, a - way!

nim-ble, nim-ble, quick, a - way!

42

1 2

f *mp*

quick, quick, quick, quick, a - way, a - way, a - way, An ho - li - -way!

f *mp*

quick, quick, quick, quick, a - way, a - way, a - way, An ho - li - -way!

f *mp*

quick, quick, quick, quick, a - way, a - way, An ho - li - -way!

f *mp*

quick, quick, a - way, a - way, An ho - li - -way!

f

quick, quick, quick, quick, a - way, a - way, - way!

f

quick, quick, quick, quick, a - way, a - way, - way!

36
NO HASTE BUT GOOD!
(The second part)

MICHAEL EAST

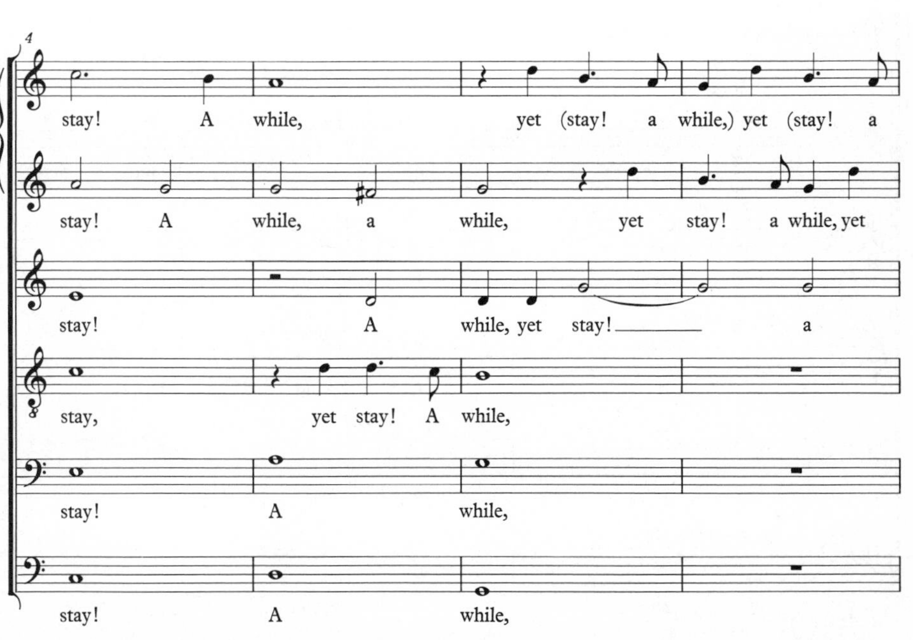

8

while,) yet (stay! a while)

stay! a while

while, yet stay! a while

yet stay! a while, yet (stay! a while,) a while

yet stay! a while, yet stay! a while

yet stay! a while

12

mf sustained

of free I bound must

mf sustained

of free, of free I bound must

mf sustained

of free I bound must

mf sustained

of free I bound must be,

mf sustained

of free I bound must

mf sustained

of free I bound must

17

be, But bound to him,

be, I bound must be,

be, I bound must be, But bound to him,

I bound must be, But bound

be, I bound must be, But bound

be, I bound must be,

22

but (bound to him)

But bound to him that's

but (bound to

to him, to him that's bound

to him

But bound to

27

dim.

that's bound to me;

dim.

bound to me;

dim. *p*

him,) to him that's bound to me;

dim. *p*

to me, to me;

dim. *p*

that's bound to me, that's bound to me;

dim. *p*

him that's bound to me, to me;

[← o = o. →]

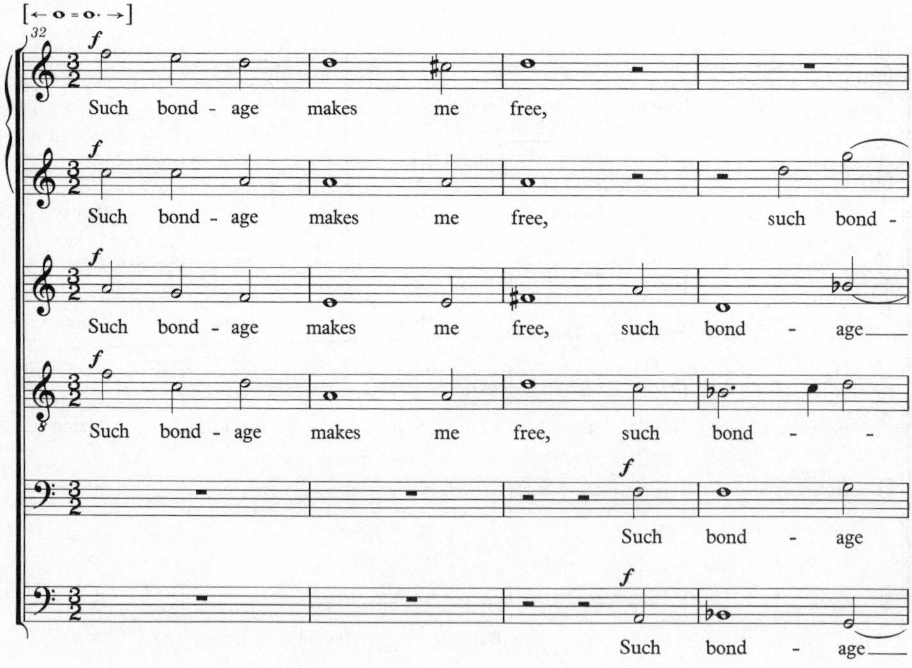

32

f

Such bond - age makes me free,

f

Such bond - age makes me free, such bond -

f

Such bond - age makes me free, such bond - age

f

Such bond - age makes me free, such bond - -

f

Such bond - age

f

Such bond - age

36
[← o· = o →]
mp
makes me free. An ho - li - day, a hap - py
- age makes me free. An ho - li - day, a hap - py
makes me free. An ho - li - day, a hap - py
- age makes me free. An ho - li - day, a hap - py
makes me free.
makes me free.
40
ff
day, an (ho - li - day, a hap - py day,) a mer - ry, mer - ry,
day, an (ho - li - day, a hap - py day,) a mer - ry, mer - ry,
day, an (ho - li - day, a hap - py day,) a mer - ry, mer - ry,
day, an ho - li - day, a hap - py, hap - py day,
An ho - li - day, a mer - ry, mer - ry,
An ho - li - day, a hap - py day,

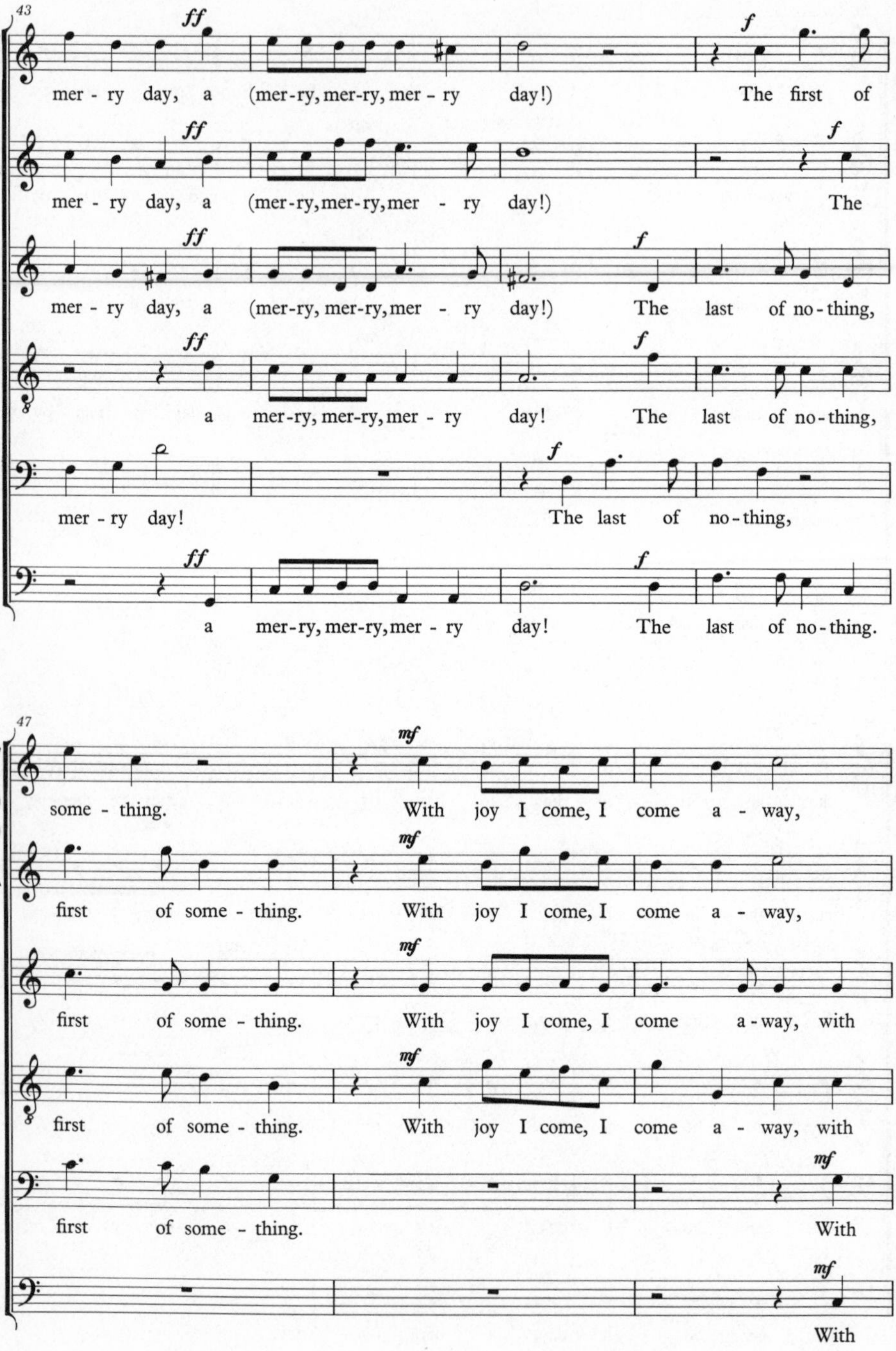

43

ff

mer - ry day, a (mer-ry, mer-ry, mer - ry day!) The first of

mer - ry day, a (mer-ry, mer-ry, mer - ry day!) The

mer - ry day, a (mer-ry, mer-ry, mer - ry day!) The last of no-thing,

a mer-ry, mer-ry, mer - ry day! The last of no-thing,

mer - ry day! The last of no-thing,

a mer-ry, mer-ry, mer - ry day! The last of no-thing.

50

f
I come, I come a - way,

f
I come, I come a - way,

f
joy I come, I come a - way, I come, I come a - way,

f
joy I come, I come a - way, I come, I come a - way,

joy I come, I come a - way,

joy I come, I come a - way,

53

1 2

mp
I come, I come a - way, I come a - way! An ho - li- - way!

mp
I come, I come a - way, I come a - way! An ho - li- - way!

mp
I come, I come a - way, a - way! An ho - li- - way!

mp
I come, I come a - way! An ho - li- - way!

I come, I come a - way, a - way! - way!

I come, I come a - way, a - way! - way!

37
SEE, SEE THE SHEPHERDS' QUEEN

THOMAS TOMKINS

Happily and with crisp rhythm

8
fa la la la la, fa la la la la, fa la la la
la, fa la la la la la, fa la la la la
la la, fa la la la la, fa la la la
la, fa la la la la la, fa la la
la la la, fa la, fa la la, fa la la, fa la
12
p
la, See, see the shep - herds' queen, Fair Phyl - lis
p
la, See, see the shep - herds' queen, Fair Phyl -
p
la, See, see the shep - herds' queen, Fair Phyl -
p
la, See, see the shep - herds' queen, Fair Phyl - lis
p
la, See, see the shep - herds' queen, Fair Phyl -
17
all in green, fa la la la la, fa la la la la, fa la la la
- lis, all in green, fa la la la la, fa la la la
- lis all in green, fa la, fa la la la la la,
all in green, fa la,
- lis all in green, fa la la la,

21

f

la la, fa la la la la la, The

la, fa la la la la, fa la la la la, The

fa la la la la, fa la la la la, The

fa la la la la, fa la la la, The

fa la, fa la la, fa la la, fa la la, The

25

shep - herds home her bring - ing With pip - ing and with sing - ing, sing - ing.

shep - herds home her bring - ing With pip - ing and with sing - ing, sing - ing.

shep - herds home her bring - ing With pip - ing and with sing - ing, sing - ing.

shep-herds home her bring - ing With pip - ing and with sing - ing. *p* Fa

shep - herds home her bring-ing With pip - ing and with sing-ing, with sing-ing.

29

p Fa la la la la la la,

p Fa la la la la, fa la la la la

p Fa la la, fa la, fa la la la, fa la la la la

la la la la la la la la la, fa la la la la la la la la la, fa

p Fa la la la la la la la la la, fa la la

33

fa la la la la la la la la la, fa la la la la la, fa

la la, fa la la la la la la la la la, fa la la

la la la la la, fa la la la la la la, fa la la la,

la la la la la la la la,

la (la la la la,) fa la la la,(fa la la la la

37

la la la la, *mp* The shep - herds home her bring - ing With

la la la, *mp* The shep - herds home her bring - ing With

fa la la la, *mp* The shep - herds home her bring - ing With

la la la la la la la la la la, *mp* The shep-herds home her bring - ing With

la,) fa la la, *mp* The shep - herds home her bring - ing With

41

pip - ing and with sing - ing, sing - ing. Fa la la la

pip - ing and with sing - ing, sing - ing. Fa la la la la la

pip - ing and with sing - ing, sing - ing. Fa la la, fa la, fa

pip - ing and with sing - ing. Fa la la la la la la la la la, fa la la

pip - ing and with sing-ing, with sing-ing. Fa

45
cresc.
la, fa la la la la la, fa
cresc.
la, fa la la la la la la la la la la la,
cresc.
la la la, fa la la la (la la la la,) fa la la, fa la
cresc.
la la la la la la la, fa la la la, fa la la la
la la la la la la la la la, fa la la la (la la la la,)
49
f
la la la la la la la la la, fa la, fa la la la.
f
fa la la la, fa la la la la.
f
la la la, fa la la la, fa la la la.
f
la, fa la la la la la la la la la la.
f
fa la la la, (fa la la la la la,) fa la la.
53
mp
Then dance we on a row, And chant it as we
mp
Then dance we on a row, And chant it as we
mp
Then dance we on a row, And chant it as we
mp
Then dance we on a row, And chant it as we
mp
Then dance we on a row, And chant it as we

58
go. Fa la la,
go. Fa la la,
go. Fa la la la la la, fa
go. Fa la la la la la la, fa la la la la
go. Fa la la la la la la la la
62
fa la la la la la, fa la la la la
fa la la la la la la la, fa la la la la la la,
la la, fa la la la la la, fa
la, fa la la la,
la la la, fa la la la la
cresc.
66
la, fa la la la la, fa la la
fa la la la la la la la,
la la la, fa la la, fa la la la
fa la la la la la la la,
la la la, fa la la la la la, fa la la
cresc.

70
la la, fa la la la la la,
fa la la la la la la la,
la la la, fa la la, fa la la la, fa la la,
fa la la la la la la la la,
la, fa la la la la la, fa la la la la,
75
Then dance we on a row, And chant it as we
Then dance we on a row, And chant it as we
Then dance we on a row, And chant it as we
Then dance we on a row, And chant it as we
Then dance we on a row, And chant it as we
80
go. Fa la la,
go. Fa la la,
go. Fa la la la la la, fa
go. Fa la la la la la la, fa la la la la
go. Fa la la la la la, fa la la

84
fa la la la la la la la la la la la la la la,
cresc.
fa la la la la la, fa la la la la
la la, fa la la la la la, fa
la, fa la la la,
la la la, fa la la la la
88
cresc.
fa la la la la la la la,
la la, fa la la la, fa la la
la la la, fa la la, fa la la la
cresc.
fa la la la la la la la,
cresc.
la la la, fa la la la la la, fa la la
92
f
fa la la la la la la la.
f
la la, fa la la la la la.
f
la la la, fa la la la la la la, fa la la.
f
fa la la la la la la la la.
f
la, fa la la la la la, fa la la la la.
[𝄐]

38
SINCE ROBIN HOOD

THOMAS WEELKES

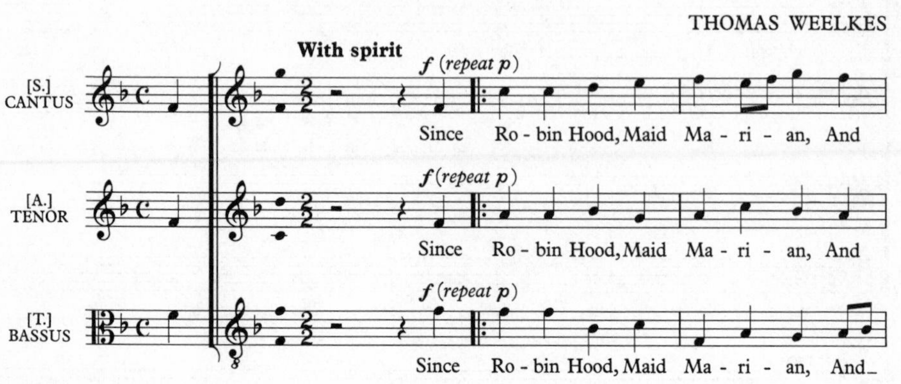

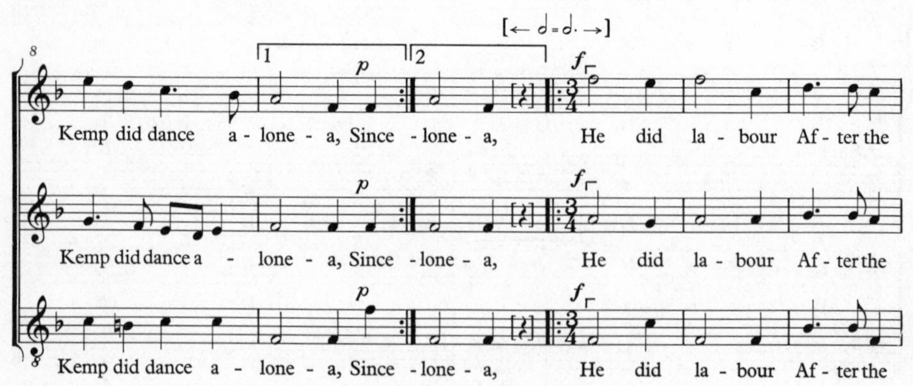

13

ta - bor. For to dance Then in - to France, for (to dance

ta - bor. For to dance Then in-to France, for (to dance

ta - bor. For to dance Then in - to France, for (to dance then

19

[← 𝅗𝅥. = 𝅗𝅥 →]

then in - to France.) He took pains To skip, (to skip,) to

then in - to France.) He took pains, took pains To skip, (to skip,) to skip

in - to France.) He took pains To skip, to skip, (to skip,) to

24

skip it in hope of gains, of gains. He will trip it, trip it, trip it on the

it in hope of gains, (in hope of gains.) He will trip it, trip it, (trip it) on the

skip it in hope of gains, of gains. He will trip it, trip it, trip it on the

29

1 2

toe, Did-dle did-dle did-dle doe, (did-dle did-dle did-dle doe.) doe.)

toe, Did-dle did-dle did-dle doe, (did-dle did-dle did-dle doe.) doe.)

toe, Did-dle did-dle did-dle doe, (did-dle did-dle did-dle doe.) doe.)

39
SEE WHAT A MAZE OF ERROR

GEORGE KIRBYE

8
cresc.
-rinth of ter - ror (and la - by-rinth of ter - ror,) of
mf
ter - - ror, (and la - by-
cresc.
ter - - ror, (and la - by-rinth of ter - ror,) of
p cresc.
and la - by - rinth of ter - ror (and la -
p cresc.
and la - by-rinth of
12
f
ter - - - ror, my love hath trac - - -
-rinth of ter - ror,)
f
ter - - - ror, my love hath trac - - -
f
- by-rinth of ter - ror,) my love hath trac - - - - -
f
ter - - - ror, my love hath trac - - - - -
16
mp
- ed, my love hath trac - - - - - ed,
mp
my love hath trac - - - - - ed,
mp
f
- ed, (my love hath trac - - - - - ed,) my love hath
f
- ed, my love hath
f
- ed, my love hath

20
f
my love hath trac'd hath trac - - ed.
p
f
my love hath trac - - - - - - ed.
p
trac - - - - - - ed hath trac - ed. wretch - ed
p
trac - - - ed, (my love hath trac - ed.) wretch - ed
p
trac - - - - - - - - ed. wretch - -
25
wretch - - ed I, whom
wretch - - ed I, wretch - - ed I,
I, wretch - - ed
I, wretch - - ed I, whom love pain
- - ed I, wretch - - ed I,
31
love pain - - eth, whom love pain - eth,
mf
whom love pain - - eth, (whom love pain - eth,) and true faith
mf
I, whom love pain - - eth, and true faith
mf
- eth, (whom love pain - eth,) and true faith
whom love pain - - eth, whom love pain - eth,

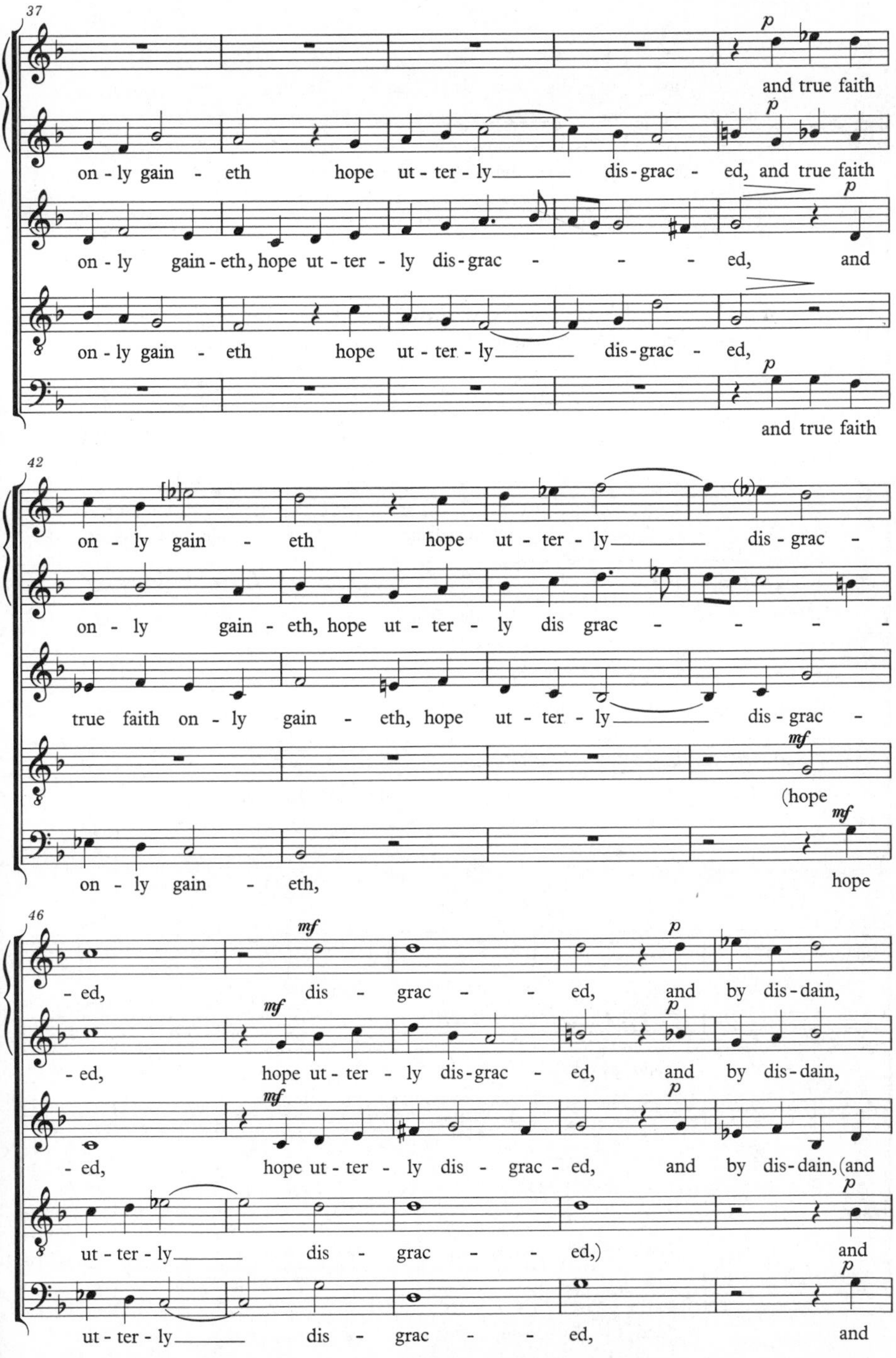
37
p
and true faith
on - ly gain - eth hope ut - ter - ly dis - grac - ed, and true faith
p
on - ly gain - eth, hope ut - ter - ly dis - grac - - - ed, and
on - ly gain - eth hope ut - ter - ly dis - grac - ed,
p
and true faith
42
on - ly gain - eth hope ut - ter - ly dis - grac -
on - ly gain - eth, hope ut - ter - ly dis grac - - - -
true faith on - ly gain - eth, hope ut - ter - ly dis - grac -
mf
(hope
mf
on - ly gain - eth, hope
46
mf
p
- ed, dis - grac - - ed, and by dis - dain,
mf
p
- ed, hope ut - ter - ly dis - grac - ed, and by dis - dain,
mf
p
- ed, hope ut - ter - ly dis - grac - ed, and by dis - dain, (and
p
ut - ter - ly dis - grac - - ed,) and
p
ut - ter - ly dis - grac - - ed, and

51
and by dis - dain de - fac - ed, (and by dis - dain de -
and by dis - dain de - fac - ed, and by dis - dain de -
by dis - dain,)
and by dis -
by dis - dain, and by dis - dain de - fac - ed, (and by dis -
by dis - dain, and by dis - dain de -
55
f
- fac - ed,) and by dis-dain, and by dis-dain de -
- fac - ed, and by dis-dain, and by dis-dain de -
- dain de - fac - ed, and by dis-dain,(and by dis-dain,)and by dis-dain de -
- dain de - fac - ed,) and by dis-dain,
- fac - ed, and by dis-dain,
60
- fac - ed, and by dis - dain de - fac - ed.
- fac - ed, and by dis - dain de - fac - ed.
- fac - ed, and by dis-dain de - fac - ed.
and by dis - dain de - fac - ed.
and by dis - dain de - fac - ed.

40
SING WE AND CHANT IT

8
v. 1 p (both times)
v. 2 f (both times)
la.
Not long youth last - eth, And old age
Hence, care, be pack - ing! No mirth be
v. 1 p (both times)
v. 2 f (both times)
la.
Not long youth last - eth, And old age
Hence, care, be pack - ing! No mirth be
v. 1 p (both times)
v. 2 f (both times)
la.
Not long youth last - eth, And old age
Hence, care, be pack - ing! No mirth be
v. 1 p (both times)
v. 2 f (both times)
la.
Not long youth last - eth, And old age
Hence, care, be pack - ing! No mirth be
v. 1 p (both times)
v. 2 f (both times)
la.
Not long youth last - eth, And old age
Hence, care, be pack - ing! No mirth be
12
hast - eth. Now is best lei - sure To take our
lack - ing! Let spare no trea - sure To live in
hast - eth. Now is best lei - sure To take our
lack - ing! Let spare no trea - sure To live in
hast - eth. Now is best lei - sure To take our
lack - ing! Let spare no trea - sure To live in
hast - eth. Now is best lei - sure To take our
lack - ing! Let spare no trea - sure To live in
hast - eth. Now is best lei - sure To take our
lack - ing! Let spare no trea - sure To live in

16
plea - sure.
plea - sure.
Fa la la la la
plea - sure.
plea - sure.
Fa la la la la la la la la,
plea - sure.
plea - sure.
Fa la la la, fa la
plea - sure.
plea - sure.
Fa la la la la la, fa la
plea - sure.
plea - sure.
Fa la la la la la la la, fa la
1.
2.
20
la, fa la la la la. la.
fa la la la, fa la la la. la.
la la la la la la, fa la la la la. la.
la la la la la, fa la la la la. la.
la la la la la la ___ la. la.

41
STRIKE IT UP, TABOR

THOMAS WEELKES

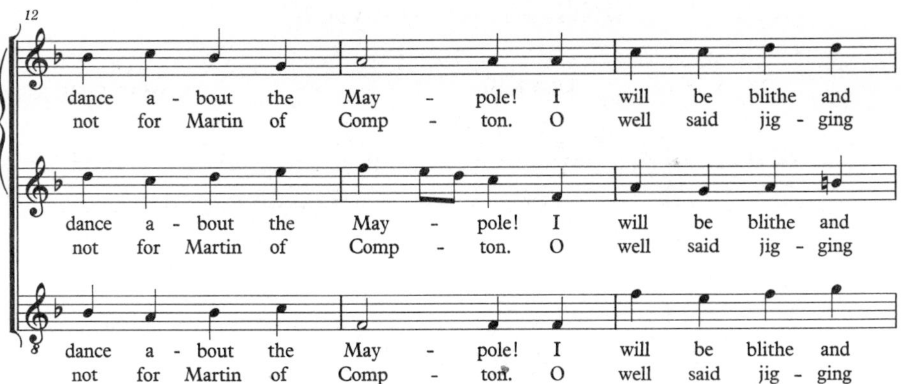
12
dance a - bout the May - pole! I will be blithe and
not for Martin of Comp - ton. O well said jig - ging
dance a - bout the May - pole! I will be blithe and
not for Martin of Comp - ton. O well said jig - ging
dance a - bout the May - pole! I will be blithe and
not for Martin of Comp - ton. O well said jig - ging

15
brisk! Leap and skip, Hop and trip, Turn a - bout In the rout, Un -
Al'ce, Pret-ty Jill Stand you still! Dap-per Jack Means to smack. How
brisk, blithe and brisk! I'll leap and skip, Hop and trip, Turn a-bout In the rout, Un-
Al'ce, jig-ging Al'ce, O pret-ty Jill Stand you still! Dap-per Jack Means to smack. How
brisk! Leap and skip, Hop and trip, Turn a - bout In the rout, Un-til
Al'ce, Pret-ty Jill Stand you still! Dap-per Jack Means to smack. How now?

18
1
2
ff
- til ve - ry wea - ry, wea - ry joints can scarce frisk. I frisk.
now? fie! fie! fie! fie! fie! fie! fie! you dance false. The false.
ff
- til ve - ry wea - ry, wea - ry joints can scarce frisk. I frisk.
now? fie! fie! fie! fie! fie! fie! fie! you dance false. The false.
ve - ry wea - ry, joints can scarce frisk. frisk.
fie! fie! fie! fie! fie! you dance false. false.

42
SING WE AT PLEASURE

With gaiety THOMAS WEELKES

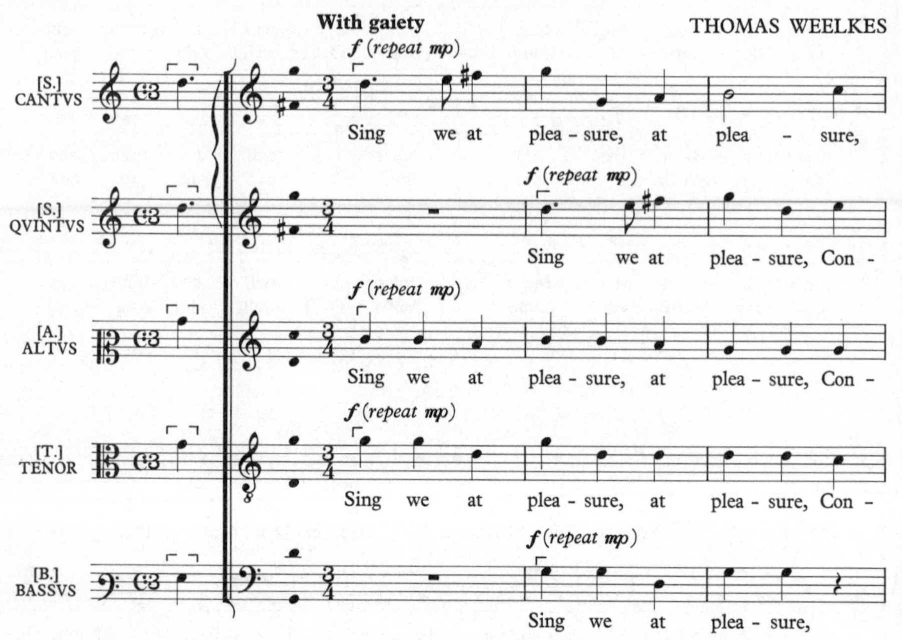

9
Fa la la la la, fa
Fa la la la la la la la la la la
la la la la la la la la la la la la la la la la
la la la la la la la la la la, fa la la la
la la la la la la, fa la la la la la
14
la la la la la la la la la la la la la la
la, fa la la la la la la la la
la la la la la la la la la la la la la la la
la la la la la la la la la la la la, fa la la
la la la la la la la la, fa la la la
19
1
2
f
la la la la la la la la. la. Sweet
la la la la la la la la. la. Sweet
la la la la la la la la la la. la. Sweet
la la la la la la la la la la. la. Sweet
la, fa la la la la la la. la. Sweet

23
Love shall keep the ground, Whilst we his prai-ses
Love shall keep the ground, Whilst we his
Love shall keep the ground, shall keep the ground, Whilst
Love shall keep the ground, Whilst we his prai-ses sound,
Love shall keep the ground, Whilst we his prai-ses sound,
27
sound, (whilst we his prai-ses sound,) his
prai-ses sound, (whilst we his prai-ses sound,) his
we his prai-ses sound, (whilst we his
(whilst we his prai-ses sound, whilst we his prai-ses sound,) his
(whilst we his prai-ses sound,) his
30
prai - ses sound. All shep - herds in a ring Shall,
prai - ses sound. All shep - herds in a ring, in a
prai - ses sound.) All shep - herds in a ring Shall,
prai - ses sound. All shep - herds in a ring Shall,
prai - ses sound. All shep - herds in a ring

dan - cing,— e - ver sing, (shall, dan - cing,—
ring Shall, dan - cing,— e - ver sing,
dan - cing, e - ver sing, (shall, dan - cing, e - ver
dan - cing,— e - ver sing, (shall, dan - cing,—
Shall, dan - ing,— e - ver sing,
e - ver sing,) e - ver sing: Fa la la la
(shall, dan - cing,— e - ver sing:) Fa la la la
sing, shall, dan - cing, e - ver sing:) Fa la la
e - ver sing,) e - ver sing: Fa la la la la la la la
(shall, dan - cing,— e - ver sing:) Fa la la la la la
la la la la la la la la la la la la la
la la la la la la la la la la la la la
la la la la la la la la la la la la
la la la la la la, fa la la la la la la la la la la la, fa la la
la, fa la la la la la la la la la la, fa la la la la la la

50
la la la la la la la la la. Sweet Love shall
la la la la la la la la la. Sweet Love shall
la la la la la la la. Sweet Love shall
la la la la la la la la la la la. Sweet Love shall
la la, fa la la la, fa la la la la. Sweet Love shall
mp
55
keep the ground, Whilst we his prai-ses sound,
keep the ground, Whilst we his prai-ses sound, (whilst
keep the ground, shall keep the ground, Whilst we his prai-ses
keep the ground, Whilst we his prai-ses sound, (whilst we his
keep the ground, Whilst we his prai-ses sound, (whilst we
cresc.
59
(whilst we his prai - ses sound,) his prai - ses
we his prai - ses sound,) his prai - ses
sound, (whilst we his prai - ses
prai - ses sound, whilst we his prai - ses sound,) his prai - ses
his prai - ses sound,) his prai - ses

62
f
sound. All shep - herds in a ring, in a ring
sound. All shep - herds in a ring Shall, dan - cing,
sound.) All shep - herds in a ring Shall, dan - cing,
sound. All shep - herds in a ring Shall, dan - cing,
sound. All shep - herds in a ring
67
Shall, dan - cing, e - ver sing, (shall,
e - ver sing, (shall, dan - cing, e - ver
e - ver sing, (shall, dan - cing, e - ver sing, shall,
e - ver sing, (shall, dan - cing, e - ver
Shall, dan - cing, e - ver sing, (shall,
72
p
dan - cing, e - ver sing:) Fa la la la la la la
sing,) e - ver sing: Fa la la la la la
dan - cing, e - ver sing:) Fa la la la la la
sing,) e - ver sing: Fa la la la la la la la la la la la la la
dan - cing, e - ver sing:) Fa la la la la la la, fa

77
la la la la la la la la la la la
la la la la la la la la la la la la
la la la la la la la la
la, fa la la la la la la la la la la la, fa la la
la la la la la la la, fa la la la la la la la la la la

81
cresc.
la la la la la la la la la.
la la la la la la la la la.
la la la la la la la la.
la la la la la la la la la la la.
la la, fa la la la, fa la la la la.
f

43
SLEEP, FLESHLY BIRTH

ROBERT RAMSEY

10
mp
- - ful earth,
peace - - - ful earth, And
- - ful earth, And let thine ears,
peace - ful earth, And let thine
peace - ful earth,
peace - ful earth,
15
And let thine ears, (and let thine ears)
let thine ears list to the mu - sic of the
(and let thine ears)
ears, (and let thine ears) list to the mu - sic of the
And let thine ears
And let thine

20
list to the mu-sic of the spheres,
spheres, and (let thine ears) list (to the
list to the mu-sic of the spheres, the spheres, list (to the
spheres, and let thine ears list to the
list to the mu - sic of the spheres, list (to the
ears list to the
25
p
While we a - round
mu - sic of the spheres,) While we a -
mu - sic of the spheres,) While we a - round this
mu - sic of the spheres, While we a - round this
mu - sic of the spheres,) While we a - round, while
mu - sic of the spheres, While we a - round

30
this fai - - - ry ground
-round this fai - ry, fai - - - ry ground Thy
fai - ry ground, this (fai - - - ry ground)
fai - - - ry, fai - - - ry ground
we a - round this fai - - - ry ground
this fai - - - ry ground
35
Thy dole - - - ful o - bit
dole - - - ful o - bit, thy (dole - - ful o -
Thy dole - - - ful o - - - bit
Thy
Thy
Thy dole - - - ful, thy dole - - ful

40
keep - - ing, thy dole - - - ful o - - -
- - bit) keep - ing, thy (dole - - ful o -
keep - ing, thy (dole - - - ful o - - -
dole - - ful o - bit, thy (dole - - -
dole - - - ful, dole - - - ful o - - -
o - - - bit keep - - ing, thy (dole - ful
45
mp
- - bit keep - - ing,) Make mar-ble melt with
mp
- - bit keep - - ing,) Make mar-ble melt with weep - -
mp
- - bit keep - - ing,) Make mar-ble melt with
- - ful o - bit) keep - - - ing,
- - bit keep - - ing,
o - bit keep - - ing,)

weep - - - ing,

- - - ing,

weep - - ing,

mp
Make mar-ble melt with weep - - -

mp
Make mar-ble melt with weep - -

mp
Make mar-ble melt with weep - -

(make mar-ble melt) with weep - ing.

make(mar-ble melt with weep - - - ing.)

- ing, (make mar-ble melt with weep - - - ing.)

- - ing, (make mar-ble melt with weep - - - ing.)

- ing, (make mar-ble melt with weep - - - ing.)

[← o = o. →]
60
p
With num-'rous feet we'll part and meet.
p
With num-'rous feet we'll part and meet.
p
With num-'rous feet,
pp
with num-'rous
pp
With num-'rous
pp
With num-'rous
65
feet we'll part and meet.
feet we'll part and meet,
ppp
with (num-'rous feet.)
feet,
ppp
with num-'rous feet
ppp
With num-'rous feet

70

[← o· = o →]

f

Then cho - rus - like in a ring thy

Then cho - rus - like in a ring thy prais -

Then cho - rus - like in a ring thy

Then cho - rus - like in a ring thy

we'll part and meet. Then cho - rus - like in a ring thy

we'll part and meet. Then cho - rus - like in a ring thy

75

prais - es sing, While showers of flowers be - strew thee, (while

- - es sing, While showers of flowers be -

prais - - - es sing, ——— While

prais - es sing, While showers of flowers be - strew thee,

prais - es sing, While showers of

prais - es sing, While showers ——— of

79
showers of flowers be - strew thee,) be - strew thee, while
- strew thee, (while showers of flowers be - - strew thee,) be - strew thee,
showers of flowers be - strew thee, while
while (showers of flowers be - strew thee,)
flowers be - strew thee, (while showers of flowers be -
flowers be - strew thee, (while showers of flowers be -
83
(showers of flowers be - strew thee,) while (showers of flowers be - strew
while (showers of flowers be - strew thee,) be - strew
(showers of flowers,) while (showers of flowers be - strew
while showers of flowers, while (showers of flowers be - strew
- strew thee,) (while showers of flowers be - strew thee,) we'll
mf
- strew thee,) be - strew thee,

87

mf

thee,) we'll thus with tears be -

mf

thee, we'll thus with tears, with tears

mf

thee,) we'll thus with tears

mf

thee,) we'll thus with tears be - dew thee, with

thus with tears, (we'll thus with tears,) we'll thus

mf

we'll thus with tears, with tears

92

p

- dew thee. Rest

p

be - dew thee. Rest in

p

be - dew thee. Rest

p

(tears be - dew thee.) Rest

p

with tears be - dew thee. Rest

p

be - - - dew thee. Rest

97
in soft peace, sweet youth,
soft peace, sweet youth, and
in soft peace, sweet youth,
in soft peace, sweet youth, and
in soft peace, sweet youth,
in soft peace, sweet youth,
102
and there re - main
there re - main
and there re - main
there re - main Till soul and bo - dy meet to join
and there re - main Till soul and bo - dy meet to join
and there re - main

107
Till soul and bo - dy meet to join a - - -
Till soul and bo - dy meet to join a -
mp
To join a - gain, till
a - gain,
a - gain,
mp
till
mp
Till
112
- gain,
mp
(till soul and bo - dy
mp
- gain, till (soul and bo - dy meet to join a -
soul and bo - dy meet to join, to join a -
mp
till (soul and bo - dy meet to
(soul and bo - dy meet to join a - gain,) (till
soul and bo - dy meet to join a - gain,

116
meet to join a-gain,)(till soul and bo - dy meet to join a -
- gain, till soul and bo - dy meet to join a -
- gain, till (soul and bo - dy meet) to (join a -
join a - gain, to join a - gain,
soul and bo - dy meet to join, to join a - gain,
(till soul and bo - dy meet to join a - gain,)
121
mf dim. (second time)
- gain,) meet to join, to join a - gain. - gain.
- gain,) meet to join a - gain. Rest - gain.
- gain,) to join a - gain. - gain.
meet to join a - gain. - gain.
meet to join a - gain. - gain.
to join a - gain. - gain.
p
pp

44
SWEET HONEY-SUCKING BEES
(The first part)

JOHN WILBYE

Flowing but with tenderness

7
still,) why do you still Sur - feit on ro - - ses,
still, why do you still) Sur - feit on ro - - ses,
why do you still,) Sur - feit on ro - ses, pinks and
(why do you still,) Sur - feit on ro - - ses,
10
pinks and vi - o - lets, As if the choic - est nec - tar lay in
pinks and vi - o - lets, As if the choic - est nec -
vi - o - lets, As if the choic - est nec - tar
pinks and vi - o - lets, As if the choic - est nec - tar lay in
14
them where-with you store, (where-with you store,
- tar lay in them
lay in them where-with you store your cu-rious
them, where-with you store your cu - rious ca - bin -

17
f
where with you store) your cu-rious ca - bin - ets? Ah, make your
where with you store your cu - rious ca - bin -
f
ca - bin - ets? Ah, make your
- ets? your cu-rious ca - - - bin -
f
Ah,
20
flight, (ah, make your flight,)
f
- ets? Ah, make your flight to Me - li - sua - via's
flight to Me - li - sua - via's
f
- ets? Ah, make your flight, ah, (make your
make your flight to Me - li - sua - via's
23
ah, make your flight, (ah, make your flight) to
lips, ah, make your flight to
lips, ah, make your flight;
flight,) your flight to Me - li -
lips, ah, make your flight to

26
Me - li - sua - via's lips;
Me - li - sua - via's lips;
mf
There may you re - vel, (there may you re - vel,) there,
mf
- sua - via's lips; There may you re - vel, there (may you re - vel,
Me - li - sua - via's lips;
29
mf
There, there may you re - vel in am - bro - sian cheer, Where
mf
There may you re - vel, there may you re - vel in am - bro - sian cheer, Where
there may you re - vel,
there may you re - vel) in am - bro - sian cheer, Where
mf
There may you re - vel,
33
smil - ing ro - ses and sweet lil - ies sit,
smil - ing ro - ses and sweet lil - ies sit,
there may you
smil - ing ro - ses and sweet lil - ies sit,

37
there may you re - vel,
there may you re - vel,
re - vel, (there may you re - vel) in am - bro - sian cheer, Where
there may you re - vel, (there may you re - vel) in am - bro - sian cheer, Where
(there may you re - vel) in am - bro - sian cheer, Where
41
p
Keep-
smil - ing ro - ses and sweet lil - ies sit, Keep-
smil - ing ro - ses and sweet lil - ies sit, Keep-
smil - ing ro - ses and sweet lil - ies sit,
45
p
Keep - ing their Spring - tide,
- ing their Spring - tide gra - ces,
- ing their Spring - tide gra - ces, keep - ing their
- ing their Spring - tide gra - ces, (keep - ing their

48

keep - ing their Spring - tide gra - ces, keep - ing

(keep - ing their Spring - tide gra - ces,) keep - ing

Spring - tide gra - es, keep - ing their Spring -

Spring - tide gra - es,) all the year,

Keep - ing their Spring -

51

their Spring - tide gra - ces all the year,

their Spring - tide gra - ces all the year,

- tide,) Spring - tide gra - ces, (keep - ing their Spring - tide

their Spring - tide gra - ces all the year, all the

- tide, Spring - tide gra - ces all the year,

54

keep - ing their Spring - - - tide gra - - - ces

keep - ing their Spring - - - tide gra - -

gra - ces,)

year, keep - ing their Spring - - - tide gra - - - ces

57
all the year,
ces all the year,
keep - ing their Spring - tide
all the year, keep - (ing their Spring -
keep - ing their Spring - tide
61
(keep - ing their
keep - ing their Spring - tide,
gra - ces all the year, (keep - ing their Spring - tide
- tide gra - ces all the year, keep - ing their
gra - ces all the year, (keep - ing their
65
Spring - tide gra - ces all the year.
Spring - tide gra - ces all the year.
gra - ces all the year.
Spring - tide gra - ces all the year.)
Spring - tide gra - ces all the year.

45
YET, SWEET, TAKE HEED
(The second part)

JOHN WILBYE

At the same speed

8
mp
Sting not, sting not her
not, sting not her soft lips,
not her soft lips, (sting not her soft
not her soft lips, her soft
Sting not, sting not her
13
mf
soft lips, O be - ware of that,
mf
O be-ware of that, (O be -
mf
lips, O be-ware of that, (O
mf
lips, O be - ware of that, (O
mf
soft lips, O be-ware of
16
(O be-ware of that,) O be - ware of that,
- ware of that,) (O be-ware of that,) O be -
be - - - ware of that,
be - - - ware of
that, (O be - ware of that, O be-ware of

19

(O be-ware of that,) O, O be - ware
- ware, O (be-ware of that,) O be -
(O be - ware of that,)
that, be - ware of that, (be -
that,) O be - - ware

23

of that, *f* For if one flam - - ing
- ware of that, *f* For if one flam - - ing
f For if one flam - - ing
- ware of that,)
of that,

27

dart come from her eye, come (from her eye, come from her
dart come from her eye, (come from her eye, come from her
dart come from her eye, (come from her eye,) Was

30
dim.
eye,) Was ne - ver dart so sharp, ah, then you die, you
dim.
eye,) Was ne - ver dart so sharp, ah, then you die,
dim.
ne - ver dart so sharp, ah,
34
p
die, (ah, then you die, then you die, you die!)
p
then you die, (then you die,)(then you die,) ah, then you die!
p
ah, then you die, ah, then you die, you die!
38
f
For if one flam - ing dart come from her eye, (come from her
f
For if one flam - ing dart come from her eye, (come from her
f
For if one flam - ing dart come from her eye,

42
eye, come from her eye,) Was ne - ver dart so sharp, ah,
eye, come from her eye,) Was ne - ver dart so sharp, ah,
come (from her eye,) Was ne - ver dart so sharp, ah,
46
dim.
then you die, (then you die, then you die, then you die,) ah, then you
dim.
then you die, you die, (ah, then you die, then (you die, you
dim.
ah, then you die, ah, then you die, you
50
f
For if one flam - ing dart come from her
f
For if one flam - ing dart come from her
p
die.
p
die.) For if one flam - ing dart
f
p
die.

54
eye, (come from her eye, come from her eye,) was ne - ver dart so
eye, (come from her eye, come from her eye,) was ne - ver dart so
come from her eye, (come from her eye,) was ne - ver dart so
58
dim.
sharp, ah, then you die, then you die, (then you die,) ah,
dim.
sharp, ah, then you die, then you die, then you die, ah,
dim.
sharp, ah, then you die, then you die, ah,
62
p
then you die,(then you die,) you die.
p
then you die, then you die.
f
Was ne - ver dart so sharp,
p
f
then you die. Was ne - ver dart,
f
Was ne - ver dart so

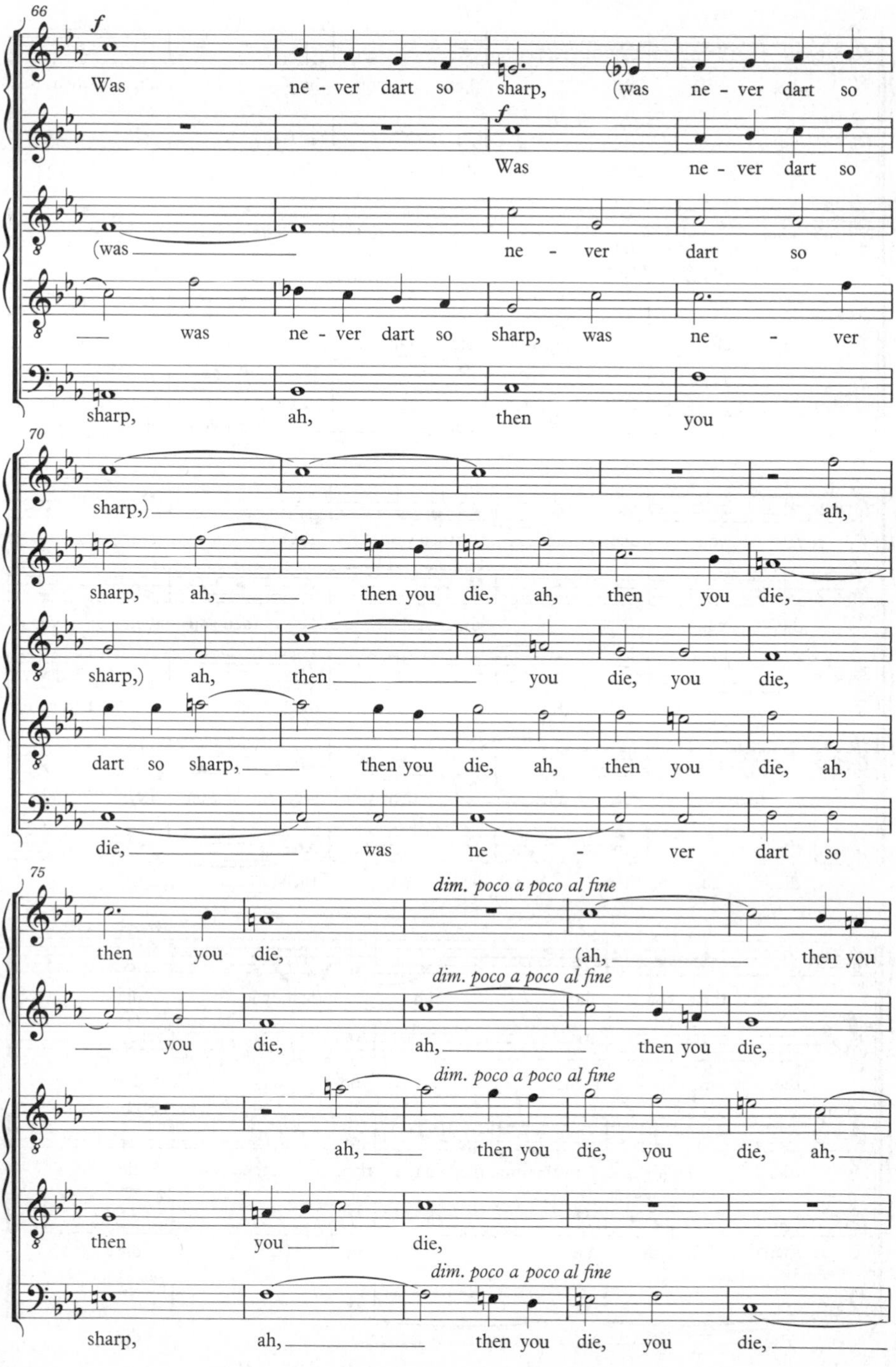

66

f
Was ne - ver dart so sharp, (was ne - ver dart so
f
Was ne - ver dart so
(was ne - ver dart so
was ne - ver dart so sharp, was ne - ver
sharp, ah, then you

70

sharp,)
ah,
sharp, ah, then you die, ah, then you die,
sharp,) ah, then you die, you die,
dart so sharp, then you die, ah, then you die, ah,
die, was ne - ver dart so

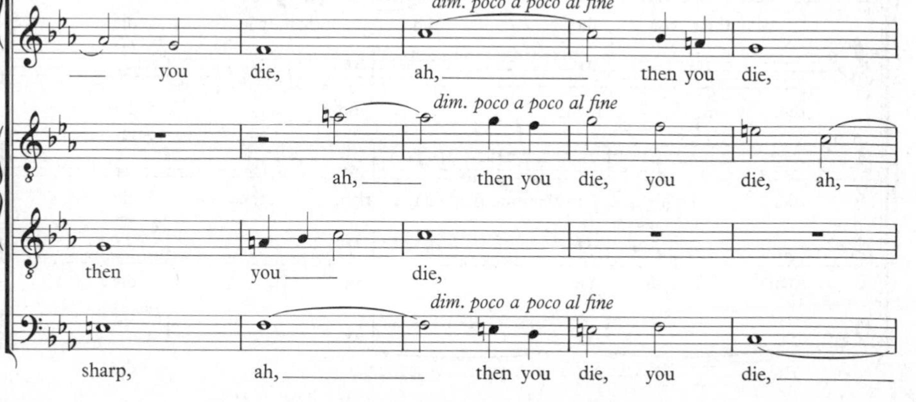

80
die, ah, then you die,) ah, then
(ah, then you die,) ah, then you
then you die,
dim. poco a poco al fine
ah, ah, then you die, (ah, then you die, ah,
ah, then you die, you
85
you die, (ah, then you die,) ah,
die, you die, ah, then you die, you
(ah, then you die,) ah, then you
then you die,) ah, then you die, you die, (ah,
die, ah, then you die, ah, then
90
pp
then you die, ah, then you die.
die, ah, then you die.
die, (ah, then you die,) ah, then you die.
then you die, you die.)
you die.

46
SWEET SUFFOLK OWL

THOMAS VAUTOR

10
Suf - folk owl, so trim - ly dight With fea-thers like a la - dy bright,
(Suf - folk owl,) so trim - ly dight With fea-thers like a la - dy bright,
Suf - folk owl, so trim - ly dight With fea-thers like a la - dy bright,
(Suf - folk owl,) so trim - ly dight With fea-thers like a la - dy bright,
(Suf - folk owl,) so trim - ly dight With fea-thers like a la - dy bright,
14
f
sweet (Suf-folk owl,) so (trim - ly dight With fea-thers like a la - dy bright,)
sweet (Suf-folk owl, so trim - ly dight With fea-thers like a la-dy bright,) Thou,
sweet (Suf - folk owl,) so (trim - ly dight With fea-thers like a la-dy bright,) Thou,
sweet (Suf - folk owl, so trim - ly dight With fea-thers like a la-dy bright,) Thou,
sweet (Suf - folk owl, so trim - ly dight With fea-thers like a la-dy bright,) Thou,
18
mf
dim.
pp
Thou sing'st a - lone, sit - ting by night, Te
thou sing'st a - lone, sit - ting by night, Te
sit - ting by night, sit - ting by night, Te
sit - ting by night, (sit - ting by night,) Te
sit - ting by night, (sit - ting by night,) Te

23
whit, te whoo, te (whit, te whoo,) te (whit, te whoo,) te whit, te whoo,
whit, te whoo, te (whit, te whoo,) te (whit, te whoo,) te (whit,) te (whit,)
whit, te whoo, te (whit, te whoo,) te (whit, te whoo,) te whit, te whoo,
whit, te whoo, te (whit, te whoo,) te (whit, te whoo,) te whit, te whit, te
whit, te whoo, te (whit, te whoo,) te (whit, te whoo,) te (whit, te whoo,) te
27
te whoo, te whit, te whoo,
te whoo, te whit, te
te (whit, te whoo,) te whit, te whit, te whoo,
whoo, te whoo, te (whit, te whoo,) te
whit, te whoo, te (whit,
31
te whit, te whit, te whit, te whoo.
whoo, te whit, te whoo.
te (whit, te whoo,) te (whit, te whoo.)
whit, te whoo, te whit, te whoo.
te whoo,) te (whit, te whoo.)
f
f
f
f
f

35
mf
Thy note, that forth so free - ly rolls,
mf
Thy note, that forth so free - ly rolls,
mf
Thy note, that forth so free - ly rolls, thy (note, that
mf
Thy note, that
mf
Thy note, that
40
f
With
f
With
cresc.
f
forth so free - ly rolls,) rolls, With
cresc.
forth so free - ly rolls,
cresc.
f
forth so free - ly rolls, With
44
shrill com - mand The mouse con - trols, with (shrill com - mand The mouse con -
shrill com - mand The mouse con - trols, with (shrill com - mand The mouse
shrill com - mand The mouse con - trols, with (shrill com - mand The
f
With shrill com - mand The mouse con - trols,
shrill com - mand The mouse con - trols, with (shrill com - mand The

48
dim.
p
-trols,) And sings a dirge for dy-ing souls,
con-trols,) And sings a dirge for dy-ing souls,
mouse con-trols,) And sings a dirge for dy-ing souls,
And sings a dirge for dy-ing souls,
mouse con-trols,) And sings a dirge for dy-ing souls,
52
mf
and sings a dirge, and (sings a
and sings a dirge, and (sings a dirge)
and (sings a dirge for dy - - - ing souls,)
and sings a dirge, and (sings a dirge) for dy-
and (sings a dirge for dy - ing souls,) for
56
dirge) for dy-ing souls, for dy-ing
for dy-ing souls, for (dy - ing souls,)
for dy-ing, for dy-ing souls, for (dy-ing souls,) for
- - ing souls, for (dy - ing,) for (dy - ing
(dy - ing souls,) for (dy - ing souls,) for

60
[← o· = o →]
mp p pp mp cresc.
souls, (for dy - ing souls,) souls, souls, souls,
for (dy - ing souls,) souls, souls, souls, Te
(dy - ing souls,) souls, souls, souls, Te
souls,) for (dy-ing souls,) souls, souls, souls, Te
(dy - ing souls,) souls, souls, souls, Te
65
Te whit, (te whit,) te whoo,
whit, (te whit,) te whoo, te whit, te
whit, te whoo, te (whit, te whoo,) te (whit, te whoo,)
whit, (te whit,) te whoo, te (whit, te whoo,) te
whit, te whoo, te (whit, te whoo,)
69
te whit, te whoo,
whoo, te
te (whit, te whoo,) te (whit, te whoo,)
(whit, te whoo,) te whit, te whoo,
te (whit, te whoo,)

73
f
mf
te (whit, te whoo,) te whit, (te
whit, te whit, te whoo, te whit, te (whit,)
te (whit, te whoo,) te (whit, te whoo,) te
te (whit, te whoo,) te (whit, te
te (whit, te whoo,) te whit, te whoo, te
76
dim. al fine
whit,) te whoo, (te whoo,)
te whoo, te (whoo,) te whit, te
whoo, te (whit, te whoo,) te (whit, te whoo,) te
whoo,) te whit, te (whit, te whoo,) te (whit, te whoo,) te
(whit, te whoo,) te (whit, te whoo,) te whoo, te
80
te whit, te whoo, (te whit, te whoo.)
whoo, te whit, te whoo.
whoo, te whit, te whoo, te whit, te whoo.
(whit, te whoo,) te (whit, te whit, te whoo.)
whit, te whoo, te (whit, te whoo,) te whoo.

47
THE SILVER SWAN

ORLANDO GIBBONS

5
death ap-proached un - locked her si - lent throat;
mf
locked her si - lent throat; Lean - ing her
mf
death ap-proached un - locked her si - lent throat; Lean -
mf
- proached un - locked her si - lent throat; A -
mf
un - locked her si - lent, si - lent throat; Lean - ing her
8
mf
Lean - ing her breast a - gainst the reed - y
breast a - - - gainst the reed - y shore, Thus
- ing her breast a - gainst the reed - y shore,
- gainst the reed - y shore, Thus sung her
breast a - gainst the reed - y shore,
11
shore, Thus sung her first and last, and sung no
sung her first and last, and sung no more, no
Thus sung her first and last, and sung no
first and last, and sung no more, and sung no
Thus sung her first and last, and sung no

14
p
more: Fare - well, all
p
more: Fare - well, all joys; O
p
more: Fare - well, all joys; O
p
more: Fare - well, all joys; O
p
more: Fare - well, all joys; O
16
joys; O death, come close mine eyes; More
death, come close mine eyes; More geese than swans now
death, come close mine eyes; More geese than swans
death, come close mine eyes; More geese than
death, come close mine eyes; More geese than
19
dim.
pp
geese than swans now live, more fools than wise.
dim.
pp
live, more fools than wise, than wise.
dim.
pp
now live, more fools than wise.
dim.
pp
swans now live, more fools than wise.
dim.
pp
swans now live, more fools than wise.

48
THIS SWEET AND MERRY MONTH OF MAY

WILLIAM BYRD

6

May, of May, While Na -

mer - ry month of May, of May,

month, (and mer-ry, mer-ry month) of May, While Na - ture wan - tons,

mer-ry, mer-ry month) of May,

f While Na - ture wan - tons, wan - tons in her

f While Na - ture wan - tons, wan - tons

10

- ture wan - tons in her prime, wan - tons in her

While Na - ture wan - tons, wan - tons in her prime,

wan - tons in her prime, while Na - ture wan - tons in

While Na - ture wan - tons, wan - tons in her prime, in her

prime, wan - tons in her prime, in her

in her prime, while Na - ture wan - tons, wan - tons in

14
mf
prime,
And birds do sing,
in her prime,
And birds do sing,
her prime, (in her prime,)
And birds do sing,
prime, And birds do sing,
(and birds do
prime,
And birds do sing,
(and
her prime,
And birds do
18
f
(and birds do sing,)
and birds do sing,
(and birds do sing,)
and beasts do play, do
(and birds do sing,) do sing,
and beasts do
sing,)
and birds do sing,
and
birds do sing,)
and beasts do play, do
sing,
(and birds do sing,)
and beasts

22
f
and beasts do play, do play, do play,
play, (and beasts do play, do play,)
play, (and beasts do play,) do play, and beasts do play, do play,
beasts do play, (and beasts do play,) do play, and beasts do play,—
play, (and beasts do play, do play,) and beasts do
do play, do play, (and beasts do play,— do play,)
26
(and beasts do play,) do play
do play, and beasts do— play
(and beasts— do play, do play)
— do play, and beasts— do play
play, do play,— do— play, do— play, do— play
and beasts do play,— do play,— do— play, do play, (do play)

[← o = o. →]

30

mp For plea - sure of the joy - ful

mp For plea - sure of the joy - ful time,

mp For plea - sure, (for plea - sure) of the joy - ful time, the joy - ful

mp For plea - sure of the joy - ful

mp For plea - sure of the joy - ful time, the joy - ful

mp For plea - sure of the joy - ful time,

34

[← o. = o →]

time, (of the joy - ful time,)

(of the joy - ful time,) the joy - ful time, f I choose the first for

time, (the joy - ful time,) f I choose the first for ho -

time, the joy - ful time, (the joy - ful time,)

time, of the joy - ful time, f I choose the

of the joy - ful time, the joy - ful time, f I choose the first for

38
f
I choose the first for ho - li-day,
ho - li-day, for ho - li - day, (for ho - li-
- li - day, for ho - li-
f
I choose the first for ho - li-day, for ho - li-
first for ho - li - day, for ho - li-
ho - li-day, (I choose the first for ho - li - day,)
42
mp
for ho - li - day, (for ho - li - day,) And greet E - li -
- day,) (for ho - li - day,)
- day, (for ho - li - day,) (for ho - li - day,)
mp
- day,(for ho - li - day,) (for ho - li - day,) And greet E - li-
mp
- day, (for ho - li - day,) And greet E-
mp
for ho - li - day, (for ho - li - day,) And greet E - li -

46
mp
- za, E - li - za with a rhyme, with a rhyme,
And greet E - li - za, E -
And greet E - li - za, E - li - za with a rhyme,
- za, E - li - za with a rhyme, (and greet E - li - za,)
- li - za, E - li - za with a rhyme, (and greet E -
- za, E - li - za with a rhyme, with a rhyme,
50
and greet E - li - za, E - li - za with a
- li - za with a rhyme, with a rhyme, (with a rhyme,)
(with a rhyme,) and greet E - li - za, E - li - za with a
E - li - za, and (greet E - li - za)
- li - za with a rhyme,) (and greet E - li - za
and greet E - li - za, E - li -

54

rhyme, with a rhyme, (with a

(with a rhyme,)(with a rhyme,) with a

rhyme, with a

with a rhyme, (with a rhyme,) with a

with a rhyme,) with a rhyme, with a

-za with a rhyme, with a rhyme, with a

58

f

rhyme:) O beau - te - ous Queen of se -

rhyme: O beau - te - ous Queen,

rhyme: O beau - te - ous Queen,

rhyme: O beau - te - ous Queen of se - cond

rhyme: O beau - te - ous Queen of se - cond

rhyme: O beau - te - ous Queen of

64

- cond Troy,

(O beau - te - ous Queen)

O beau - te - ous Queen of se -

Troy, (O beau - te - ous Queen of se -

Troy, (O beau - te - ous Queen of

se - cond Troy, (O beau - te - ous Queen of

69

Take well in worth,

of se - cond Troy, Take

- cond Troy, Take well in worth a sim - ple toy, a

- cond Troy,) of se - cond Troy, Take well in worth,

se - cond,) of se - cond, (of se - cond Troy,) Take well in worth a

se - cond Troy,) Take well in worth, (take

74

take well in worth a sim - ple toy,—

well in worth a sim - ple toy, a sim - ple toy,

(sim - ple toy,) (a sim - ple toy,) take

(take well in worth a sim - ple toy, (a sim - ple toy,)

sim - ple toy, (take well in worth a

well in worth) a sim - ple toy, take well in worth a

78

a sim - ple toy, take well in worth a

take *well in worth a sim - ple toy,* a sim - ple toy,

(well in worth a sim - ple toy,) a sim - ple toy,

take well in worth a sim - ple toy,

sim - ple toy,) a sim - ple toy, take

sim - ple toy, a sim - ple toy, (a

82
sim - ple toy, a sim - ple toy,
take well in worth a sim - ple
dim. al fine
take (well in worth a sim - ple toy,) a sim - ple
(take well in worth a sim - ple
dim. al fine
well in worth a sim - ple toy, (take well in
dim. al fine
sim - ple toy,) (a sim - ple toy,) take well in
86
dim. al fine
a sim - ple toy, a sim - - ple toy.
p [𝄐]
dim. al fine
toy, (a sim - ple toy,) (a sim - ple toy.)
p [𝄐]
toy, (a sim - ple toy,) (a sim - ple toy.)
p 𝄐
dim. al fine
toy,) a sim - ple toy, a sim - ple toy.
p [𝄐]
worth a sim - ple toy,) a sim-ple toy, a sim - ple toy.
p [𝄐]
worth a sim - ple toy, a sim - ple toy.
p 𝄐

49
THOUGH AMARYLLIS DANCE

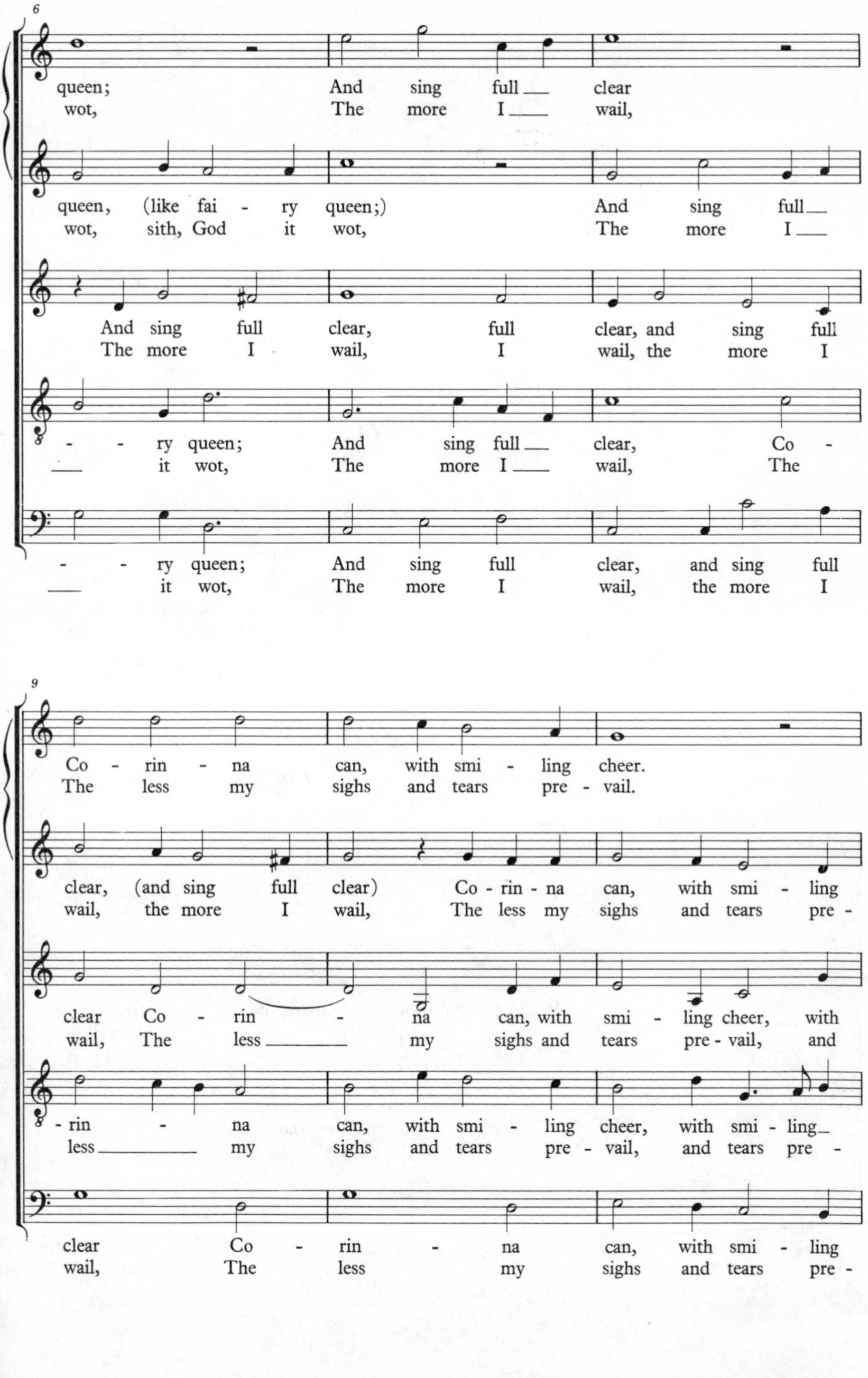

6

queen; And sing full clear
wot, The more I wail,

queen, (like fai - ry queen;) And sing full
wot, sith, God it wot, The more I

And sing full clear, full clear, and sing full
The more I wail, I wail, the more I

- - ry queen; And sing full clear, Co -
it wot, The more I wail, The

- - ry queen; And sing full clear, and sing full
it wot, The more I wail, the more I

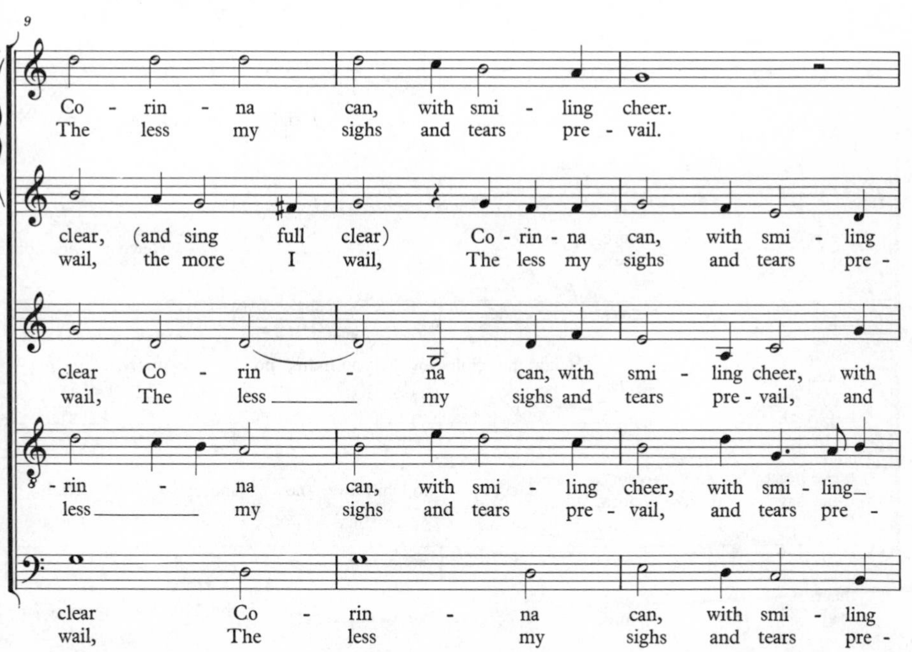

12
mp
Yet since their eyes make
What shall I do but
mp
cheer, with smi - ling cheer. Yet since their eyes make
- vail, and tears pre - vail. What shall I do but
mp
smi - ling cheer. Yet since their eyes make heart so
tears pre - vail. What shall I do but say there -
mp
cheer, with smi - ling cheer. Yet since their eyes
- vail, and tears pre - vail. What shall I do
mp
cheer, with smi - ling cheer. Yet since their eyes make
- vail, and tears pre - vail. What shall I do but

15
p
heart so sore, Heigh ho, 'chill love no
say there - fore,
heart so sore, Heigh ho, 'chill
say there - fore,
p
sore, Heigh ho, 'chill love no more, no more,
- fore,
p
make heart so sore, Heigh ho, 'chill love no more, (heigh
but say there - fore,
p
heart so sore, Heigh ho, 'chill love no more,
say there - fore,

19
cresc.
more, (heigh
cresc.
love, heigh ho, 'chill love no more, 'chill love no
cresc.
'chill love no more, no more, (heigh ho, 'chill love
cresc.
ho, 'chill love no more,) no more, heigh
cresc.
'chill love no more, heigh ho, 'chill love no more,
22
mf
f
ho, 'chill love no more,) 'chill love no more, ('chill love no
mf
more, no more, 'chill love no more, ('chill love no more,)
mf
f
no more,) no more, 'chill love no more, ('chill love
mf
f
ho, 'chill love no more, 'chill love no more, no more, 'chill love no
mf
f
(heigh ho, 'chill love no more,) 'chill love no more,
26
more,) no more.
f
p
'chill love no more. Heigh ho, 'chill love no
p
no more,) no more. Heigh ho, 'chill love no
p
more, no more. Heigh
no more.

29

p Heigh ho, 'chill love no more,

more, 'chill love no more, *cresc.* 'chill love no

more, no more, heigh ho, 'chill love, *cresc.* heigh

ho, 'chill love no more, (heigh ho, *cresc.* 'chill love no

p Heigh ho, 'chill love no more, *cresc.* 'chill love no more,

32

cresc. (heigh ho, 'chill love no

more, no more, heigh ho, 'chill love no more,

ho, 'chill love no more, 'chill love no more, no more,

more,) no more, heigh ho, 'chill love no

heigh ho, 'chill love no more, *mf* (heigh

35

more,) *mf* 'chill love no more, *f* ('chill love no

no more, *mf* 'chill love no more, *f* ('chill love

mf 'chill love no more, *f* ('chill love no more,)

more, *mf* ('chill love no more, no more,) *f* 'chill love no

ho, 'chill love no more,) *f* 'chill love no more,

2. My sheep are lost for want of food,
And I so wood,
That all the day
I sit and watch a herdmaid gay,
Who laughs to see me sigh so sore,
Heigh ho, 'chill love no more.

3. Her loving looks, her beauty bright
Is such delight,
That all in vain
I love to like and lose my gain,
For her that thanks me not therefor,
Heigh ho, 'chill love no more.

4. Ah, wanton eyes, my friendly foes,
And cause of woes,
Your sweet desire
Breeds flames of ice and freeze in fire.
Ye scorn to see me weep so sore,
Heigh ho, 'chill love no more.

50
THOUGH PHILOMELA LOST HER LOVE

THOMAS MORLEY

21
ff
He is a fool that lov - ers prove, And leaves to sing
ff
He is a fool that lov - ers prove, And leaves to sing
ff
He is a fool that lov - ers prove, And leaves to sing
26
to live in pain.
p
Fa la la la la la la la
to live in pain.
p
Fa la la la la la la la
to live in pain.
p
Fa la la la la la la la
31
la la la la la la la la la la la la la la, fa la
cresc. (second time)
la la la la la la la la la la la, fa la la la, fa
cresc. (second time)
la la la la la la la la la la la la la, fa la la
cresc. (second time)
36
la la la la la la la. la.
1
2
f
la la la la la, fa la la la la. la.
f
la la la la la la. la.
f

51
THOSE SWEET DELIGHTFUL LILIES

THOMAS BATESON

8
(na - ture gave my Phyl - lis,) which (na - ture
- lis, which (na - ture gave my Phyl-lis,) which na - ture gave my
- lis, my Phyl - lis,) which (na - ture gave,) which (na - ture gave)
- lis, which na - ture gave my Phyl - lis, which
gave my Phyl - lis,) which (na - ture gave,) which (na - ture
11
p
gave my Phyl - lis,) Those sweet de - light - ful li -
Phyl - - lis, Those sweet de - light - ful li -
my Phyl - lis, Those sweet de - light-ful li -
na-ture gave my Phyl - lis, Those sweet de - light - ful li -
gave) my Phyl - lis, Which
15
- lies, Which (na - ture gave,) which (na - ture gave,) which (na - ture
- lies, Which na - ture gave my Phyl-lis, which (na - ture gave my
- lies, Which na-ture gave my Phyl - lis, which (na - ture
- - lies, Which na - ture gave my Phyl -
na - ture gave my Phyl - lis,

18
cresc.
gave) my Phyl - lis, which (na - ture gave my Phyl-lis,) which
f
cresc.
Phyl - lis, which na - ture gave my Phyl - lis,)
cresc.
gave my Phyl - lis,) which (na - ture gave my Phyl -
cresc.
- lis, my Phyl - lis, which na - ture gave my
cresc.
which (na - ture gave my Phyl - lis,) which (na - ture
21
(na - ture gave my Phyl - - - lis,) Ay me, (ay
p
cresc.
f
(which na - ture gave my Phyl - lis,) Ay me, (ay
- lis,) which (na - ture gave) my Phyl - lis, Ay me, ay
Phyl - lis, which na-ture gave my Phyl - lis, Ay me, (ay
gave,) which (na - ture gave) my Phyl - lis, Ay
25
me, ay me, ay me,) my Phyl - lis, each
mf
me,) ay me, my Phyl - lis,
me, ay me, my Phyl - lis, my Phyl - lis, each
me, ay me,) ay me, my Phyl - lis, each hour
me, (ay me,) my Phyl - - - lis, each

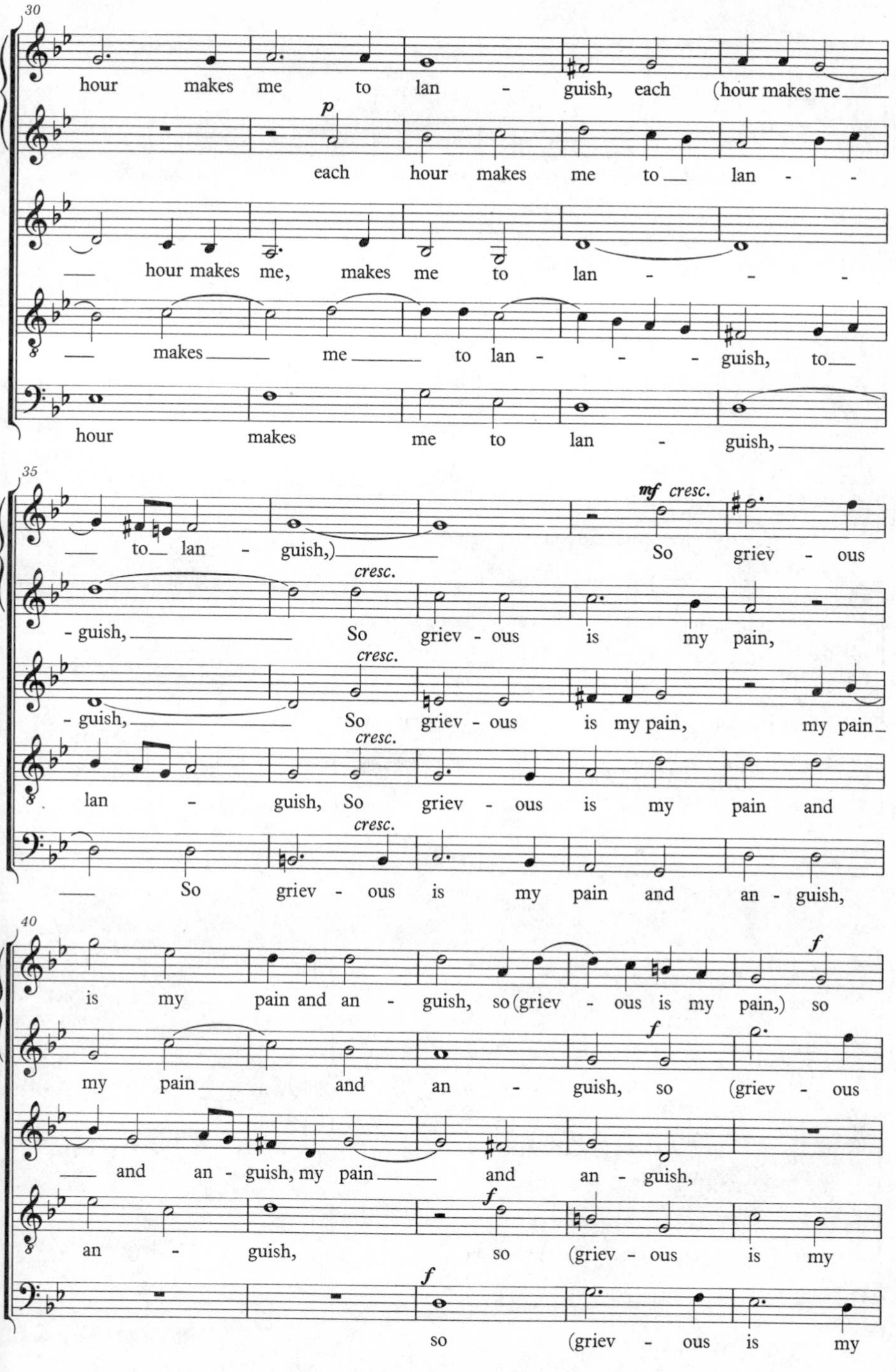
30
hour makes me to lan - guish, each (hour makes me
p
each hour makes me to lan - -
hour makes me, makes me to lan - - -
makes me to lan - - - guish, to
hour makes me to lan - guish,
35
mf cresc.
to lan - guish,) So griev - ous
cresc.
- guish, So griev - ous is my pain,
cresc.
- guish, So griev - ous is my pain, my pain
cresc.
lan - guish, So griev - ous is my pain and
cresc.
So griev - ous is my pain and an - guish,
40
f
is my pain and an - guish, so (griev - ous is my pain,) so
f
my pain and an - guish, so (griev - ous
and an - guish, my pain and an - guish,
f
an - guish, so (griev - ous is my
f
so (griev - ous is my

45
dim.
(griev - ous is my pain) and an - guish, so (griev - ous
dim.
is my pain and an - - - guish,) so
f
dim.
so (griev - ous is my pain,) so (griev - ous is my
dim.
pain,) so (griev - ous is my pain) and an - guish,
dim.
pain,) my pain, my
50
p
is my pain and an - guish,) and an - guish. Ay
p
(griev - ous is my pain and an - guish. Ay
p
pain and an - guish,) my pain and an - - - guish. Ay
p
so (griev - ous is my pain and an - guish.) Ay
pain and an - - - guish.
55
cresc.
mf
me, ay me, ay me, my Phyl -
cresc.
mf
me, (ay me, ay me, ay me,) my Phyl -
cresc.
mf
me, ay me, ay me, my Phyl - lis, my Phyl -
cresc.
mf
me, (ay me, ay me,) ay me, my Phyl -
p cresc.
mf
Ay me, (ay me,) my Phyl - - -

60
p
- lis, each hour makes me to
p
- lis, each hour makes me to lan - guish, (each
p
- lis, each hour makes me, makes me to lan -
p
- lis, each hour makes me to lan - - -
p
- lis, each hour makes me to lan -
65
cresc.
lan - - - guish, So griev - ous
hour makes me to lan - guish,)
cresc.
- - - guish, So griev - ous
cresc.
- guish, to lan - - guish, So griev - ous
cresc.
- guish, So griev - ous is my
69
is my pain, my pain and
mf cresc.
So griev - ous is my pain and an -
is my pain, my pain and an - guish, my pain
is my pain and an - guish,
pain and an - guish,

73
f
an - guish, so (griev - ous is my
f
- guish, so griev - ous is my pain, so (griev - ous
f
and an - guish, so (griev - ous
f
so (griev - ous is my pain,) so (griev -
f
so (griev - ous is my pain,) my
77
dim.
pain and an - - - - guish,) so
dim.
is my pain and an - guish,) so (griev - ous
dim.
is my pain,) so (griev - ous is my
dim.
- ous is my pain) and an - guish,
dim.
pain, my
81
pp [𝄐]
(griev - ous is my pain and an - guish.)
pp [𝄐]
is my pain and an - guish,) and an - guish.
pp [𝄐]
pain and an - guish,) my pain and an - - guish.
pp [𝄐]
so (griev - ous is my pain and an - guish.)
pp 𝄐
pain and an - - guish.

52
THULE, THE PERIOD OF COSMOGRAPHY
(The first part)

THOMAS WEELKES

9

- mo - gra - phy,) Thu - - - le, the

(the pe - riod of cos - mo - gra - phy,)

Thu - - - le, the pe - riod of cos - mo - gra - phy, of

of cos-mo - gra - phy,) cos - mo - gra - phy, the pe - riod of cos-mo - gra -

pe - riod of cos - mo - gra - - phy, the pe - riod of cos-mo -

- le, _____ the pe - riod of cos - mo - gra - phy, (the

13

pe - riod of cos - mo - gra - phy, (the pe - riod of cos -

Thu - - le, the pe - riod

cos - mo - gra - phy, Thu - - - le, the

- phy, of cos - mo - gra - phy, the pe - riod of cos-mo - gra -

- - gra - phy, of _____ cos - mo - gra - phy,

pe - riod of cos - mo - gra - phy,) of _____

17
- mo - gra - phy,) of cos - mo - gra - phy,
f
of cos-mo - gra - phy, Doth vaunt of Hec - la,
f
pe - riod of cos - mo - gra - phy, Doth vaunt of Hec - -
f
- phy, of cos - mo - gra - phy, Doth vaunt of
the pe - riod of cos-mo - - gra - - - phy,
f
cos - mo - - gra - phy, Doth
21
f
Doth vaunt of Hec - la, (doth
of Hec - - la, (doth vaunt of Hec - - - la,)
- la, of Hec - - - la, (doth vaunt of
Hec - la, (doth vaunt of Hec - la,) of Hec - la,
f
Doth vaunt of Hec - la, (doth vaunt of Hec - -
vaunt of Hec - la, (doth vaunt of Hec - la,)

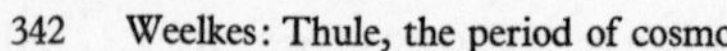

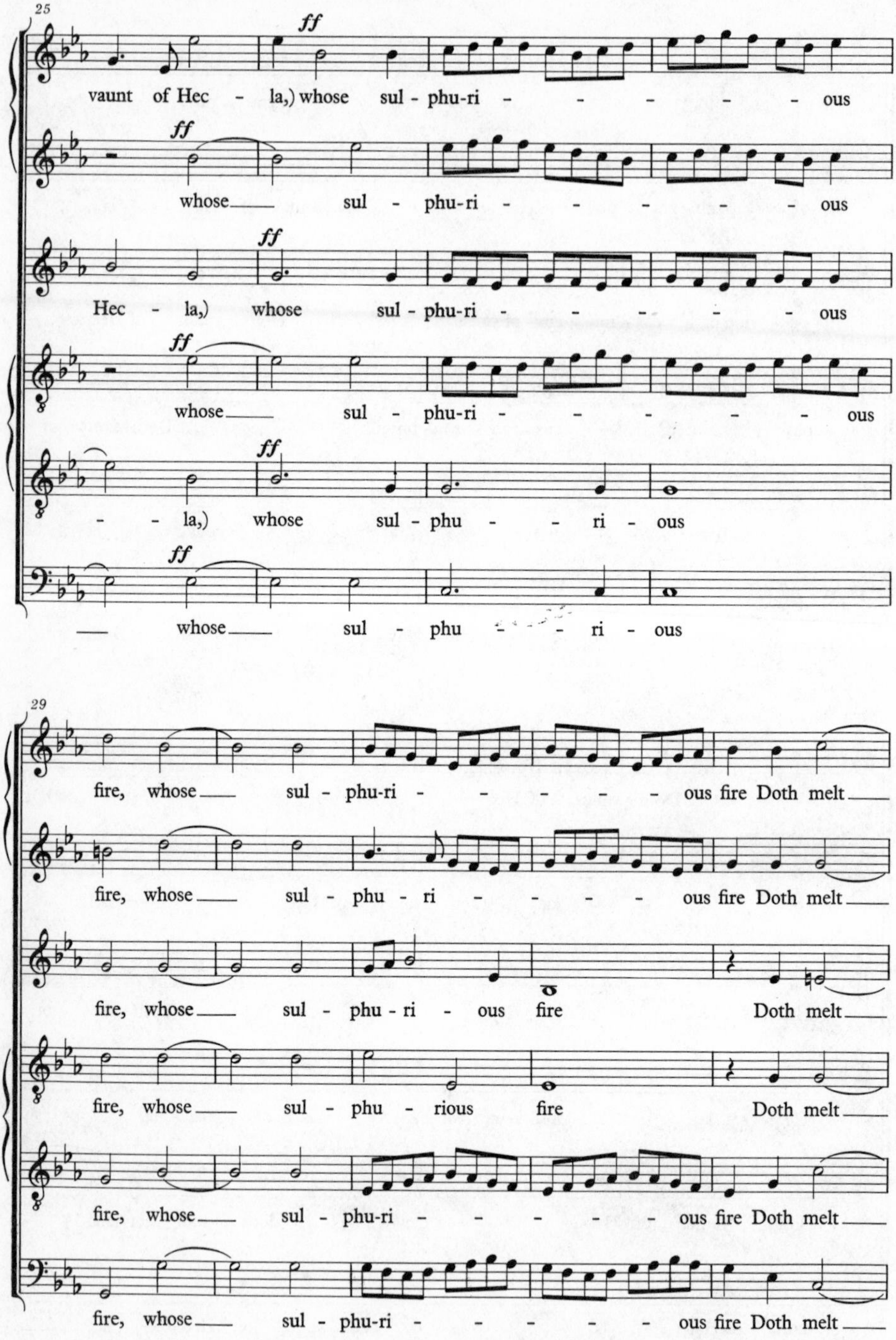

25

vaunt of Hec - la,) whose sul - phu-ri - - - - - ous

whose sul - phu-ri - - - - ous

Hec - la,) whose sul - phu-ri - - - - - ous

whose sul - phu-ri - - - - ous

- - la,) whose sul - phu - ri - ous

whose sul - phu - - ri - ous

29

fire, whose sul - phu-ri - - - - - ous fire Doth melt

fire, whose sul - phu - ri - - - - ous fire Doth melt

fire, whose sul - phu - ri - ous fire Doth melt

fire, whose sul - phu - rious fire Doth melt

fire, whose sul - phu-ri - - - - - ous fire Doth melt

fire, whose sul - phu-ri - - - - - ous fire Doth melt

34
mf
the fro - zen clime and thaw the sky, (and thaw the
the fro - zen clime and thaw the sky, and thaw the
the fro - zen clime
the fro - zen clime and thaw the sky,
the fro - zen clime and thaw the sky, the
the fro - zen clime;
38
[← 𝅗𝅥 = 𝅗𝅥. →]
f
sky,) (and thaw the sky,) the sky; Trin -
sky, (and thaw the sky,) (and thaw the sky,) the sky; Trin -
and thaw the sky, and thaw the sky, the sky; Trin -
and thaw the sky, the sky; Trin -
sky, the sky; Trin -
Trin -
3
4

41
[← 𝅗𝅥. = 𝅗𝅥 →]
-a - cri-an Æt - na's flames as - cend, as - cend not
-a - cri-an Æt - na's flames
-a - cri-an Æt - na's flames as - cend not high - er, as -
-a - cri-an Æt - na's flames as - cend,
-a - cri-an Æt - na's flames as - cend not
-a - cri-an Æt - na's flames as - cend not high - er,
45
high-er, (as - cend not high-er,)(as - cend not high -
as - cend not high-er, (as - cend not high-er,)(as - cend not high - er.)
- cend not high - er, (as - cend not high - er,) (as -
as - cend not high - er, as - cend not high - er, (as -
high-er, (as - cend not high - er,) as - cend not high - er.
as - cend not

49
- - er.) These things seem won - - - drous,
These things seem won - - - drous,
- cend not high-er.) These things seem won - - - drous,
- cend not high - er.) These things seem won - - - drous,
These things seem won - - - drous,
high-er, not high - er. These things seem won - - - drous,
53
mf
yet more won - - - drous I, more won -
yet more won - - - drous I, yet more
yet more won - - - drous I, yet more
yet more won - drous I, yet more won -
yet more won - - - drous I, (yet more
yet more won - - - drous I, (yet more

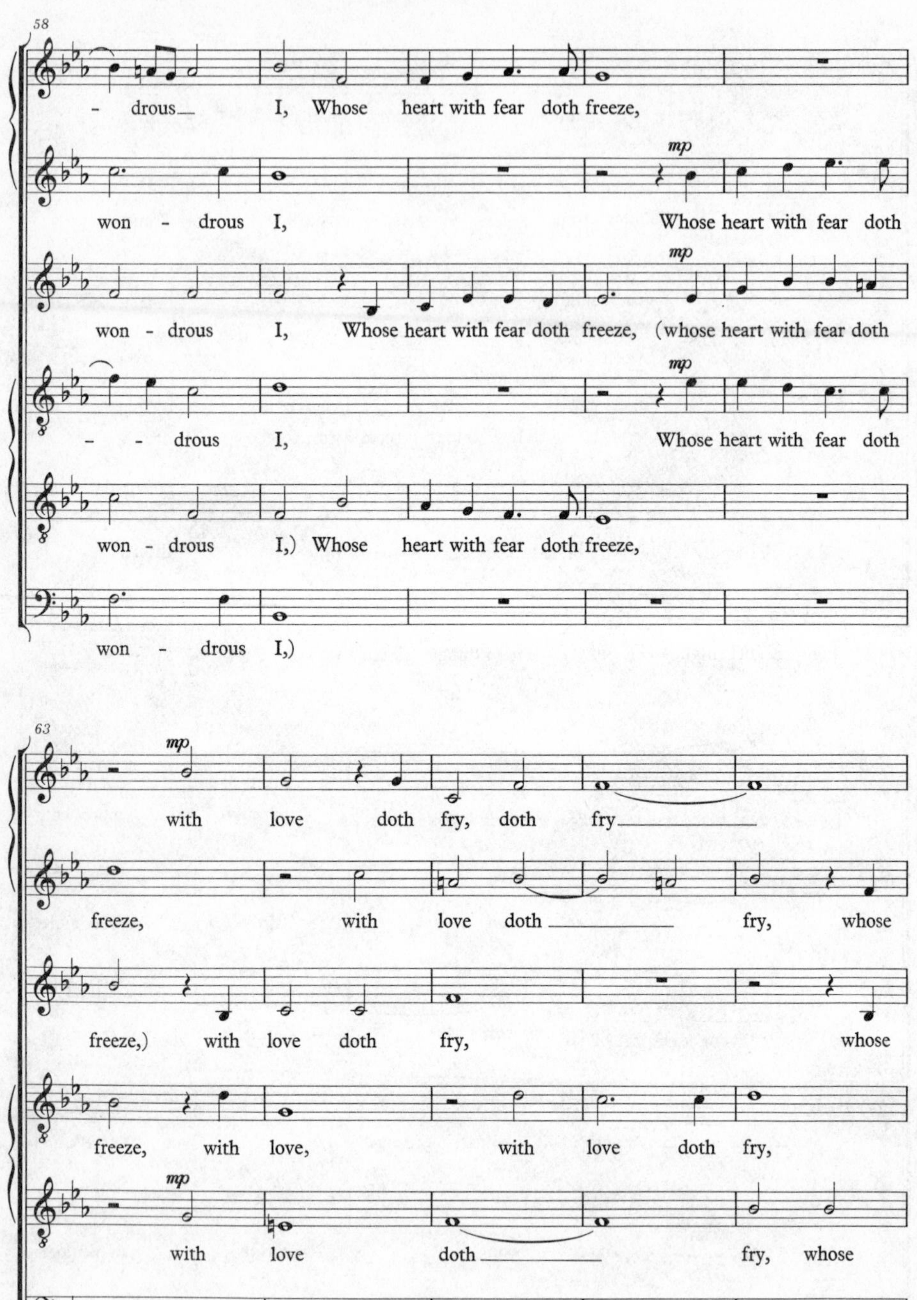
58
mp
- drous I, Whose heart with fear doth freeze,
won - drous I, Whose heart with fear doth
won - drous I, Whose heart with fear doth freeze, (whose heart with fear doth
- - drous I, Whose heart with fear doth
won - drous I,) Whose heart with fear doth freeze,
won - drous I,)
63
with love doth fry, doth fry
freeze, with love doth fry, whose
freeze,) with love doth fry, whose
freeze, with love, with love doth fry,
with love doth fry, whose

68
p
with love,
heart with fear doth freeze,
p
with
heart with fear doth freeze, whose heart with fear doth freeze, with love doth
p
whose heart with fear doth freeze,
p
with
heart with fear doth freeze,
p
with love,
mp
Whose heart with fear doth freeze,
p
with
73
with love doth fry, doth fry.
love doth fry, with love doth fry.
fry, with love doth fry.
love doth fry, with love doth fry.
with love doth fry, with love doth fry.
love doth fry, doth fry.

53
THE ANDALUSIAN MERCHANT
(The second part)

THOMAS WEELKES

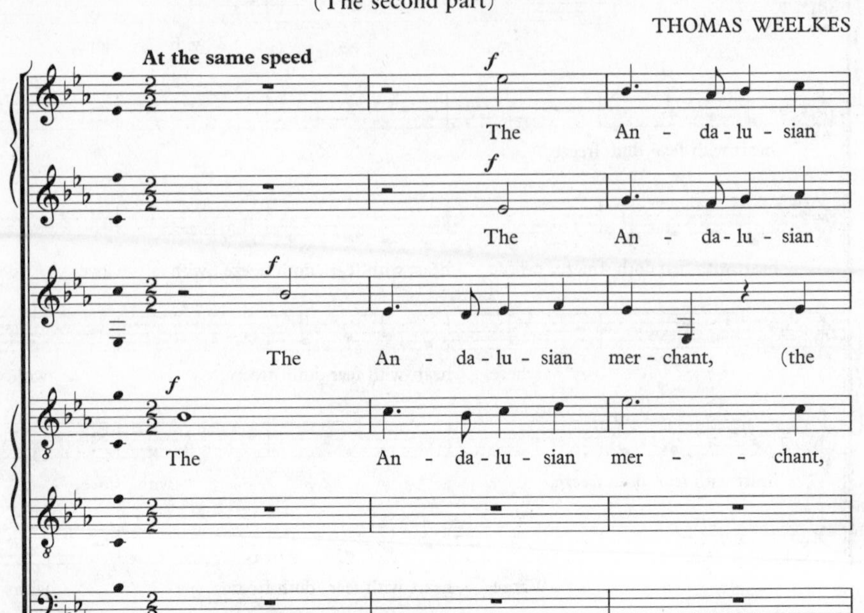

4

mer - - - chant, that re - turns, that re - turns

mer - chant, that re - turns La - den with

An - da-lu - sian mer-chant,) that re - turns, that re - turns, re -

that re - - turns, that re - turns

f
The An - da-lu - sian mer-chant, that re - turns, that re -

f
The An - da-lu - sian mer - chant, that re - - -

8
La - den with co - chi-neal and Chi - na dish-es, and
co - chi-neal and Chi - na dish-es, la - den with co - chi - neal and Chi - na
- turns La - den with co - chi-neal and Chi - na dish-es,
La - den with co - chi-neal and Chi - na dish - es, (la - den with
- turns La - den with co - chi-neal and Chi - na dish-es, (la - den
- turns La - den with co - chi-neal and Chi - na dish-es, (la -
12
Chi - na dish - es, (la - den with co - chi-neal and Chi - na
dish-es, (la - den with co - chi-neal and Chi - na dish - es,) Chi - na dish-es,
la - den with co - chi-neal and Chi - na dish - es, (la - den
co - chi-neal and Chi - na dish-es,) la - den with co - chi - neal and Chi - na
with co - chi-neal and Chi - na dish-es,) (la - den with
- den with co - chi - neal and Chi - na dish-es,) and Chi - na dish-es, (la -

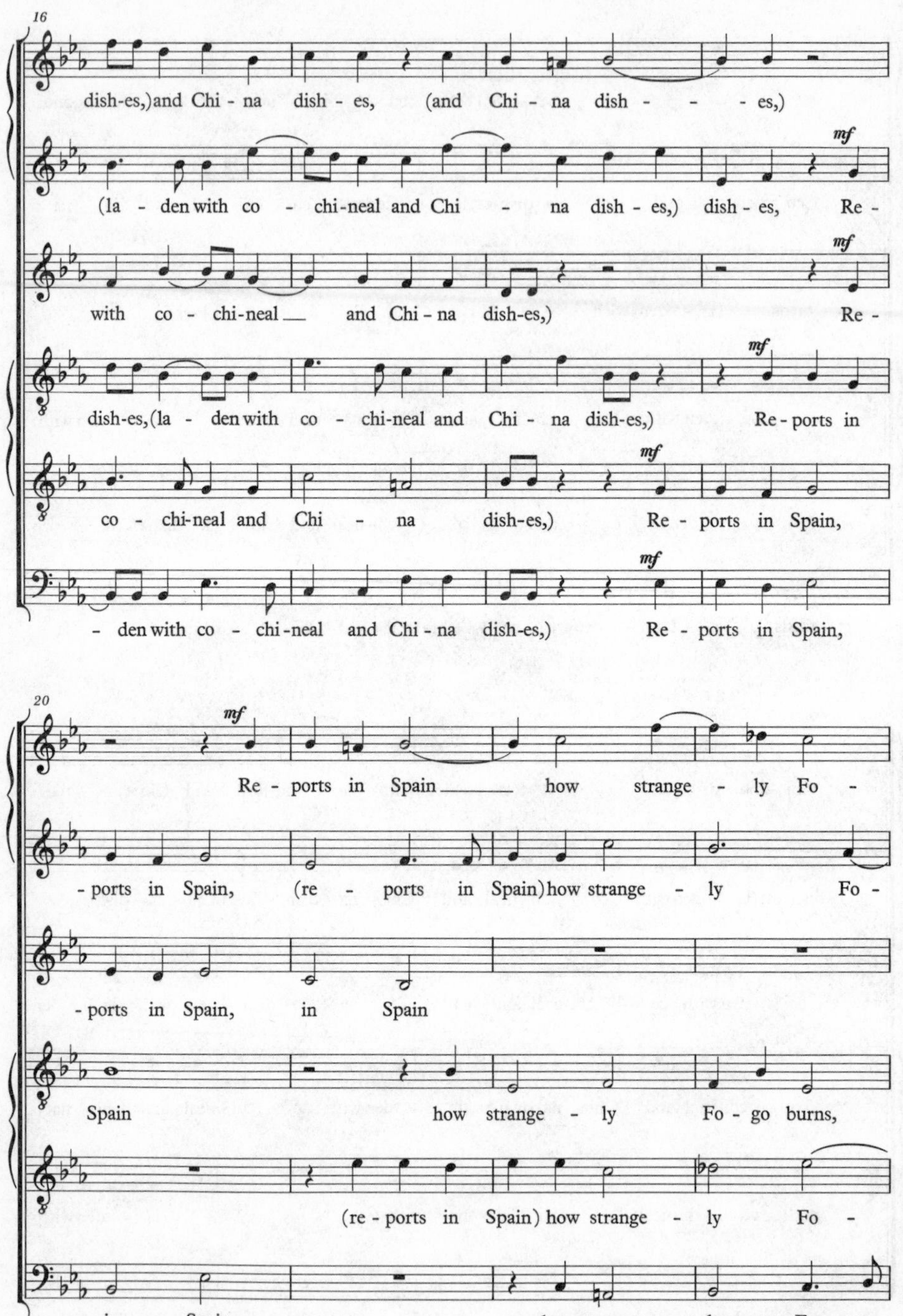
16
dish-es,) and Chi - na dish - es, (and Chi - na dish - - - es,)
mf
(la - den with co - chi-neal and Chi - na dish - es,) dish - es, Re -
mf
with co - chi-neal and Chi - na dish-es,) Re -
mf
dish-es, (la - den with co - chi-neal and Chi - na dish-es,) Re - ports in
mf
co - chi-neal and Chi - na dish-es,) Re - ports in Spain,
mf
- den with co - chi-neal and Chi - na dish-es,) Re - ports in Spain,
20
mf
Re - ports in Spain how strange - ly Fo -
- ports in Spain, (re - ports in Spain) how strange - ly Fo -
- ports in Spain, in Spain
Spain how strange - ly Fo - go burns,
(re - ports in Spain) how strange - ly Fo -
in Spain how strange - ly Fo - go

24

- go burns, how___ strange - ly Fo - - go burns, (how___

- - go burns, how strange-ly Fo - - go burns,

how___ strange - ly

(how___ strange - ly Fo - go burns,) how

- - go burns, how___ strange - ly Fo - - go

burns, (how___ strange - ly Fo - go burns,)

28

___ strange - ly Fo - go burns,) how strange, how

(how___ strange - ly Fo - go burns)

Fo - go burns, how strange-ly Fo -

strange-ly Fo - go burns, (how___ strange - ly Fo - go burns,)

burns, how strange - ly_______ it burns, how

(how strange-ly Fo - go burns,) how

32

strange-ly Fo - - go burns *f* A - midst an

f A - midst an

- - go burns, Fo - go burns *f* A - midst an

(how strange-ly Fo - go burns) *f* A - - midst an

strange-ly Fo - go burns *f* A - - midst an

strange-ly Fo - go burns *f* A - - midst an

36

o - cean full of fly-ing fish - es, fly-ing fish - es, full of fly-ing

o - cean full of fly-ing fish - es, full of fly-ing fish -

o - - cean full of fly-ing fish - es, full of

o - - - - - cean full of fly-ing fish - es,

o - - cean full of fly-ing fish - es, full of fly-ing

o - - cean full of fly-ing fish - es, full of fly-ing fish - es,

39
fish - es, (full of fly-ing fish - es,) (full of fly-ing fish - es.)
- - es, full of fly-ing fish, full of fly-ing fish - - es. These
fly-ing fish - es, (full of fly-ing fish - es,) fly - ing fish - es.
full of fly-ing fish - es, of fly - ing fish - es.
fish - es, (full of fly-ing fish - es,) (full of fly-ing fish - es.) These
(full of fly-ing fish - es,) (full of fly-ing fish - - es.) These
42
mf
These things seem won - drous, yet more won - -
things seem won - drous, yet more won - -
These things seem won - drous, yet more won - -
These things seem won - drous, yet more won - drous
things seem won - drous, yet more won - -
things seem won - drous, yet more won - -

48

- drous I, (yet more won - drous I,)

- drous I, more won - drous___ I, Whose heart with fear doth

- drous I, yet more won - drous I, Whose heart with fear doth

I, yet more won - drous___ I,

- drous I, (yet more won - drous I,) Whose heart with fear doth

- drous I, yet more won - drous I,

53

mp Whose heart with fear doth freeze, with love doth___

freeze, *mp* with love, with love doth

freeze, *mp* (whose heart with fear doth freeze,) with love doth fry,

mp Whose heart with fear doth freeze, with love, with

freeze, *mp* with love doth___

58
fry, whose heart with fear doth freeze,
fry,
whose heart with fear doth freeze, (whose heart with fear doth
love doth fry, whose heart with fear doth
fry, whose heart with fear doth freeze,
mp
Whose heart with fear doth
63
p
with love doth fry.
p
with love, with love doth fry.
p
freeze,) with love doth fry, with love doth fry.
p
freeze, with love, with love doth fry.
p
with love, with love doth fry.
p
freeze, with love doth fry.

54
THUS SINGS MY DEAREST JEWEL

THOMAS WEELKES

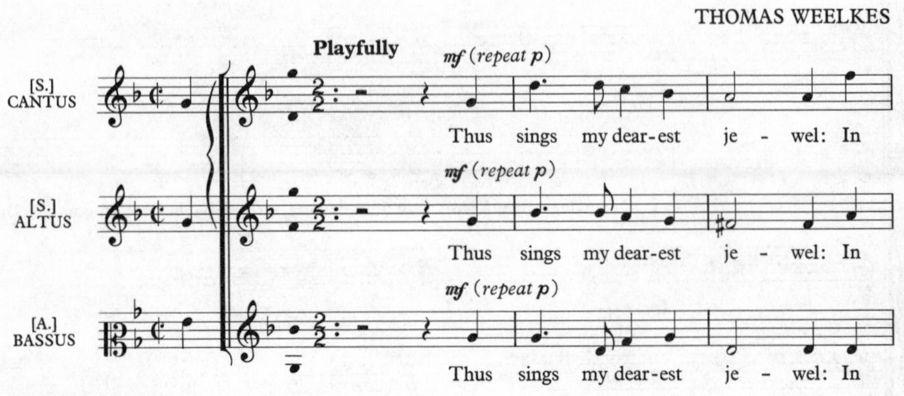

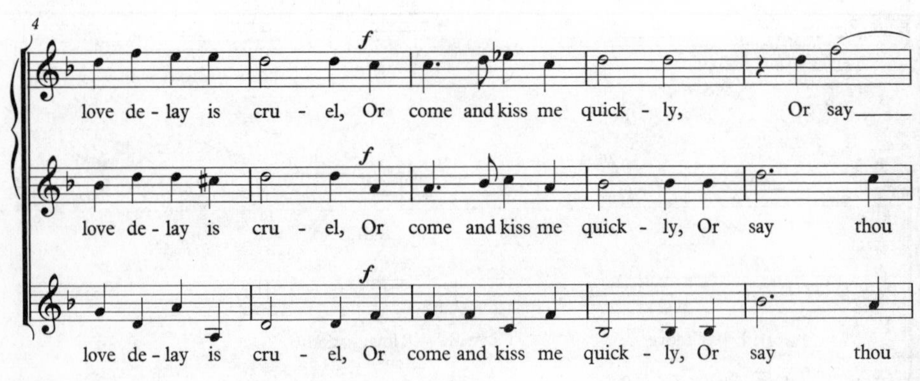

[← 𝅗𝅥. = 𝅗𝅥 →]
mf
la, fa la la la la la, fa la la) la. Now sings my love -
mf
la, fa la la la la la, fa la la) la. Now sings my love - ly
mf
la la la, fa la la la) la. Now sings my love - ly
- ly trea - sure: In love a kiss, (a kiss) is a harm - less plea -
trea - sure: In love a kiss is a harm - less plea - sure.
trea - sure: In love a kiss is a harm - less plea - - -
dim. (second time)
- sure. Fa la la, fa (la la, fa la la, fa la la, fa la la, fa la la, fa la la,
dim. (second time)
Fa la la la, (fa la la la, fa la la la, fa
dim. (second time)
- sure. Fa la la la la la la
fa la la la, fa la la la) la. la.
la la la, fa la la la la.) Now la.
la la la la la. Now la.
1
2

55
TOO MUCH I ONCE LAMENTED

THOMAS TOMKINS

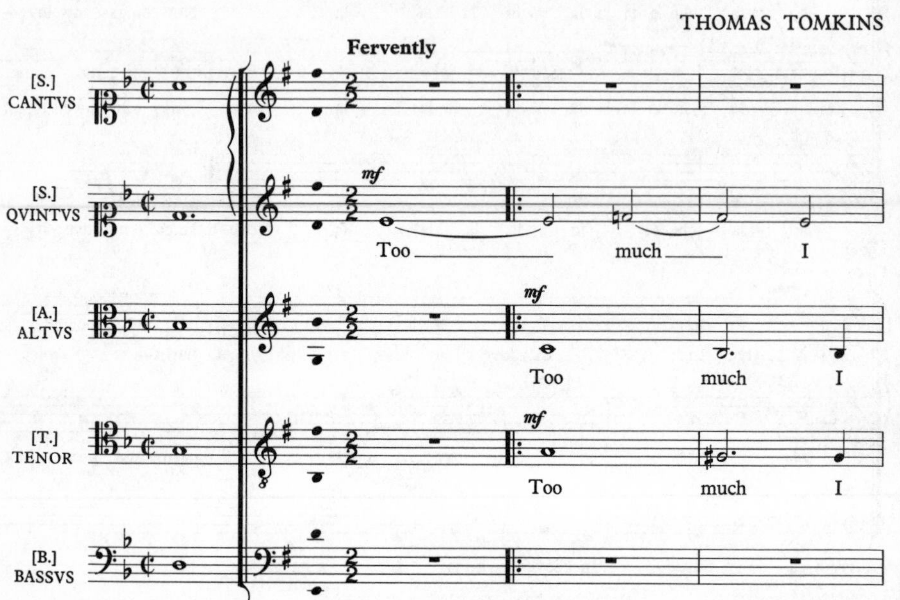

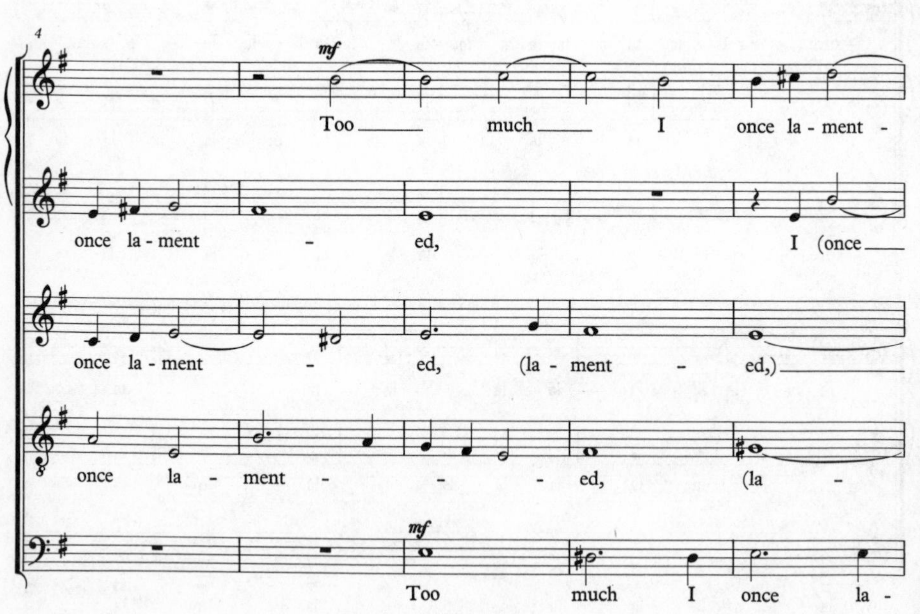

9

- - ed, (la - ment - ed,)

la - ment - ed, While

I once la - ment - -

- ment - ed,) la - ment - ed, While

- ment - ed, (la - ment - ed,)

14

While love my heart tor - ment - - ed, (tor -

love my heart tor - ment - ed, (tor-ment - - - ed,) (tor -

- ed, While love my heart tor - ment - ed, while (love my heart tor -

love my heart tor - ment - - ed,

While love my heart tor -

18

- ment - ed,) tor - ment - ed, (tor -

- ment - ed,) tor - ment - ed, (tor - ment -

- ment - ed,) tor - ment - ed, (tor - ment - -

(tor - ment - - ed,) (tor - ment -

- ment - ed, (tor - ment - ed,)

★ In the repeat C and Q exchange parts.

36
p
A - las, Ay me,
p
A - las,
- - las, and Ay me, and (Ay
p
A - las, and Ay
p
A -
41
(a - las, and Ay me,) ay me,
and Ay me, a -
me,) a - las,
me, (a - las, and Ay me,) Ay me,
- las, and Ay me,
46
sat I wring - - -
- las, (and Ay me,) sat I wring - - -
(and Ay me,) sat I wring -
and (Ay me, ay me,) sat I
sat I wring -

62i3: Small notes to be sung second time

* In the repeat C and Q exchange parts

56
TRUST NOT TOO MUCH, FAIR YOUTH

ORLANDO GIBBONS

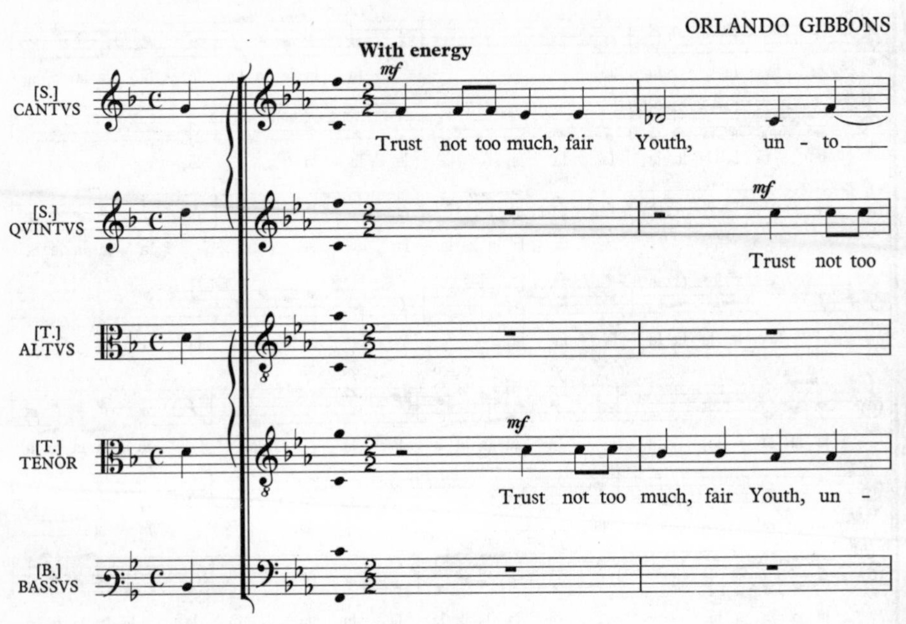

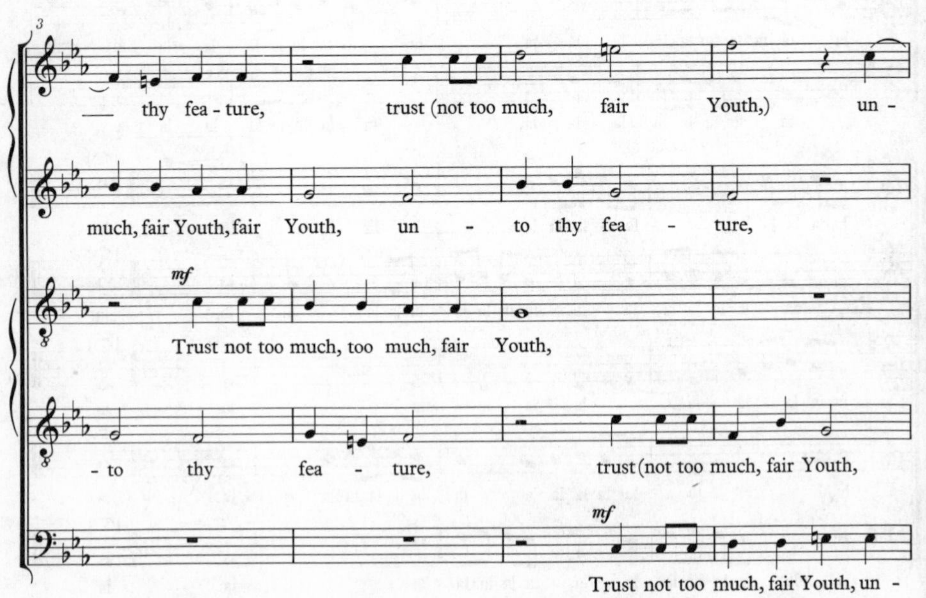

7

- - to thy__ fea - ture, trust (not too much, fair Youth, un - to thy

trust (not too much, fair Youth, un - to [♭] thy fea - ture,)

trust (not too much, fair Youth, un - to thy fea -

un - to thy fea - ture,) trust (not too

- to thy fea - ture, trust not too much, too much, fair

11

fea - ture,) trust (not too much, fair Youth, fair Youth, un - to thy fea - ture, trust (not too

trust not too much, fair Youth, un - - to

ture, trust__ (not too much, fair Youth, un - to thy

much, fair Youth, un - to thy fea - ture,)

Youth, trust not too much, un - to thy

15

much, fair Youth, un - to thy fea - ture,) un - - to thy fea -

thy fea - - ture,) trust not, (fair Youth,________ un - to

fea - ture,)____ un - to____ thy fea - - -

trust (not too much, fair____ Youth, un - to thy fea -

fea - - - ture, trust (not__ too much, un - to thy fea -

19

mp

- ture; Be not en - a - mour - ed, be (not en - a - mour -

fea - ture; Be not en - a - mour - ed, be (not en - a - mour -

- ture; Be not en - a - mour-ed, be (not en - a - mour-ed,) en -

- ture;)

- ture;)

22

- ed,) be not en - a - mour-ed of thy

- ed,) be (not en - a - mour - ed,) be not en - a - mour - ed of thy blush - ing

- a - - moured of thy blush - ing hue,

Be not en - a - mour - ed, be (not en - a - mour - ed) of thy

Be not en - a - mour-ed, be (not en - a - mour-ed) of thy

25

blush - ing, blush - ing hue.

hue, thy blush - ing hue, of (thy

be not en - a - - moured of thy blush -

blush - ing hue, en - a - - moured of thy

blush - ing hue, of (thy blush - - ing

29

f
Be game-some whilst thou art a good - ly crea - ture,

blush - ing hue.) *f* Be game-some whilst thou art a good -

- - ing hue. *f* Be game-some whilst thou

blush - ing hue. *f* Be

hue.) *f* Be game-some whilst thou art

32

thou (art a good - ly crea - ture,)

- - ly crea - - - ture, whilst (thou

crea - - - ture, be game-some whilst thou

game-some whilst thou art a good - - - ly crea - - -

a good - ly crea - ture, thou

34

be (game-some whilst thou art a ____

art a good - ly crea - - -

art a good - - ly crea - - ture,

- ture, be (game-some whilst thou

art a good - ly crea - - - ture, thou

36
good ly crea - ture,) whilst thou art a
- ture,) be (game-some whilst thou
a good - ly crea - ture, thou (art a good - ly crea - - -
art a good - ly crea - ture,) be (game-some whilst thou
(art a good-ly crea - ture,)
39
good - ly crea - - - ture, be (game-some whilst thou
art a good - ly crea - - -
- ture,) be (game-some whilst thou art a good - ly crea - ture,)
art a good - ly crea - - - ture,)
be (game-some whilst thou
41
art a good-ly crea - - - - - ture;)
- ture,)
be game - some
be (game-some whilst thou art a good-ly crea-ture,) thou art a good-ly crea - -
art a good - ly crea - - - ture,) thou art a good-ly

44
a
whilst thou art a good - - - ly, good - - - ly
- ture, be game-some whilst thou art a good - -
crea - - - ture, be (game-some whilst thou art a
46
p
The flowers will fade that in thy gar - den
good - ly crea - ture; The flowers will fade that in thy gar - den
crea - ture; The flowers will fade that in thy gar-den
- ly crea - ture;
good - ly crea - - - ture.
50
grew, the(flowers will fade that in thy gar - den
grew, that (in thy gar - den grew.)
grew, that in thy gar - den grew, (that in
In thy
Sweet

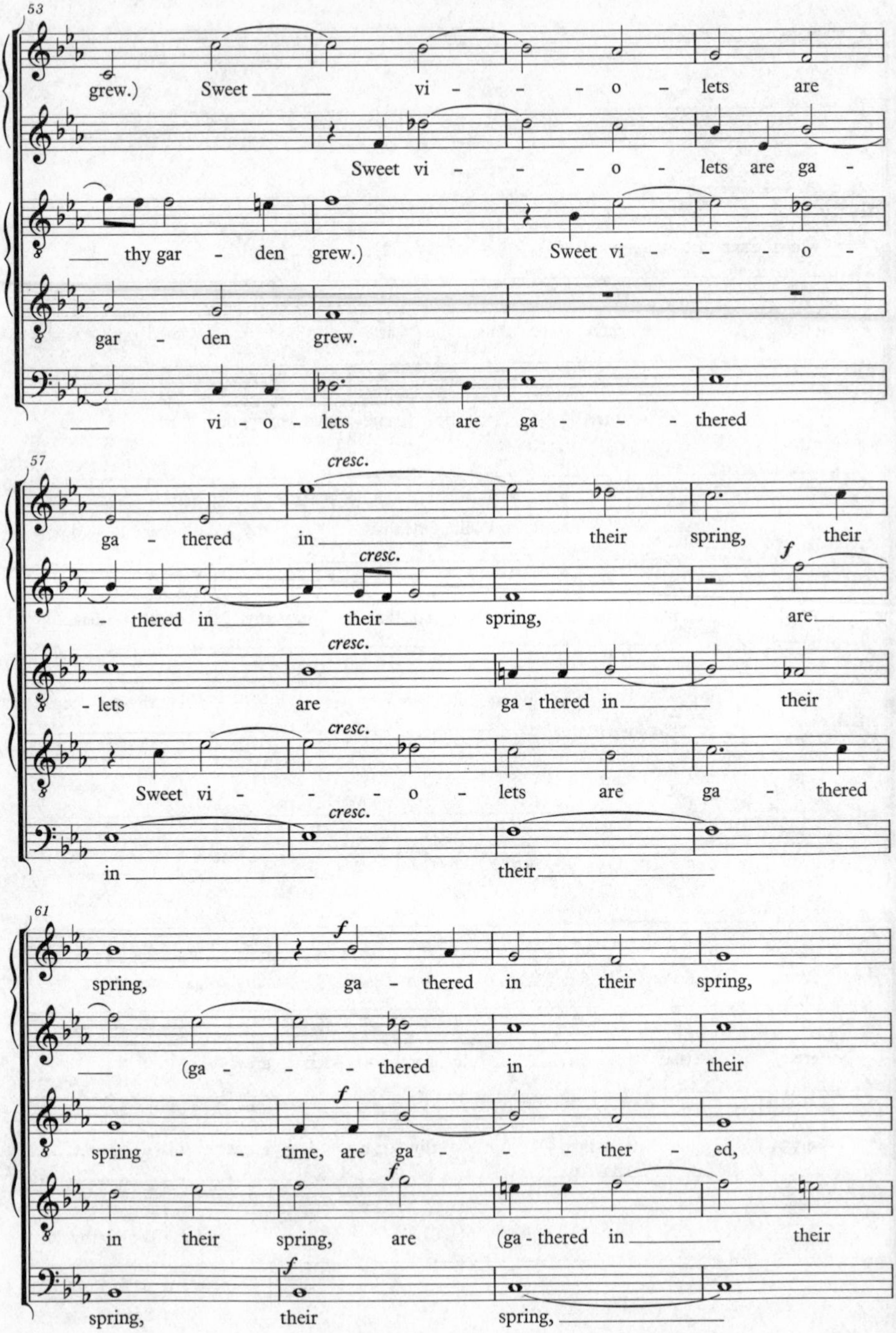
53
grew.) Sweet vi - - o - lets are
Sweet vi - - o - lets are ga -
thy gar - den grew.) Sweet vi - - o -
gar - den grew.
vi - o - lets are ga - - thered
57
cresc.
ga - thered in their spring, their
cresc.
f
- thered in their spring, are
cresc.
- lets are ga - thered in their
cresc.
Sweet vi - - o - lets are ga - thered
cresc.
in their
61
f
spring, ga - thered in their spring,
(ga - - thered in their
f
spring - - time, are ga - - ther - ed,
f
in their spring, are (ga - thered in their
f
spring, their spring,

65

mf in their spring, sweet vi - - - o - lets

spring,) mf in their spring, are ga - - - thered

mf in their spring, sweet (vi - - - o - lets

spring,) mf sweet (vi - - - o - lets are ga - -

mf in (their spring,) sweet (vi - - - o -

68

are ga - thered, are (ga - thered in their

in their spring, sweet (vi - o - lets are ga - - - thered

are ga - thered,) are ga - thered in their spring,

- thered in their spring,)

- lets are ga - thered in their spring,) their

71

spring,) White pri - mit falls with-out-en pi-ty -

in their spring,) ga - thered in their spring,

their spring, White pri - mit falls with-out - en

White pri - mit falls with-out-en pi-ty - ing, white (pri - mit falls with - out - en

spring, their spring, White pri - mit

75
-ing, white (pri - mit falls with - out - en pi - ty - ing,) falls
White pri - mit falls with-out - en pi - ty - ing, white (pri-mit falls with-
pi - ty - ing, white (pri - mit falls with-out - en
pi - ty - ing,)
falls with - out - en
78
with-out - en pi - ty - ing, white pri - mit falls, (white
-out - en pi - ty - ing,) white pri - mit falls with - out-en pi - ty-
pi - ty - ing,) white pri - mit falls
white pri - mit falls, white pri - mit falls with-out - en
pi - ty - ing, white pri - mit
82
pri-mit falls) with - out - en pi - ty - ing.
-ing, white (pri - mit falls with-out - en pi - ty - ing.
with - out - en pi - ty-ing, with-out - en pi - ty - ing.
pi - ty-ing, with - out - en pi - ty, pi - ty - ing.
falls with - out - en pi - ty - ing.

57
WEEP, O MINE EYES

JOHN BENNET

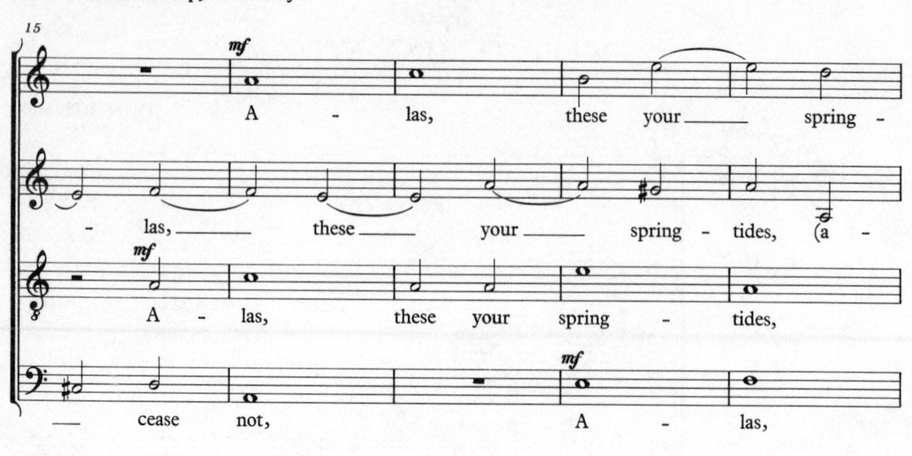
15
mf
A - las, these your spring -
- las, these your spring - tides, (a -
mf
A - las, these your spring - tides,
mf
cease not, A - las,

20
- tides, (a - las, these your spring -
- las, these your spring - tides,) me-thinks, in - crease
(a - las, these your spring -
these your spring - tides in - crease

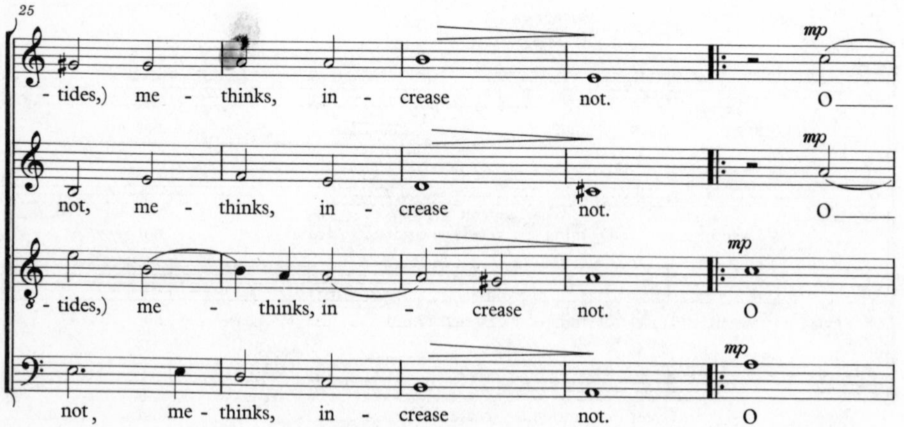
25
- tides,) me - thinks, in - crease not. O
mp
not, me - thinks, in - crease not. O
mp
- tides,) me - thinks, in - crease not. O
mp
not, me - thinks, in - crease not. O
mp

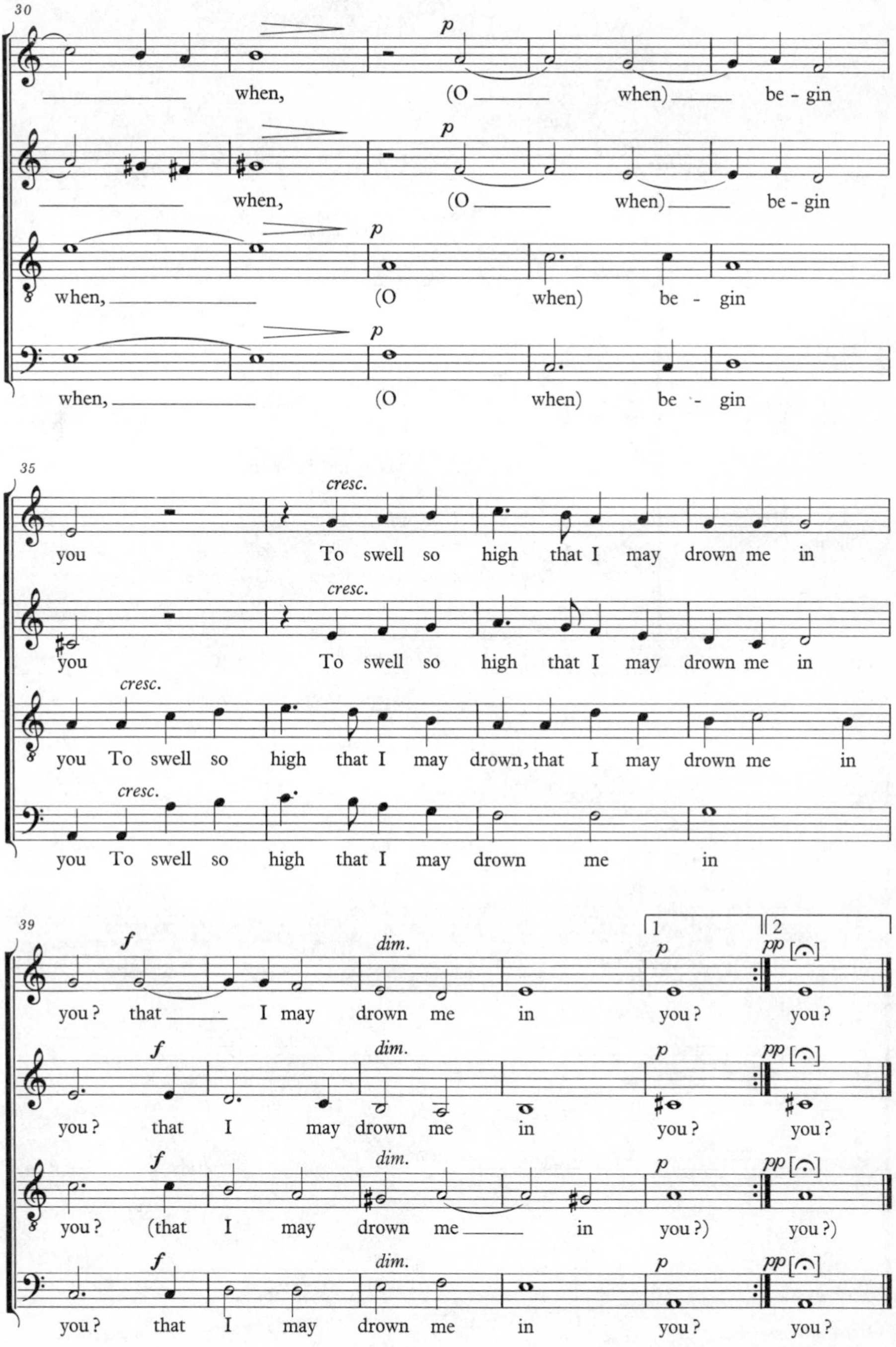

30
p
when, (O when) be - gin
p
when, (O when) be - gin
p
when, (O when) be - gin
p
when, (O when) be - gin
35
cresc.
you To swell so high that I may drown me in
cresc.
you To swell so high that I may drown me in
cresc.
you To swell so high that I may drown, that I may drown me in
cresc.
you To swell so high that I may drown me in
39
1
2
f dim. p pp
you? that I may drown me in you? you?
f dim. p pp
you? that I may drown me in you? you?
f dim. p pp
you? (that I may drown me in you?) you?)
f dim. p pp
you? that I may drown me in you? you?

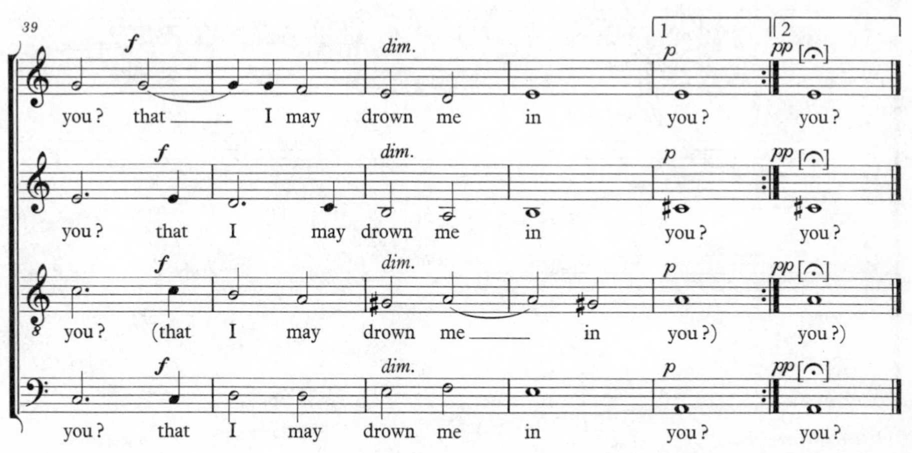

58
WEEP, WEEP, MINE EYES

JOHN WILBYE

10
weep, weep, my heart, mine eyes shall
weep, weep, my heart, mine eyes shall
weep, my heart, mine eyes shall ne'er be
weep, weep, O my heart, mine eyes shall ne'er be
weep, weep, my heart, mine eyes shall ne'er
15
ne'er be blest. Weep *eyes*, weep, *heart*, and
ne'er be blest. Weep eyes, weep heart, and both this
blest. Weep eyes, weep heart, and both this ac - cent
blest. Weep eyes, weep heart, and
be blest. Weep eyes, weep heart, and both
20
both this ac - cent cry: A
ac - cent cry:
cry: A thou-sand deaths I die, (a thou - sand
both this ac - cent cry, and both this ac - cent
this ac - cent cry: A thou - sand
mp
mp
mp
mp
mp

24
thou - sand deaths I die,
A thou - sand deaths I
deaths I die,) a thou - sand, thou- sand deaths I
cry: A thou - sand, thou - sand deaths I die, (a thou - sand
deaths I die, I die, Fla -
28
a thou - sand, thou - sand
die, I die, a
die, I die, a thou - sand, thou - sand deaths
deaths I die,) a thou - sand, thou - sand deaths, a
-min - ia, I die, a thou - sand
32
deaths I die, I die, a thou - (sand, thou - sand
thou - sand deaths I die, (a thou - sand
I die, a thou-sand,(thou - sand deaths) I
thou - sand, thou - sand deaths I
deaths I die, I die, a thou - (sand

36
deaths I die.) Ay me, ah, ah cru-el For-tune!
deaths I die.) Ay me,
die. Ay me, ah, ah cru-el For-tune!
die. Ay me, ah, ah cru-el For-tune!
deaths I die.) Ah, ah cru-el For-tune!
41
ay me. Now, Le - an - der, to die I
ay me. Now, Le - an - der, to
ay me, ay me. Now, Le - an - der, to die
ay me. Now, Le - an - der,
ay me.
47
fear not. Death, do thy worst! I care not, (Death, do thy
die I fear not. Death, do thy worst! I care
I fear not. Death, do thy worst! I
to die I fear not. Death, do thy worst! I care
Death, do thy

52
worst! I care not,) (Death do thy worst! I
not, (Death, do thy worst! I care not,) I
care not, (Death, do thy worst! I care
not, (Death, do thy worst! I care not!)
worst! I care not, Death, do thy worst! I
56
mp cresc.
care not! I hope, I hope
mp cresc.
care not! I hope, I hope
mp cresc. f
not! I hope when
mp cresc.
I hope when I am dead, I hope
mp cresc.
care not! I hope when I am dead
61
f
when I am dead in E-ly-sian plain, (in E-
f
when I am dead in E-ly-sian plain, (in E-ly-sian
I am dead in E-ly-sian plain, (in E-ly-sian
f
when I am dead in E-ly-sian plain, (in E-ly-sian
f
when (I am dead)

66
-ly - sian plain,) (in E-ly - sian plain) To meet, and there
plain,) in E - ly - sian plain To meet, and there
plain,) (in E - ly - sian plain) To meet, and there with joy, and
plain,) (in E - ly - sian plain) To meet, and there with joy,
in E - ly - sian
70
dim.
with joy, (and there with joy,) (and there
with joy, (and there with joy,) (and there
there with joy, (and there with joy,) (and
and there with joy, (and there
plain To meet, and
74
p[𝄐]
with joy,) with joy we'll love a - gain.
with joy,) with joy we'll love a - gain.
there with joy,)(and there with joy) we'll love a - gain.
with joy,) with joy we'll love a - gain, a - - - gain.
there with joy we'll love a - gain.

59
WHAT IS OUR LIFE?

ORLANDO GIBBONS

8
mf
- on,
play of pas - si - on, what
a play of pas - si - on, of pas - si -
play of pas - si - on, a play
What is our life? a
12
(what is our life,)
is our life, what (is
- on, what (is our life? a
of pas - si - on, what (is our
play of pas - si - on, what
17
what is our life? our
our life,) what (is our
play of pas - si - on.)
life? a play of pas - si -
is our life, our life? a

22
life? a play of pas - si - on.
life? a play of pas - si -
Our mirth
- on,) what (is our life? a play of
play of pas - - - si - on. Our
26
Our mirth the mu-sic of di-vi-si-on, of di-vi - si -
- on.) Our mirth the mu-sic of di -
the mu - sic, the mu - sic of di - vi - si-on,
pas - si - on. Our
mirth the mu-sic of di-vi-si-on, of di-vi-si-on, our (mirth the
30
- on.
- vi - si-on, our mirth the mu - sic of di-vi -
our (mirth the mu - sic of di-vi-si-on,) our (mirth the mu - sic
mirth the mu - sic of di-vi-si - on, our (mirth the mu - sic of di -
mu - sic of di - vi - si - on,)

34
mf
Our mo-thers' wombs the tir - ing-hou - ses be,
- si - on.)
of di - vi - si - on.) Our mo-thers' wombs, our (mo -
- vi - si - on.) Our mo - thers' wombs, our
Our mo-thers' wombs the tir - ing-hou -
38
Where we are dressed
Our mo-thers' wombs the tir-ing-hou-ses be,
- thers' wombs) the tir - ing, the tir-ing-hou-ses be, Where
mo-thers' wombs the tir - ing - hou-ses be,
- ses be, Where we are
42
for this short co - me - dy. Heaven
Heaven the ju -
we are dressed, are dressed for this short
Where we are dressed for this short co - me -
dressed, are dressed for this short co - -

46
the ju - di - cious sharp spec - ta - tor is,
- di - cious sharp spec - ta - tor is, heaven
co - me - dy. Heaven the ju -
- dy, short co - me - dy.
- me - dy. Heaven the ju - di - cious
50
That
(the ju - di - cious sharp spec - ta - tor is,) That
- di - cious sharp spec - ta - tor, spec - ta - tor is,
spec - ta - tor is, That
sharp spec - ta - tor is,
54
sits and marks still who doth act a - miss,
sits and marks still who doth act a - miss, that (sits and
That sits and marks, that (sits and marks) still who doth act a -
sits and marks, that sits and marks still who doth act a -
That sits and marks who doth a - miss, that sits and

58

that (sits and marks still who doth act a - miss.)

marks still who doth act a - miss,) still who doth act a - - -

- miss, that sits and marks, marks still who doth act a -

- miss, still who doth act a-miss, that (sits and marks still who doth act a -

marks still who doth act a - miss, still who doth act a -

62

p

Our graves, (our graves) that

- miss. *p* Our graves that hide us

- miss. *p* Our graves that hide us

- miss. *p* Our graves that hide us

- miss. *p* Our graves that hide, that

67

hide us from the

from the search - ing sun, that (hide us

from the search - ing

from the search - ing sun, from the search-ing

hide us from the search - ing

71
search - ing sun Are like drawn cur -
from the search - ing sun) Are like drawn cur - tains
sun Are like drawn
sun, the search - ing sun Are like drawn cur - tains,
sun Are like drawn cur - tains
76
- tains when the play is done,
when the play is done, are (like
cur - tains when the play is done, when (the play
drawn cur - - tains
when the play is done, when (the
80
drawn cur - tains when the play is
is done,) when the play
when the play is
play is done.)

84

when ___ the _ play ___ is _ done, ___ the _ play ___

done,)

___ is done, ___ is ___ done, are (like drawn

done, the _ play is _ done, are _ like drawn

88

___ is done, ___ are _ like drawn cur - tains _ when the play is

are (like drawn cur - tains when ___ the _ play is

cur - tains when the _ play is done,) the play is ___

cur - tains when the _ play is done.

f Thus

92

done. *f* Thus march we, play - ing,

done. *f* Thus march we, play -

done. *f* Thus march ___ we, play - ing, thus

f Thus march ___ we, play - ing, thus

march we, play - ing, to our lat - est rest,

96
thus (march we, play - ing,) thus march we,
- ing, thus (march we, play - ing,) thus march we,
(march we, play - ing,) thus march we, play - ing,
march we, play - ing, thus (march we, play - ing,) thus
thus (march we, play - ing, to our
100
play - ing, to our lat - est rest, thus march we, play - ing,
play - ing to our lat - est rest, our lat - est rest,
thus (march we, play - ing,) thus
march we, play - ing, to our lat - est rest, thus (march we, play - ing
lat - est rest,) our lat - est rest,
104
thus march we, play - ing, to our lat - est
thus (march we, play - ing,)
march we, play - ing, to our lat - est rest, thus (march we, play - ing, to our
to our lat - est rest,) thus (march we, play -
thus march we play - ing, thus

108

rest, thus (march we, play - ing, to our lat - est

thus march we, play - ing, to our lat - est rest, On - ly

lat - est rest,) thus (march we, play - ing,

- ing,) thus (march we, play - ing, to our

(march we, play - ing, to our lat - est rest,)

112

dim.

rest,) On - ly we die, we die in ear -

dim.

we die in ear - - nest, that's no

dim.

to our lat - est rest,) On - ly we die in ear - nest, that's

dim.

lat - est rest,) On - ly we die,

dim.

On - ly we

116

p

- nest, that's no jest, we die in ear - nest, that's no jest.

p

jest, in ear - nest, that's no jest.

p

no jest, we (die in ear - nest, that's no jest.)

p

we die in ear - nest, that's no jest.

p

die, in ear - nest, that's no jest, no jest.

60

WHITHER AWAY SO FAST?

THOMAS MORLEY

12
love ap - prov - ed, ap - prov - ed? What haste, I say, what
love ap - prov - - ed? O say
- - - ed? What haste, I say, what haste? Tell me, what
15
haste, I say, (what haste, I say,) mine own best dar - ling dear be-lov -
sweet, what haste a-way, what haste? Tell me, my dar - ling
haste, what haste. Tell me, my dar - - - ling
18
- ed, dear be-lov - ed?
dear be-lov - ed. Then will we try Who best runs, thou or
dear be - lov - ed. Then will we try Who fast - er runs, thou or
22
Then lo, I come! dis - patch thee! I come, I come, I come, I come, I come, lo, I
I. Now, now I come! dis - patch thee! I come, I come, I
I. See then, I come! dis - patch thee! I come, a-way, a-way, a-way, a -

25
come! dis-patch thee! I come! Hence I say, a-way, a - way, hence a-way, a-way, a -
come, a - way, a - way, lo, I come! Hence a - way, I come, I come, haste thee hence a -
- way, lo, I come, I come, I come! dis - patch
28
mf
- way, a - way, or I catch, I catch, or I catch thee. Think,
mf
- way, or else I catch thee. Think, think not
mf
thee! Haste thee hence a - way, or else I catch thee, I
31
think not thus a-way to 'scape all a - lone with - out
thus a-way to 'scape, to 'scape, my dear, with - out
catch thee. Think, think not thus a-way to 'scape with - out
34
me, no, think not thus a-way to 'scape with - out me,
p
me, with-out me, no, think not thus a-way to 'scape with-out me, no,
p
me, to 'scape thus with - out, with - out me, no, think not

38

p
no, think not, thus a-way to 'scape, to 'scape with - out ___

think not thus a - way to 'scape, to 'scape with - out ___

thus a-way to 'scape with - out me, to 'scape with - out

41

f
me. But run! You need ___ not doubt ___

f
me. But run! You need ___ not doubt ___

f
me. But run! You need not doubt

45

mf
me. What now! What! faint you? Of ___ your sweet feet for -

mf
me. What now! What! faint you? Of ___ your sweet

mf
me. What now! What! faint you, faint you? Of your sweet feet

49

mp
- sak - - - - - en? O well I see you

mp
feet for - sak - - en, for - sak - en? O

mp
for - sak - en, for - sak - en? O well I

53
cresc.
f
mean to mock me. Run, I say, or else I catch — you. What? — You halt?
cresc.
f
well I see you mean to mock me. Run, or else I catch you. What? You
cresc.
f
see you mean to mock me. Run, or else I catch you. What? You
57
O do — you so? A - lack — the while! what! are — you down? — Pret-ty maid, well
halt? O do you so? A - lack the while! what! are you down? Fair
halt? O do you so? A - lack the while! what! are you down? Pret-ty
61
mf
o - ver - tak - - - - - en! What
mf
maid, then well o - ver - tak - - en! What now! what now fair
maid, well o - ver - tak - - - en!
64
now! What! faint you? Of your sweet, of your sweet
maid, What now! What! faint you? Of your sweet
mf
What now! What! faint you, faint you? Of your sweet

Process-engraved by
Michael L. Rowe

Critical commentary by Andrew Parker

Sources

Printed Sources

A Bateson (Thomas)
The first set of English Madrigales: to 3. 4. 5. and 6. voices . . . Printed by Thomas Este. 1604
B Bennet (John)
Madrigalls To Fovre Voyces . . . Printed in little Saint Hellens by William Barley, the Assigne of Thomas Morley. Cum Priuelegio. 1599
C Byrd (William)
Psalmes, Sonets, & songs of sadnes and pietie . . . Printed by Thomas Este, the assigne of W. Byrd . . . 1588
D East (Michael)
The Third Set Of Bookes . . . to 5. and 6. parts: Apt both for Viols and Voyces . . . Printed by Thomas Snodham . . . 1610
E East (Michael)
The Fovrth Set Of Bookes . . . To 4. 5. and 6. Parts: Apt for Viols and Voyces . . . Printed by Thomas Snodham . . . 1618
F Farmer (John)
The First Set Of English Madrigals: To Foure Voices . . . Printed in London in Little Saint Helens by William Barley, the Assigne of Thomas Morley . . . 1599
G Farnaby (Giles)
Canzonets To Fowre Voyces . . . Printed by Peter Short . . . 1598
H Gibbons (Orlando)
The First Set Of Madrigals and Mottets of 5. Parts: apt for Viols and Voyces . . . Printed by Thomas Snodham, the Assigne of W. Barley. 1612
I Greaves (Thomas)
Songs Of Sundrie kinds . . . Madrigalles, for fiue voyces . . . Imprinted by Iohn Windet . . . 1604
J Kirbye (George)
The first set Of English Madrigalls, to 4. 5. & 6. voyces . . . Printed by Thomas Este . . . 1597
K Morley (Thomas)
Madrigalls To Fovre Voyces . . . The First Booke . . . By Thomas Este in Aldersgate street . . . 1594
L Morley (Thomas)
The First Booke of Balletts To Five Voyces . . . By Thomas Este. 1595
M Morley (Thomas)
Canzonets. Or Little Short Songs To Three Voyces . . . Imprinted at London by Tho: Est, the assigne of William Byrd . . . 1593
N Morley (Thomas)
Madrigales The Triumphes of Oriana, to 5. and 6. voices: composed by diuers seuerall aucthors . . . Printed by Thomas Este, the assigne of Thomas Morley. 1601
O Tomkins (Thomas)
Songs Of 3. 4. 5. and 6. parts . . . Printed for Matthew Lownes, Iohn Browne, and Thomas Snodham. 1622
P Vautor (Thomas)
The First Set: . . . Apt for Vyols and Voyces . . . Printed by Thomas Snodham, for Matthew Lownes and Iohn Browne. 1619
Q Ward (John)
The First Set of English Madrigals To 3. 4. 5. and 6. parts apt both for Viols and Voyces . . . Printed by Thomas Snodham. 1613
R Watson (Thomas)
The first sett, Of Italian Madrigalls Englished . . . There are also heere inserted two excellent Madrigalls of Master William Byrds . . . Imprinted at London by Thomas Este . . . 1590
S Weelkes (Thomas)
Ayeres Or Phantasticke Spirites for three voices . . . Printed by William Barley . . . 1608
T Weelkes (Thomas)
Balletts And Madrigals To fiue voyces . . . Printed by Thomas Este. 1598
U Weelkes (Thomas)
Madrigals Of 5. and 6. parts, apt for the Viols and voices . . . Printed by Thomas Este, the assigne of Thomas Morley. 1600
V Wilbye (John)
The First Set Of English Madrigals To 3. 4. 5. and 6. voices . . . Printed by Thomas Este. 1598
W Wilbye (John)
The Second Set Of Madrigales To 3. 4. 5. and 6. parts, apt both for Voyals and Voyces . . . Printed by Thomas Este alias Snodham, for Iohn Browne . . . 1609

Manuscript Sources

(Libraries listed by RISM sigla)

1	Gu	Autograph Part-Books, Robert Ramsey
2	Lbl	Add. 29372-7
3	Lbl	Add. 36484
4	Lbl	Add. 15117
5	Lbl	Add. 18936-9
6	Lcm	MS 684
7	Och	MS 21
8	Och	MSS 984-8

Editorial method

Notation

All symbols in square brackets are editorial. Large accidentals in parentheses are implicit from the conventions of the source or sources but are not notated therein. Small accidentals in parentheses are cautionary. Ligatures are shown by a brace over the notes concerned; coloration is denoted by a broken brace round the groups of notes.

Text

Where repetition of text in the sources is indicated by *bis* markings the text is here placed in parentheses. While the underlay in such circumstances is, in the main, syllabic, in certain places melisma could provide alternative interpretations. Where between, for example, printed and manuscript sources an occasional word is supplied compared with a printed *bis* mark, this word is not placed in parentheses but is taken as a clear and definite indication of underlay. Text not indicated by a *bis* marking and supplied editorially appears in an italic fount. The spelling, capitalization and punctuation of text have been taken from FELLOWES, E. H.: *English Madrigal Verse 1588-1632*, revised and enlarged by Frederick W. Sternfeld and David Greer, Third Edition, O.U.P., 1967. Words in parentheses in the source are notated in angle brackets.

Time-Changes

There is no definitive and contemporary account of conventions used in the notation of *tripla* and *sesquialtera* proportion in England during the currency of the madrigal repertoire. That a convention was intended, if not followed in every instance which can be examined, is seen from the seven sources of the Altus part to Richard Deering's *Country Cries*[1]. In each case, despite divergence of time-signatures, even between individual parts of a set of books, there is unanimity in the notation of two sections in black notation and one final section in white notation. The solution to the black notation is provided in John Farmer's *Fair Phyllis I saw* (No. 16 in this volume) as well as in many keyboard manuscripts. In the Farmer madrigal there is a change to black notation at the phrase *O then they fell a-kissing* in the lower three voices while the upper voice continues with rests in ₵ time. This carries the implication that white minim is exactly equivalent to black semibreve plus black minim, or black perfect semibreve, and this interpretation works for every case of black notation in the repertoire which I have examined. Within this *tripla* there was a reluctance, if not the theoretic inability to express notes longer in duration than black perfect semibreve, and this would explain the otherwise fussy change of time from black notation for long notes at the ends of sections or pieces.

If this solution disposes of the *tripla* problem (one which was unclear, even to Morley) the white notation has no direct proof, but has been taken as the *sesquialtera* proportion and has proved successful in each application. Here duple-time breve is equivalent to triple-time dotted breve.

1. Lbl Add. 18937; Lbl Add. 17795; Lcm 2049; Lbl Add. 29373; Lbl Add. 29427; Lcm 684; T 1163.

Editorial note

As is shown in detail by the variants listed below in this commentary, the manuscript sources used of these madrigals, often held merely to be copies of the printed books, provide additional insight into the problems of underlay and use of accidentals not notated by the compositors. Indeed, some of the variants might have been difficult for the scribe to have arrived at, had he a printed copy from which he was working, unless he were insouciant towards his source. In many cases textual underlay is clarified by slurs in the manuscripts, while in some printed sources melisma is enhanced by use of additional blank stave type-sorts to align words and notes more accurately. For a printed source, where there is no manuscript concordance, when a wrong note exists I have preferred the solution which inverts the type-sort – i.e. a note on line 2 of the stave in the source should have been on line 4 – rather than imply that the compositor failed to identify a type-sort with a note on a line when he should have been handling one with a note in a space. Human error would tend to favour the misplacing of notes by a third in manuscript rather than by a tone.

In the source-list for each madrigal I have notated the printed copy or copies examined in order that any bibliographical variants between apparently identical copies of the same printed edition might be clarified.

The following are used as abbreviations in the list of variants:

TS Time-signature; *l*, *b*, *sb*, *m*, *c*, *q* for long, breve, semibreve, minim, crotchet and quaver, respectively; locations are shown in the order: bar number (Arabic), part number counting down the system (small Roman), note or symbol within the bar (Arabic); an 'a' after the bar number indicates a second-time bar; the Helmholtz system of pitch notation is used.

ANDREW PARKER

Variants

1. Bennet All creatures now
Source: N, No. IV (Cu, Lcm)
Variants: 71i-v l: *l*

2. Wilbye Adieu, sweet Amaryllis
Sources: V, No. XII (Lbl); 2; 6
Variants: Pref. Stave: TS ₵ (2, 6)/45 i-iv l: *l* (V) with pause (6)/45 i, iii & iv l: *b* with pause (2)/ 45 ii l: *l* with pause (2)

3. Tomkins Adieu, ye city-prisoning towers
To Mr. *William White*
Source: O, No. XXII (Lcm)
Variants: 48 i-v: TS 3 [A true white *tripla*: note-values halved]/54 i, ii & iv: TS ₵/54 iii & v: TS C

4. Gibbons Ah, dear heart
Sources: H, No. XV (Cu); 7 (textless)
Variants: *deere* (7)/1 iii l: *c* rest, *m* f′ (H)/25 i-v: no pause (H)/7 has repeat *signum* and does not continue after bar 25.

5. Morley April is in my mistress' face
Sources: K, No. I (Lbl); 4 (Voice & Lute); 3 (iv only)
Variants: 3 iii 3: No ♯ (3)/4 iii l: No ♯ (3)/ 11 iv l: (3 goes drastically wrong here) *m* rest, *c* rest, *c* d *And*, *q* e♭ *Ju-*, *q*f-*ly*, *q* g *in*, *q* a *hir*, *m* b♭ *eies*/13 iv l: *hir eies*(3)/14 iv l: *so deir* (3)/17 iv 2: *But in hir* (3)/19 iv l: *breist, but in hir breist* (3)/ 24 iv 2: *Within hir hart* (3)/26 iv 2: *Within hir* (3)/ 27 iv l: *m* e♭ *hart*, *m* e♭ *is* (3)/33 iv l: *breist* (3)/ 35 iv l: *m* e♭ *breist*, *m* e♭ *is* (3)/38 i l: *b* with pause (4)/38 i-iv l: *l* (K)

6. Weelkes As Vesta was
Source: N, No. XVII (Lcm)
Variants: 116 i-vi l: *l*

7. Greaves Come away, sweet love
Source: I, No. XXI (Lbl)
Variants: Pref. Stave: *m* rest, *c* rest in ii-iv only/65 i-vl: *b*

8. Cavendish Come, gentle swains
Source: N, No. XI (Lcm)
Variants: 32 i-v: TS 3/37 i-v: TS C/62 i-iv l: *l*/ 62 v l: *b* with pause

9. Ward Come, sable night
Sources: Q, No. XXVII (Cu); 2
Variants: 122 i-vi l: *l* (Q)/122 i & v l: *b* with pause (2)/122 ii-iv & vi l: *l* with pause (2)

10. Farnaby Consture my meaning
Source: G, No. XX (Lbl)
Variants: 45 i & iv l: *b* [*Consture*, pronounced cón-ster, a variant of the more usual *conster* was the common pronunciation of the word down to the nineteenth century, even after the usual spelling had changed to *construe*.]

11. Weelkes Come, sirrah Jack, ho!
Sources: S, No. VI (Cu); 5
Variants: Pref. Stave iii: clef C_2 (5)/TS Ͼ (5)/8 i 3: No ♮ (5)/10 i 2: ♭ (5)/14a i-iii: TS ₵ (5) C (S)/14a i-iii: *sim.*/14a i-iii 3: *signum* (5)/14a i-iii l: *m* dot (5)/16 i-iii 3: *it*'s (S)/16 iii 3: c′ (5)/18 ii 3: *q* c″, *q* b′♭ (5)/18 iii 3: c′ (5)/22 ii 2: *very very good for the blood, tis very* (5)/24 i & iii 3: *c, c* (5)/25a i-iii l: *m* dot with pause (5); *b* with pause (5) [No 2nd stanza in (5)]

12. Gibbons Dainty fine bird
Source: H, No. IX (Cu)
Variants: 43 i-iv l: *l*/43 v l: *b* with pause

13. Wilbye Draw on, sweet night
Sources: W, No. XXXI (Cu); 2; 6 (i, iii, v & vi only)
Variants: Pref. Stave: TS ₵ (2, 6)/34 iii l: *q* d′ *want*, *q* e′ *of*, *m* f′ *com-* (6)/41 i 4: *I consecrate it whol-* [then melisma] (6)/113 iv 3 to 114 iv l: printed slur (W)/125 iii l: *my* [melisma] to 125 iii 4, 125 iii 5 *com-*, *-plain-* (6)/126 iii 4: *bis* marking only (W, 6)/129 i-vi l: *l* (W) with pause (2)/129 i, iii, v & vi l: *l* with pause (6)

14. Farmer Fair nymphs, I heard one telling
Source: N, No XIV (Lcm)
Variants: 42 iv l: c♯ implied/68 i l: (inverted type-sort) d″/74 i-vi l: *l*

15. Wilbye Flora gave me fairest flowers
Source: V, No. XXII (Lbl)
Variants: 52 i-v l: *l*

16. Farmer Fair Phyllis I saw
Source: F, No. XV (Lbl)
Variants: 19 et seq: *wandred*/32 ii-iv: TS Ͼ/34 ii-iv: TS₵/35 i-iv: TS Ͼ/41 i-iv: TS₵/56 ii-iv: TS Ͼ/58 ii-iv: TS ₵/59 i-iv: TS Ͼ/65 i-iv: TS ₵

17. Morley Fyer, fyer!
Source: L, No. XIV (Lbl)
Variants: 2nd stanza supplied in v only because more space available than in i-iv/89 i, ii, iv l: *l*/ 89 iii l: *b*/89 v l: *b* with pause

18. Morley Hard by a crystal fountain
Source: N, No. XXIII (Cu, Lcm)
Variants: 12 iii 3: c′/82 i-vi: TS 3/82 i 2: *Mymphs* (Lcm only)/82 iii 2: *Mymphs* (Cu only)/ 89 i-vi: TS C/128 i-iii, v & vi l: *l*/123 iv l: *b*

19. Weelkes Hark, all ye lovely saints
Source: T, No. VIII (Lcm)
Variants: 35a i-v l: *l*

20. Wilbye Lady, when I behold
Source: V, No. X (Lbl)
Variants: 70 i-iv l: *l*

21. Morley I love, alas, I love thee
Source: L, No. XVII (Lbl, *two copies*)
Variants: 57 i-v l: *l* (K.3.i.5.)/57 v l: *b* with pause (K.3.i.4.)

22. Morley Leave, alas, this tormenting
Sources: L, No. XIX (Lbl) (K.3.i.4.); 2
Variants: Pref. Stave i-v: TS ₵ (2)/14 v 2: *bis* (L)/ 38 iii 2: *bis* (L)/ 40 i-v: TS 3 (L, 2)/43 i-v: TS C (L), ₵ (2)/48 ii l: ♮ 1st time only (2)/50 v

2: ♮ (L)/55 ii l: ♮ 1st time only (2)/ 58 v l: ♮ 2nd time only (2)/61a i-v: *b* with pause (2)/ 61a i l: *b* with pause (L)/ 61a ii-v l: *l* (L)

23. Byrd Lullaby, my sweet little baby
Sources: C, No. XXXII (Lbl); 8 (Down one tone, text in ii only)
Variants: l iv l: *b* dot (8)/lvl: *sb* dot (8)/2 iii 2: *sb*, *m* g (8)/3 v l: *sb* dot (8)/4 i 2: *m* dot, *c* g′ (8)/ 4 iii l: *b* dot (8)/6 v l: *sb* (8)/7 iv l: *b* dot (8)/8 iii l: *sb* (8)/ll i 2: *m* dot, *c* c″ (8)/ 13 iii 2: *sb* (8)/ 15 i l: *sb* (8)/15 iv l: *sb* dot (8)/16 i 2: *m* (8)/16 v 2: *m* (8)/17 v l: *sb* dot (8)/19 iii 2: *c* rest (8)/21 iii 2: *m* dot (8)/22 iv l: *m*, *c* rest (8)/22 v l: *sb* (8)/23 iii 2: *sb* (8)/25 i 2: *m* b♭ (8)/25 iii l: *b* dot (8)/ 33 v 3: *sb* dot, *sb* g (8)/36 iii l: *c*, *c* (8)/37 iv l: *sb*, *sb* g dot (8)/40 v 2: g (8)/41 iv 2: *m*, *c* (8)/ 46 i l: *sb* (8)/48 i 2: *m* (8)/48 iv 2: *m*, *m* g, *m* rest, *b* g with pause (8)/49 ii 3: *-by*, *lul-*, *-la-* (8)/52 i-v: TS $^{\mathrm{C}}_{3}$ (C), C (8)/53 v 2: No ♮ (8)/54 i l: *m* c′dot, *q* b′♭, *q* a′, m b′♭ (8)/54 iv 3: *sb* dot (8)/ 55 iii 2: *m* dot (8)/55 iv 2: *sb* dot (8)/58 v l: *sb* dot (8)/59 v l: *sb* (8)/60 iii 2: *sb* dot (8)/ 61 i 3: *m* g′ (8)/62 iv 2: *c* d, *c* e♭ (8)/65 iv l: *sb* b♭ (8)/66 i l: *sb* (8)/66 v 2: *m* B♭ (8)/68 iii l: *m* f′ dot, *c* e♭ (8)/69 i l: *sb* b′♭, *m* d″ (8)/69 iii 2: *sb* (8)/7 l i l: *sb* dot (8)/7 l iv l: *sb* b♭ dot, *m* b♭, *sb* g (8)/71 v l: *sb* dot (8)/73 iii l: *sb* dot (8)/73 iv l: *sb* dot, *m* rest (8)/76 iii l: *m* rest (8)/76 iv l: *sb* b♭ dot, *m* b♭, *sb* b♭ dot (8)/76 v l: *sb* dot (8)/78 iii l: *m* dot (8)/79 v l: *sb* (8)/81 iii l: No ♮ until 81 iii 3 (8)/ 84 v 3: *m* (8)/85 v 2: *sb* (8)/86 iv l: *sb* dot (8)/87 iii l: *m* d′, *sb* d′ (8)/87 iv 2: *sb* dot (8)/88 iii l: No ♮ until 88 iii 3 (8)/89 iii l: *sb* dot (8)/90 iv l: *sb* dot (8)/92 iii l: *sb* dot (8)/92 iv l: color (C)/ 95: *signa* in (8); repeat in full (C)/96 i l: color (C)/97 iii l: No ♮ (8)/98 i 2: No ♮ (8)/ 98 iii l: color (C)/99 iii l: *sb* dot (8)/100 i 3: *sb* (8)/100 iii 2: *sb* dot (8)/101 ii l, 2: slur (8)/101 v 2: *sb* (8)/102 i 2: *m* b′♭, *m* b′♭ dot, *c* g′ (8)/102 v l: *m* e♭, *m* e♭ (8)/103 iv 5: No ♮ (8)/107 iv l: *sb* dot (8)/110a i-iv l: *b* with pause (C)/110a v l: *l* (C)/110a i-iv l: *sb* dot with pause (8)/110a v l: *sb* dot (8)
[As is seen, the majority of these variants refer to notes not repeated because of the instrumental intentions of (8).]

24. Vautor Mother, I will have a husband
Source: P, No. IV (Lbl)
Variants: 10 iii 2: *shuld a*/40 i-v: TS 61/56 i-v: TS ¢/67 i-iv l: *l* /67 v l: *b* with pause

25. Tomkins Music divine
To Mr. Doctor *Heather*
Source: O, No. XXIV (Lcm)
Variants: 5 iv l: *b* - i.e. dot missing/54 ii 2: *When*/103 i-vi l: *l*

26. Morley My bonny lass she smileth
Source: L, No. VII (Lbl)
Variants: 18 i-v: TS 3/27 i-v: TS C/28 i-v l: *l*

27. Morley Now is the month of maying
Source: L, No. III (Lbl)
Variants: 18 i-v l: *l*

28. Weelkes O care, thou wilt despatch me
Source: U, No. IV (Lbl)
Variants: 8 iv l: ô/27 ii & iii l: *thou dost*/31 iii 2: *thou dost*/58 i-v l: *l*

29. Weelkes Hence, Care, thou art too cruel
Source: U, No. V (Lbl)
Variants: 7 iv 2: ♮ inked in to ♭/58 i-v: *l*

30. Ward Out from the vale
Sources: Q, No. XXI (Cu); 2
Variants: Pref. Stave iii: No b′♭ (Q)/53 ii 2: *which* plus *bis* mark (2)/89 i-vi l: *l* (Q)

31. Wilbye O what shall I do?
Source: W, No. VI (Cu)
Variants: 38 i-iii l: *b*/88 i-iii l: *b*

32. Tomkins O yes! Has any found a lad?
To Master *Iohn Coprario*
Source: O, No. IX (Lcm)
Variants: 68 i-iv l: *l*

33. Gibbons O that the learned poets
Sources: H, No. II (Cu); 7 (textless)
Variants: 28 v 3: *m* g, *c* rest, *c* a♭ (7)/30 i 2: *c* rest, *c* b′♭ (7)/30 v l: *c* rest, *c* b♭, *c* g, *c* g, (7)/ 32 i 2: *m* rest, *c* rest, *c* e″♭ (7)/62 iii l: *c* rest (7)/ 70 v l: *sb* F with pause (7)/70 i-iv l: *l* with pause

34. East Poor is the life
Source: D, No. XV (Lbl, Och)
Variants: 14 i-vi: TS $^{\Phi}_{32}$/20 i-vi: TS C/33 i-vi: TS $^{\Phi}_{32}$/39 i-vi: TS C/49 i-vi: TS $^{\Phi}_{32}$/53 i-vi l: *l*

35. East Quick, quick, away, dispatch!
A song made upon the marriage of the right worshipful, and my very good friend Edward Oldisworth of Lincoln's Inn Esquire
Source: E, No. XVII (Cu, Lcm)
Variants: 5 i: TS C3/5 ii-vi: TS C3/14 i-vi: TS C/23 iv 2: *he*/27 i-vi: *signum*

36. East No haste but good!
Source: E, No. XVIII (Cu, Lcm)
Variants: 32 i-vi: TS C3/37 i-vi: TS C/38 i-vi: *signum*

37. Tomkins See, see the shepherds' queen
Source: O, No. XVII (Lcm)
Variants: 79 i l: ♯/96 i-v l: *l*

38. Weelkes Since Robin Hood
Source: S, No. XX (Cu)
Variants: 2 i-iii l: *Roben*/10 i-iii: TS 3/20 i-iii: TS C/26 ii 3: *did*/31a i l: *b*, with pause ii & iii

39. Kirbye See what a maze of error
Sources: J, No. XVII (Lbl); 6 (i, iii-v only)
Variants: 10 iv 2: f♯ *of* g, d′ *ter-* (J)/21 i l: *trast* (J)/65 i-v l: *l* (J)/65 i, iii-v l: *l* with pause (6)

40. Morley Sing we and chant it
Source: L, No. IV (Lbl)
Variants: 24 i-v l: *l* (*white*)

41. Weelkes Strike it up, Tabor
Sources: S, No. XVIII (Cu); 5

Variants: Pref. Stave: TS 𝄴 (5)/*Strike up the* (5)/6 i 2: *q* a′, *c* g′, *c* f ′, *c* f ′, *c* e′, *c* f ′, *c* f ′ (5)/6 ii 1: *c* c″ dot, *q* c″, then as i to 8 ii 2: *c* a′ (5)/7 iii 1: *c* a, *c* b♭, *c* c′ (5)/8 i-iii: TS 𝄵 (5) C (R)/10 ii 4: *c* g′, *m* f ′, *c* f ′ (5)/15 i 1: *m* e″ *c* rest (5)/15 ii 1: melisma on *brisk* to 15 ii 4/17 ii 6: *c* a′ *rout*, *c* b′♭ *till* (5)/17 iii 5: *c* f′ *till*, *c* b♭ dot *ve-*, *q* b♭*-ry*, *c* b♭ dot *wea-*, *q* b♭*-ry* (5)/18 i 3: No ♭ (5)/19 ii 2: *c* f ′, *c* f ′ (5)/20a i-iii 1: *b* with pause (S)/20a i & ii 1: *l* with pause (5)/20a iii 1: *b* with pause (5)

42. Weelkes Sing we at pleasure
Source: T, No. XII (Lcm)
Variants: 84 i-iv 1: *l* (*white*)/84 v 1: *b* (*white*) with pause

43. Ramsey Sleep, fleshly birth
Source: 1
Variants: [Underlay frequently indicated by slurs] 35 vi 2: *Make marble melt with weeping, make* [*bis*] [all erased]/60 i-vi: TS 3/71 i-vi: TS 𝄵/96 i-vi: *signa* for repeat/102 ii 1: *so*/102 v 2: *so*/125a ii-vi 1: *b*, with pause i

44. Wilbye Sweet honey-sucking bees
Sources: W, No. XVII (Cu); 2; 6 (i, iii-v only)
Variants: Pref. Stave: TS 𝄵 (2, 6)/25 iii 3: No ♮ (2)/ 36 i 1: *sits* (6)/69 i 1: *l* (W, 2) with pause (6)/69 ii-v 1: *l* (W, 2)/69 iii-v 1: *l* with pause (6)

45. Wilbye Yet, sweet, take heed
Sources: W, No. XVIII (Cu); 2; 6 (i, iii-v only)
Variants: 12 iv 2: *sting not her lips* (6)/28 iii 1: No ♭ (W, 2)/28 ii 2: No ♭ (W, 6)/41 v 1: No ♭ (W, 2)/47 iii 1: *you die*, plus *bis* mark (W, 2)/54 i 2: No ♭ (W)/61 ii 4: No ♮ (2)/65 v 2: No ♭ (W, 2)/80 iv 2: *sb* f′ *then*, *c* e′♮ *you*, *c* d′ (W, 2)/93 i, iii-v 1: *l* with pause (2, 6)/93 ii 1: *b* with pause (2)

46. Vautor Sweet Suffolk owl
Source: P, No. XII (Lbl)
Variants: 51 i-v: TS C $\frac{\text{𝄴}}{31}$ /64 i-v: TS 𝄵/83 i-v 1: *l*

47. Gibbons The silver swan
Sources: H, No. I (Cu); 7 (textless)
Variants: No TS (7)/10 i 3: Additional voice *c* c″, *c* b′♮ (7)/10 iv 1: *m* rest, *c* rest, *m* g (7)/12 iv 3: *c* g [prev. 3 variants by implication of repeat *signum* thus also in bars 17 and 19]

48. Byrd This sweet and merry month of May
Source: R, No. XXVIII (Lbl)
Variants: 30 i-vi: TS/36 i-vi: TS/90 i, ii, iv & v 1: *l*/90 iii 1: *l* with pause /90 vi 1: *b* with pause

49. Byrd Though Amaryllis dance
Sources: C, No. XII (Cu, Lbl); 8
Variants: TS $\frac{\text{Φ}}{3}$ (8)/Text in *Superius* only (8)/Pref. Stave v clef C_5 (8)/1 iv 1: *sb* g, *m* f (8)/1 c 2: *m* e, *m* d, *m* c dot (8)/3 iii 2: *m* d′, *m* b (8)/4 iii 3: *m* c′ dot, *sb* g′ (8)/4 v 4: *m* c dot (8)/5 iv 2: *m* c′ dot (8)/6 v 1: *m* g dot (8)/6 ii 3: *m* a′ dot (8)/8 iv 1: *sb* c′ dot (8)/9 iii 2: *sb* d′, *m* d (8)/10 i 2: b′ (8)/10 ii 1: *sb* g′, *m* rest (8)/11 iii 4: *c* rest (8)/12 iv 1: *m* c′ dot, *c* a, *m* a (8)/12 v 1: *m* A (8)/13 iii 1: *sb* f′ ♯ (8)/13 iv 1: *sb* a dot (8)/13 v 1: *sb* d (8)/14 ii 1: *c* rest, *m* f′, *c*f′, *m* c′ (8)/14 iii 1: *m* a′ dot, *m* a′, *c* a′ (8)/14 v 2: *sb* f (8)/15 iv 2: *m* g′, *c* g′ (8)/16 iv 1: *sb* d′ dot (8)/17 iii 4: No ♯ (C)/18 v 1: *m* e (8)/22 iv 2: *c* d′ dot, *q* c′, *q* b, *q* a, *c* b (8)/24 iv 1: *sb* c′ (8)/ 26 ii 3: *sb* g′ (8)/28 ii 2: *m* a′ (8)/28 iv 1: *m* rest (8)/30 v 1: *m* e (8)/34 iv 2: *c* d′ dot, *q* c′, *q* b, *q* a, *c* b (8)/36 iv 1: *sb* c′ (8)/37 iii 2: *m* rest (8)/39 i & iii: No color (8)/40 ii 2: *sb* g′ (8)/40 v 2: *sb* g (8)/41 i 1: *b* with pause (C)/41 ii-iv 1: *l* with pause (C)/41 v 1: *l* (C)/41 i-iii 1: *b* with pause (8)/41 iv 1: *m* c′ *sb* g with pause (8)41 v 1: *l* with pause (8)

50. Morley Though Philomela lost her love
Source: M, No. XXIII (Lcm)
Variants: 19 i-iii: TS C, *sb* (*white*)/21 i-iii: TS 3/39 i-iii: TS C, *sb* (*white*)/39a i-iii: TS C, *l* (*white*)

51. Bateson Those sweet delightful lilies
Source: A, No. XIII (Och)
Variants: 6 iv 4: *Hhillis*/29 i 2: No ♯, but at 60 ii 2/85 i-iv 1: *l*/85 v 1: *b* with pause

52. Weelkes Thule, the period of cosmography
Source: U, 6-part section, No. VII (Lbl)
Variants: 10 v 1: *q*/31 v & vi: *-ri-* appears at 32 v 3 and 32 vi 1. In each case, these syllables are preceded by an extra 5-line blank stave sort, and would thus appear to be intended by the compositor./41 i-vi: TS 3/43 i-vi: TS C/77 i-vi 1: *l*

53. Weelkes The Andalusian merchant
Source: U, 6-part section, No. VIII (Lbl)
Variants: 68 i-vi 1: *l*

54. Weelkes Thus sings my dearest jewel
Source: 5
Variants: 11 i-iii: TS 31/18 i-iii: TS 𝄵/30a i 1: *b* with pause/ 30a ii & iii 1: *l* with pause

55. Tomkins Too much I once lamented
Source: O, No. XIV (Lcm)
Variants: 22 ii 1: tied to 23 ii 1 in C/24 ii 2: *Fa* in C/26 ii 1: *la* in C/26 ii 3: *fa* in C/30 ii 3: *fa* in Q/31 ii 2: *fa* in C/32 iii 1: *la*, *fa* 1st time/63 iv 2: d 2nd time/64 v 1: *fa* 2nd time/65 ii 2: *la* in Q/65 ii 4: *fa* in Q/65 v 2: missing 1st time and inked in by hand/67 i 3: *la* in Q/68 i 2: *fa* in Q/68 iii 1: *fa la* 1st time/69 ii 1: *fa* in C/69 v 6: *fa* 2nd time/70 ii 1: no tie in Q/71 ii O: *la* in Q/71 v 2: *la* 1st time/72 iv 4: *la* 2nd time/73 v 3: *la* 2nd time/74 v 3: *la* 2nd time/74 iv 2: *bis* 1st time/74 v 3: *la* 2nd time/75 iv 1: *fa* 1st time/76a i-v 1: *l*

56. Gibbons Trust not too much, fair youth
Source: H, No. XX (Cu); 7
Variants: 50 ii 3: ♮ (H)

57. Bennet Weep, O mine eyes
Source: B, No. XIII (Och)
Variants: *Alas* in parentheses /44 i-iii 1: *l*/44 iv 1: *b*

58. Wilbye Weep, weep, mine eyes
Sources: W, No. XXIII (Cu); 2; 6 (i, iii-v only)

Variants: Pref. Stave: TS ¢ (2, 6)/1 c 2: slur to 2 v 1 (6)/16 iii 2: *heart* (2)/17 iii 1: *eyes* (2)/ 53 iv 3, 4: slur (2)

59. Gibbons What is our life?
Sources: H, No. XIV; 7 (textless)
Variants: No TS (7)/No b♭ in Pref. Stave v (7)/ 7 i 1: *sb* (H)/10 ii 1: *m* (H)/21 iv 1: *sb* (H)/25 v 2: No ♮ (7)/29 v 2: *m* (7)/40 iii 3: *m* (7)/49 v 1: No ♯ (7)/56 iv 4: No ♭ until 57 iv 2(7)/61 v 3: *c, c* (7)/69 ii 1: *m* (7)/70 v 1: *b* (7)/73 v 1: *c* c, *c* e (7)/ 77 iv 1: *b* (7)/90 iv 1: *sb* dot, *c* q *etc.*/104 i 4: No ♮ (7)/109 ii 1: No ♯ (7)/120 i-v 1: *l* (H & 7) with pause (7)

60. Morley Whither away so fast?
Sources: M, No. VII (Lcm); 3 (iii only)
Variants: 3 iii: *Whether* (M, 3)/5 iii: *deir, whyte, sueit, bonie* (3)/18 iii: *deir* (3)/28 iii 5: *I say* (3)/82 i-iii 1: *l* [Text throughout has been punctuated and capitalized to provide consistency within a part, rather than vertically.]

The Publishers and Editors gratefully acknowledge assistance given by the following libraries: Cambridge, University Library; Glasgow, University Library; London, British Library and Royal College of Music, Parry Room Library; Oxford, Bodleian Library and Christ Church Library.

Thanks are due also to Mr Colin Hawke for his assistance in preparing manuscript copy.